IMAGERY IN EDUCATION

Imagery in the Educational Process

Editors: Anees A. Sheikh & Katharina S. Sheikh

Imagery and Human Development Series
Series Editor: Anees A. Sheikh

Baywood Publishing Company, Inc.

FARMINGDALE, N.Y.

Library of Congress Catalog Card No. 85-11229
ISBN Number: 0-89503-044-6

© 1985 Baywood Publishing Company, Inc.

Library of Congress Cataloging in Publication Data
Main entry under title:

Imagery in education
   (Imagery and human development series ; 2)
   Bibliography: p.
   Includes index.
   1. Creative thinking (Education) -- Addresses, essays,
lectures. 2. Imagery -- Addresses, essays, lectures.
3. Visual education --- Addresses, essays, lectures.
4. Education -- Curricula -- Psychological aspects --
Addresses, essays, lectures. I. Sheikh, Anees A.
II. Sheikh, Katharina S. III. Series.
LB1062.I39   1985   370.11'8   85-11229
ISBN 0-89503-044-6

To our parents
Husn-Ara and Abdul H. Sheikh
and
Gertrude and Herman Schwitan
with gratitude

Table of Contents

Preface

The faculty of fantasy and imagination was held in high esteem in the West until the Renaissance. Then a dramatic re-evaluation took place, and imagery was relegated to obscurity—where it remained until the 1960s, when a new and equally dramatic re-evaluation occurred.

During the Renaissance, as the emphasis on rationalism became more and more pervasive, imagery was viewed with increasing hostility. Imagery was associated with the spiritual and the occult, and also, since the Greeks and Romans had established it as the chief memory crutch of rhetoricians, it was linked to drill and rote learning. Hence, when, in the 16th century, schooling for a larger segment of the population became an important concern in Europe, it occurred in an atmosphere of distrust and even hostility to the imaginal. Imagery was viewed as primitive, prelogical, and childish; and this orientation has prevailed among educators ever since [1].

Preschoolers have not yet learned to share this attitude and give the imagination free reign. It is the essential component in young children's most important activity—play; for, it enables them to feel, taste, smell, hear, and see whatever the situation demands—no matter how simple the props. During the initial years of schooling, concessions are made to the pupils' inclinations, and exercises which involve the imagination constitute a large portion of the curriculum. But gradually, as the children learn to read and perform simple arithmetics, exercises involving imagery are phased out of the academic subjects and relegated to those considered to be of less importance, such as shop, photography, and the arts; and from grade to grade, the neglect of the imagination becomes progressively more accentuated.

To a large extent, the educators' fascination with words and numbers is understandable. They are indeed very effective for summarizing and transmitting complex and abstract information. And, after all, the primary goal of educators has not been to nurture creativity but rather to transmit a culture's collected knowledge.

Furthermore, prior to the 1970s, the relationship between imagery and the educational process had not been explored systematically. As late as 1971, Paivio concluded, in his book, *Imagery and Verbal Processes* [2], that researchers could only speculate about the effects of imagery on learning and, therefore, could offer no clear guidelines to educators.

7

However, since then the role of imagery in learning has been explored with ever increasing enthusiasm. Already by the middle of the decade, a fair amount of research had accumulated. In 1977, Pressley [3] reviewed it, and he concluded that of the various factors which affect students' progress, mental imagery probably was the least understood and consequently the most neglected, but it was not the least important. The data indicated that imagery aids in learning and retaining the material in most and perhaps all subjects. That is, by this time, investigators had progressed to the point of being able to make "better guesses as to the effect of pictures and imagery on children's learning" [3, p. 615].

Much remained to be done. But researchers did not hestitate to take up the challenge, and a multitude of studies soon demonstrated the importance of imagery in learning. It became clear that imagery can be useful not only in the secondary subjects but in all areas of the curriculum—as it is in the business of daily living. Arnheim observes that visual thinking is utilized regularly by all: by chess players planning their strategy, by moving-men steering a piano through confined spaces, and by housewives rearranging the furniture in their living room [4].

Imagery is a very versatile learning aid. It is effective in creating the appropriate environment and mental set for learning. Although the presence of some anxiety promotes the learning process, a high level of anxiety impedes it, and imagery exercises were found to be instrumental in reducing tension.

Imagery activities promote learning in the language arts. In fact, it is imagery which renders prose and poetry memorable. Bettelheim proposed that the fairy tales which have endured, have done so due to the profound images which they evoke [5]. Also, imagery exercises are easily incorporated in this area because "the structure of language itself reflects its imaginal roots" [6, p. 165].

In the teaching of mathematics and the sciences, too, the use of imagery can make a difference. Gowan maintains, "It is here, in the area of scientific invention, that we feel the strongest case for right-hemisphere imagery" [7, p. 26].

Even in the area of sports, mental imagery has proven its worth. Suinn demonstrated that positive attitude and mental practice made an appreciable difference in athletes' performance [8].

The prestige of imagery was enhanced not only by the data produced by scientific investigations, but also as a result of the concurrent focus on the testimony of numerous creative individuals. Many artists have testified that their imagination remained a valuable resource throughout their lives. For example, Thomas Wolfe spoke of the "power of memory to evoke and bring back odors, sounds, colors, shapes and feel of things with concrete vividness" [9, p. 210].

That artists should pay tribute to the imagination is probably not surprising. But philosophers, such as Nietzsche and Singer, too, have valued it. Singer revealed that he found auditory images particularly helpful, especially a little imp who conversed with him [9].

Scientists, also, attest to the central role of imagery in their discoveries. For example, Einstein reported that visual and kinesthetic images assisted him in formulating mathematical and scientific concepts, and Kekule's discovery of the "benzene ring" was aided by a vision of a snake taking hold of its own tail. In fact, Gowan asserts "that in the case of every historic scientific discovery and invention which is researched carefully enough, we find that it was imagery, either in dreams or in a waking state, which produced the breakthrough" [7, p. 26].

This link between imagery and creativity prompted investigators to suppose that increased focus on mental imagery might stimulate creativity. Indeed, Gowan found that enriched art and music programs designed to encourage creativity led to improvement in students' performance in general [7]. Gowan explains that the right hemisphere of the brain continually generates imagery, which leads to creative thought. But this imagery generally is obscured by the activities of the dominant left hemisphere. To become aware of the imagery requires special attention and represents "a new educational challenge, if we are to educate both halves of the brain and hence stimulate creativity in young people" [7, pp. 24-25].

Since imagery revealed itself to be a useful teaching tool and even to promote the supreme human function, creation, educators could no longer afford to dismiss it as a faculty unworthy of nurture, especially since declining academic achievement continued to plague American schools and remedies did not abound. Already in 1969, Debes had campaigned vigorously on behalf of "visual literacy," insisting that visual skills should be as actively promoted as language skills [10, pp. 25-27]. In 1977, Sless reiterated this plea more strongly: "At all levels our education system is dominated by two skills: literacy and numeracy. A third area of skill which can be described as visual thinking should be given equal priority in the curriculum" [11, p. 4].

Since 1977, much more evidence has accumulated to support this view. However, perhaps the terms "visual literacy" and "visual thinking" should be replaced by "imaginal literacy." Although visual imagery is the most prevalent type, it is, obviously, not the only one, or even, for some individuals, the most important one.

Of course, the incorporation of imagery techniques into the curriculum should be a gradual process; for, at the present time, there are few teachers who possess the theoretical background and the practical training to implement them effectively. Furthermore, the techniques should be used with caution and tested and retested to ascertain their effects. Also they probably should not be globally applied. Most students undoubtedly would benefit from judiciously chosen mental-imagery activities: They would become more aware of their imagery and learn to recognize it as the fountainhead of many new adventures. But there are a few students who, like Virginia Woolf, have a fantasy "furnished with an accelerator and no brakes" [12, p. 148] and who need no further stimulation.

Educators cannot afford to ignore the potential of the imagination. The exclusive emphasis on literacy and numeracy does not lead to optimal academic performance, it discourages creativity, and, furthermore, there may well be truth in a prediction advanced by C. Ward and F. Chippendale: "The visually illiterate children of one generation become the arrogantly insensitive adults of the next" [1, p. 54].

This volume contains discussions of some of the most outstanding recent studies on the relationship of mental imagery to education. The book's purpose will have been well served if it plays a role in dispelling the suspicion that has surrounded imagery and in reinstating it as a legitimate and valuable human function in the educational process.

We wish to cordially thank all contributors for their excellent chapters—each one constitutes a vital segment of the puzzle.

The work on this book was completed while the first editor was an Alumni-in-Residence Fellow at the East-West Center in Honolulu, Hawaii, and he wishes to express his sincere gratitude for the support provided by the Center.

Anees A. Sheikh
Katharina S. Sheikh

REFERENCES

1. R. Sommer, *The Mind's Eye: Imagery in Everyday Life*, Delacorte, New York, 1978.
2. A. Paivio, *Imagery and Verbal Processes*, Holt, Rinehart and Winston, New York, 1971.
3. M. Pressley, Imagery and Children's Learning: Putting the Picture in Developmental Perspective, *Review of Educational Research, 47*, pp. 585-622, 1977.
4. R. Arnheim, *Visual Thinking*, University of California Press, Berkeley, 1969.
5. B. Bettelheim, *The Uses of Enchantment: The Meaning and Importance of Fairy Tales*, Vintage Books, New York, 1976.
6. I. Begg, D. Upfold, and T. D. Wilton, Imagery in Verbal Communication, *Journal of Mental Imagery, 2*, pp. 165-186, 1978.
7. J. C. Gowan, Incubation, Imagery, and Creativity, *Journal of Mental Imagery, 2*, pp. 23-32, 1978.
8. R. M. Suinn, Imagery and Sports, in *Imagery: Current Theory, Research, and Application*, A. A. Sheikh (ed.), Wiley, New York, 1983.
9. B. L. Forisha, Mental Imagery and Creativity, *Journal of Mental Imagery, 2*, pp. 209-238, 1978.
10. J. L. Debes, The Loom of Visual Literacy, *Audiovisual Instruction, 14*, pp. 25-27, 1969.
11. D. Sless, Visual Thinking in Education, *Pivot: A Journal of South Australian Education, 4*, pp. 4-9, 1977.
12. Q. Bell, *Virginia Woolf: A Biography*, Harcourt Brace Jovanovich, New York, 1972.

CHAPTER 1

The Ebb and Flow of Mental Imagery in Education

GISELA E. SPEIDEL
AND MARK E. TROY

Albert Einstein is universally recognized as the preeminent example of a scientific genius. That scholars should explore Einstein's writings and interviews for clues to his cognitive processes is, therefore, no surprise. What they have uncovered, however, is a surprise to many. Einstein reported that he first worked out his ideas as "more or less clear images" [1, p. 126]. Prime examples are his "Gedanken" experiments. In one of them he imagined himself traveling alongside a beam of light at 186,000 miles per second. Thus began a reformulation of electromagnetic theory.

The mental processes which in Einstein yielded such extraordinary achievements have caught the attention of philosophers, scholars, and educators for nearly twenty-five centuries. Nevertheless, a description of the nature of mental imagery has remained elusive. Nearly everyone is familiar with mental images through their own experience of them. This familiarity leads to an impression of understanding their nature. Yet, whenever mental images are subjected to study, controversy arises. Images have been studied under many different names and in conjunction with many related phenomena. Holt's taxonomy of imagery includes events such as thought imagery, synesthesia, the phantom limb, eidetic imagery, and more [2].

Because of the subjective nature of images, most writers have avoided definitions, preferring, instead, to use metaphors. Plato compared images to an imprint in wax. Thomas Aquinas described them as "corporeal similitudes." Contemporary writers tend to call them "pictures in the head." All of these metaphors emphasize vision in imagery. Although many people have attempted to identify images associated with other sensory modalities, the visual images seem to be dominant in subjective experience.

The picture metaphor implies that the object being imagined is a replica of the object of perception, just as a photograph is a copy of the external object. This metaphor limits the image to specific, concrete content. However, most people recognize that images do not behave like pictures. They are not necessarily isomorphic with a specific external object, but they may be more abstract or a combination of similar objects. For instance, when imagining a horse, most of us would not imagine a particular horse but an abstraction of the many horses we have seen. The question whether images can have abstract content in addition to concrete content has been an important issue historically. The imprint or picture metaphors, however, are inadequate for describing the abstract nature of images.

Shepard proposes an alternative to the picture metaphor [1]. He likens an image and its external referent to a lock and a key. The external object serves as the key to operate the internal image or the lock. This conceptualization gets away from the one-to-one correspondence of the external object to its internal representation. It points the way to an image consisting of more generalized abstract content. Such a conception of an image shifts the emphasis of study from the structure of imagery to the function of imagery in thought. We will return to Shepard's lock and key metaphor at the conclusion of this chapter, when we attempt to show what implications past conceptions of imagery have for research on imagery in education.

Our purpose in this introductory chapter is to outline some of the conceptions of imagery held before the recent reawakening of interest in mental imagery and to describe some of the educational practices generated by these conceptions.

Within the larger issue of the nature of knowledge, the questions, what are images and how are they connected to knowledge, become central to education. As Attneave points out, these embrace the question of the form in which knowledge is represented in the mind [3]. Although numerous solutions have been offered by philosophers and psychologists, they fall into two general classes: One class of solutions postulates abstract, logical entities, sometimes called propositions, as the form of representation; the other class of solutions postulates impressions derived from sensory data.

CLASSICAL TIMES

Images already appear in Plato's theory. In fact, the first recorded mention of the imprint metaphor is in Plato's *Theaetetus*.

> Let us call it the gift of the Muses' mother, Memory, and say that whenever we wish to remember something we see or hear or conceive in our own minds, we hold this wax under the perceptions or ideas and imprint them on it as we might stamp the impression of a seal-ring [4, p. 191d].

Plato considered these impressions to be the results of uncritical perceptions and to represent the lowest grade of cognition. Plato did not deem images to be important in human cognition; rather, he thought of them as *counterfeits of knowledge*. Plato believed that true knowledge did not derive from sense impressions but was latent in memory. For him, true knowledge occurred when the imprint from sensation fit onto its basic corresponding imprint of the Form or Idea.

Knowledge, according to Plato, is knowledge of the Forms which are the true objects of knowledge. In the *Theaetetus*, Plato reaches the conclusion that perception is not knowledge at all, because, although infallible in a sense, it cannot apprehend existence and truth [4, pp. 184b-186e].

The theory of Forms, according to Taylor, is a logical doctrine of the importance of universal propositions [5]. The Forms are members of a supraphysical world of eternal and immutable entities which are the objects of science and knowledge. The relation between the world of concepts and the world of everyday sensible experience is that the things of the sensible world are approximate and imperfect resemblances of the corresponding conceptual entities from which they derive their class names.

In contrast to Plato, Aristotle, his student, held that the only way to knowledge was by abstraction from sense impressions. Aristotle's theory of memory and reminiscence may be found in the *De Anima* [6] and the *Parva Naturalia* [7]. In Aristotle's theory, memory and reminiscence are distinct: Memory is a part of perception, and reminiscence is a part of intellect. The basic principles are that perceptions brought in by the five senses are first processed by the faculty of imagination and that images formed in this manner become the material for the intellectual faculty. According to Aristotle, "The intellectual faculty therefore understands forms in phantasm" and "never understands apart from phantasms," so, "what does not perceive by sensation acquires no knowledge or understanding at all; and when thinking occurs there must be at the same time a phantasm as its object" [6, pp. 431a, 431b, 432a, Book III, Chapter VII]. All knowledge and thought, therefore, are derived inductively from memory images formed from sensations.

Memory, in Aristotle's theory, is similar to imagination: It is a collection of mental pictures based on sense impressions, but a time element is added. He, too, uses the metaphor of a wax impression in explaining the formation of mental images. Such impressions are the basic source of all knowledge; they are refined and abstracted by the intellect, but there could be no knowledge without the impressions.

Reminiscence, unlike memory, is not confined to a starting point in present experience. Instead, it requires a voluntary act to find a starting point. Finding a starting point is sometimes difficult and a search process may be necessary. Once the starting point has been chosen, reminiscence works on the memory images by means of Aristotle's famous principles of association: contiguity, similarity, and contrast. Order also is important in reminiscence, and in this respect reminiscence is no different from memory; just as orderly arrangement of objects greatly facilitates memory, so also does it facilitate reminiscence. Contiguity and order are the most powerful principles. They explain why reminiscence may continue involuntarily from the starting point.

Thus, for Aristotle, the phenomenological aspects of sensation provide the raw materials of cognition, and the most important sensations are visual. It is the images which provide the continuity between perception and thought.

Method of Loci

The use of mnemonic techniques, particularly by orators, was widespread in the ancient world, and the mnemonics were based on images. Because he thought images were mere copies of knowledge, Plato disparaged the use of such methods. Indeed, he discouraged note-taking for the same reasons. On the other hand, mnemonic techniques were congruent with Aristotle's theory, although this was not recognized until the Middle Ages.

How did the mnemonics work? "Now let me turn to the treasure house of the ideas supplied by Invention, to the guardian of all the parts of rhetoric, the Memory" [8, III, XVI, p. 28]. With these words, the anonymous author of the classic Roman textbook on rhetoric (ca. 86-82 B.C.), introduces a practical guide to the use of mental images. The author's use of a treasure house as a metaphor for memory is very apt and one that is used frequently by other teachers of rhetoric. The artifacts to be stored in the treasure house are none other than mental images of the ideas which an orator wishes to discuss in a speech. The *Ad Herennium* sets out, in handbook fashion, the rules to follow in using this mnemonic technique. Other classical authors, notably Cicero in *De Oratore* [9] and Quintilian in his *Institutio Oratoria* [10], also discuss the method.

The method by which the images are to be constructed, stored, and retrieved is known as the method of *loci* or mnemotechnics. It probably originated with Simonides of Keos (556-468 B.C.), a Greek lyric poet and teacher of rhetoric. In this method, one constructs an image to represent each separate topic in a speech and then arranges them in some orderly fashion, usually by imagining them in familiar places (*loci*), such as the rooms of one's home. The images are then retrieved by taking a mental stroll through the imagined place during the course of speech.

An example of the mental stroll can be found in A. R. Luria's detailed case study of a man who, in modern times, independently reinvented a system like that of Simonides [11]. The man, S., had a memory of virtually unlimited capacity. Luria, who studied him for nearly thirty years, found that he used a variety of methods for converting information into images for storage in memory and subsequent retrieval. In the description that follows, S. is clearly making use of the method as it is prescribed in the *Rhetorica ad Herennium*.

When S. read through a long series of words, each word would elicit a graphic image. And since the series was fairly long, he had to find some way of distributing these images in a mental row or sequence. Most often (and this habit persisted throughout his life) he would "distribute" them along some roadway or street he visualized in his mind. . . . Frequently, he would take a mental walk along that street . . . and slowly make his way down, "distributing" his images at houses, gates, and store windows.

This technique of converting a series of words into a series of graphic images explains why S. could so readily reproduce a series from start to finish or in reverse order; how he could rapidly name the word that preceded or followed one I'd select from the series. To do this, he would simply begin his walk, either from the beginning or from the end of the street, find the image of the object I had named, and "take a look at" whatever happened to be situated on either side of it [8, pp. 31-33].

There are two features of Simonides' technique to consider here. First, it was functional. It was a technique by which the orator could improve his memory and, thus, deliver long speeches accurately. Oratory was the highest profession to which one could aspire in the ancient world. The study of rhetoric was the equivalent of our higher education. Without books and inexpensive writing implements, however, sustained oratory would have been nearly impossible had it not been for the system of mnemonic images. Accordingly, the author of *Rhetorica ad Herennium* referred to memory as the guardian of all the parts of rhetoric.

A second feature of Simonides' system is that it places extraordinary emphasis on visual cognitive processes. Cicero credits Simonides with discovering the principle that orderly arrangement of images facilitates memory. But, most of all, he praises Simonides for the emphasis on vision.

It has been sagaciously discerned by Simonides or else discovered by some other person, that the most complete pictures are formed in our minds of the things that have been conveyed to them and imprinted on them by the senses, but that the keenest of all our senses is the sense of sight, and that consequently perceptions received by the ears or by reflection can be most easily retained in the mind if they are also conveyed to our minds by the mediation of the eyes [9, p. 357].

Nowhere does a visual cognitive strategy receive more explicit treatment than in texts devoted to the training of the minds of orators. For example, in discussing the rules for places, the author of the *Rhetorica ad Herennium* says,

It will be more advantageous to obtain background (places) in a deserted than in a populous region, because the crowding and passing to and fro of people confuse and weaken the impress of the images, while solitude keeps their outlines sharp. Further, background differing in form and nature must be secured, so that, thus distinguished, they may be clearly visible; for if a person has adopted many intercolumnar spaces, their resemblance to one another will so confuse him that he will no longer know what he has set in each background. And these backgrounds ought to be of moderate size and medium extent, for when excessively large they render the images vague, and when too small often seem incapable of receiving an arrangement of images. Then the backgrounds ought to be neither too bright nor too dim, so that the shadows may not obscure the images nor the lustre make them glitter. I believe that the intervals between backgrounds should be of moderate extent, approximately thirty feet; for like the external eye, so the inner eye of thought is less powerful when you have moved the object of sight too near or too far away [8, pp. 211-213].

Commenting on this passage, Yates professes astonishment at the visual precision that is credited to the "inner eye" in these rules [12]. However, Kosslyn and his colleagues have cited a large body of evidence from laboratory experiments indicating that such visual precision in mental imagery is indeed possible [13, 14].

Further support is found in Luria's analysis of the errors made by his subject, S. The errors were of the form of omissions of items from the series to be recalled. They occurred whenever the image of the item had been placed in a spot where it was difficult for S. to discern it. If the background was poorly lit or the object did not stand out sufficiently (e.g., a white egg against a white wall), he might "walk" past it without noticing it.

Oratory was an important and prestigious activity in classical times. Since there were no modern mnemonic aids available, memory training was critical in the education of an orator. The method of *loci* was well-known to orators because of its utility and effectiveness.

The success of that system is demonstrated by the remarkable feats of memory that have been attributed to classical orators. (Pliny the Elder lists many examples in his *Natural History*.) The Greeks and Romans were in awe of the memory of orators and considered it to be of divine origin. Such memory feats are rarely seen today and are usually looked on with profound skepticism.

Because of the importance of memory to rhetoric and because of the position of rhetoric in education, Simonides' mnemonic technique, based on imagery, had a powerful influence in shaping educational practice in the ancient world.

The classical system of education was based on the seven liberal arts (grammar, rhetoric, dialectic, arithmetic, geometry, music, and astronomy); and their outline has been preserved for us by Martianus Capella.

Martianus' work, *De Nuptiis Philologiae et Mercurii* [15], was written in the 5th century A.D., at about the time of the collapse of Rome and North Africa. It describes the Latin educational system in its final form. Rhetoric occupies a prominent place among the seven liberal arts, and within rhetoric, Simonides' system of mnemonic images for enhancing memory is still in use.

The *De Nuptiis*, itself, is full of images. It is an allegory in which a wedding is taking place and the liberal arts, personified as handmaidens, are given to the bride. Grammar, for example, is an old woman with a knife with which to remove grammatical errors. Rhetoric is a tall, beautiful woman carrying weapons to wound her adversaries. The images appear to have been constructed with remarkable fidelity to the rules for images in *Ad Herennium*. They are strikingly ugly or beautiful and, thus, more memorable, according to *Ad Herennium's* author. Modern commentators on Martianus' work [15] have remarked on the lascivious nature of some of the descriptions and have wondered about the purpose for it in a serious work. However, to anyone familiar with *Ad Herennium* or Simonides' system, as were Martianus's readers, the purpose would have been clear: to facilitate memory.

The influence of *De Nuptiis Philologiae et Mercurii* extended far beyond the period in which it was written. It was the most important educational treatise in the Middle Ages. Yet it would have been difficult to comprehend, just as it is difficult for us to comprehend, had not medieval scholars been acquainted with the use of mnemonic images.

THE MIDDLE AGES

Thomas Aquinas (1225-1274) and his teacher Albertus Magnus (1193-1280) chiefly were responsible for the rebirth of interest in visual mnemonics.

Albertus Magnus in *De Bono* [16] and Thomas Aquinas in *Summa Theologica* [17] discuss the memory technique of the *Ad Herennium* and decide that it is an excellent means for remembering religious and moral precepts. Both conclude that since subtle and spiritual precepts are difficult to remember, and since concrete ideas that are products of sensation are easy to remember, the former should be linked with the latter in imagery as taught in the works of Cicero and in the *Ad Herennium*.

Aquinas likens images to sense impressions, which he considers to be the basis of knowledge. He states that "man cannot understand without images; the image is a similitude of a corporeal thing, but understanding is of universals which are to be abstracted from particulars" (cited in [12, p. 70]). Thus, Aquinas' fundamental theory of knowledge is already familiar to us as Aristotle's. And what is Aquinas' theory of memory? Basically he proposes that memory belongs to the same part of the soul, to the same cognitive processes, as imagination. Abstract concepts, according to Aquinas, are not themselves memorable, but they can be made memorable through imagery.

The Middle Ages were a period of great piety, and the virtues and ethics predominated as subjects of scholarship. Thus, Aquinas discusses images and memory under the topic of Prudence in the *Summa Theologica* [17]. In Aquinas' analysis, the virtue of prudence enables a person to apply universal knowledge to particular information derived from sense impressions. Prudence is a natural aptitude which is amenable to learning and practice. The prudent person learns from past experience and uses what has been learned to confront the present or to plan for the future. In other words, the lessons learned in the past become generalized. Furthermore, it appears that the generalization is mediated by memory images.

In describing how imagery works in learning and generalization, Aquinas adopts the main points of Aristotle's theory of reminiscence, association, and order. He agrees with Aristotle on the necessity of finding a starting point in memory from which reminiscence will proceed in an associative order. Aquinas equates the starting point and places of search mentioned by Aristotle with the *loci* of Cicero's method. Not only can we recognize in this a theory of associative learning, but we also can see the functional role attributed to imagery in the learning process.

From the above can be extracted the major points of Scholastic psychology. First, mental operations are to be viewed as a continuity of perception, memory, and thought. Second, mental images are the components of memory and the primitive elements of thought. Third, learning and generalization, which are identified with the virtue of Prudence, are mediated by memory images.

Aquinas himself developed four principles of memory based on images, order, places, and repetition and meditation. These were adopted by the Dominican order, to which Aquinas belonged, for use by their preachers. Since the Dominicans were a mendicant order, the rules spread throughout Europe. Preachers used images to remember their sermons and to make their precepts more memorable for the faithful. Given the lack of modern learning aids, mnemonic images must have been one of the most powerful learning tools of the age.

Yates [12] and Wittrock [18] have developed intriguing hypotheses about medieval art and architecture. They propose that the bizarre, grotesque, beautiful, and ugly images were created in accordance with the rules of the classical art of memory and especially in keeping with Aquinas' writings about them. According to this hypothesis, the imagery found in medieval art represented organized memory aids designed to instruct people in important Christian tenets and to facilitate their recall. Wittrock contends that if these hypotheses are correct, scholars may have completely misunderstood the character of the people of medieval Europe.

At the same time that Aquinas' memory system was being spread through Europe by the Dominicans, Ramon Lull, an eccentric Franciscan, devised a memory system based on verbal associations and abstract formulae. His system was more compatible with Plato's theory than with Aristotle's. However, it did not achieve widespread popularity until the 16th century.

THE RENAISSANCE

During the Renaissance, new concepts of cognition, especially imagination, developed. Imagination rose to the status of a divine and magically powerful faculty. It became the essence of the art of facilitating learning and memory, and more importantly, it became a means of creating new secular knowledge. Renaissance man believed that through this divine and magical faculty and with the aid of organized magical memory systems, he could understand the entire universe.

One such memory system was Guilio Camillo's memory theater [12]. This was a structure that was crowded with images, which were hierarchically organized into seven levels, which, in turn, were divided into seven gangways. Images of the seven planets were associated with each of the seven gangways. Each of the seven levels represented a dimension of knowledge. The levels carried images associated with various stages in the creation of the universe: man's soul, man's body, culture, arts, and so forth. Camillo's theater was based on the classical rules for images, and its purpose was to provide an organized system for abstracting knowledge of the universe.

Giordano Bruno created another memory system based on Aquinas' four rules for memory and on magical images from the zodiac and astrology. His system was probably the most ambitious memory system ever. However, it reflected the typical attitudes towards memory during the Renaissance. Memory systems became increasingly abstract with words replacing images in many cases. The purpose of the memory systems shifted from facilitating memory to generating knowledge.

Memory systems began to decline in influence after the Renaissance. Wittrock has attributed the decline to three possible causes [18]. Technological advances which resulted in widespread availability of inexpensive writing instruments and printed books reduced the need for holding information in memory. Neoplatonism, which rose to dominance in philosophy, emphasized the primacy of abstract ideas and de-emphasized the role of images in understanding and learning. Leaders of the Protestant Reformation disparaged the uses of imagery in sculpture, painting, and architecture and also may have discouraged the use of imagery to facilitate learning and memory in the schools.

THE PROTESTANT REFORMATION

Peter Ramus (1515-1572) was a French dialectitian and convert to Protestantism who brought about a reform of education in the 16th century. He leveled strong criticisms against Aristotelean philosophy and against the use of images in Catholic churches. He devised his own memory system in which he replaced images with a hierarchical arrangement of words. The educational methods that he introduced emphasized verbal relationships.

As was pointed out in an earlier section, the scholastics had made imagery a part of Prudence and the creative faculty. They also had made use of it to facilitate the learning and understanding of religious precepts. Ramus objected to this use of imagery. He labeled images, whether mental or artistic, as *commentitia*; that is, deceitful, frivolous, irrelevant, or arbitrary. This does not mean that he denied the existence of images; one could not deny the phenomena of perception. Rather, he deemed the use of imagery, in the form of mnemonic techniques, to aid learning, memory, and understanding to be arbitrary and misleading. Ramus substituted more "natural" classification schemes in which learning and retention would be coterminous with the method of classification. His method of classification was the dialectic in which words were cast into a hierarchical array, in which the most general categories were listed first. Each category was then subdivided into subcategories which were subdivided in turn. Some degree of spatial organization remained in the array of categories and sub-categories, but for the most part it was an abstract verbal method of representing information. There was no place in Ramus' dialectic for imagery and concrete representation. This attitude toward imagery suited the Puritan mind very well.

Ramus' prestige among the Puritans was enhanced by his murder as a Huguenot in the Massacre of St. Bartholomew in 1572. Thus, Ramus became a Protestant martyr. This combination of martyrdom and an educational reform that replaced Scholasticism turned Ramism into a movement that swept Europe, especially the Protestant countries. Although his reforms were intended for secondary schools, they produced changes in curricula in European schools at all levels. Ramism was introduced into the British Isles first at the universities in Scotland, and later, at the Puritan dominated colleges, such as Cambridge and Trinity College in Dublin. Oxford, however, retained its scholastic traditions. Ong suggests that the greatest impact of Ramism in England was felt in the preparatory schools [19].

Ramism, however, was not solely a Protestant movement: Catholics also embraced the Ramist reforms. In fact, it had a widespread grass-roots appeal among many people who, tired of the complexities of Scholasticism, welcomed Ramism as a simpler method of learning.

The educational reforms promulgated by Ramus were, on close inspection, superficial; but they contained the seeds of educational practices that emphasize verbal transmission of information, logical categorization, and linear styles of cognitive processing, and that attribute few, if any, functions to mental images.

THE INDUSTRIAL AGE

Elementary-school education of this century reflects Ramism in its reliance upon words to transmit knowledge and in its neglect of imagery. If today we were to walk into a classroom in North America (and in most other parts of the world), we probably would find the teacher talking at the children, providing them with information. He/She even might have a picture or diagram to accompany his/her talk. The children probably would be sitting at their desks, listening to the explanations of the teacher. Or, we might find the teacher asking questions, to find out what the children know [20]. Or, in this day of mimeograph and xerox machines, we might find the children hunched over work-sheets.

Montessori many years ago described such education in Italian classrooms. "In general, when we are teaching, we talk about the object which interests us, and then try to lead the scholar, when he has understood, to perform some kind of work with the object itself" [21, p. 218].

She already was aware of the inappropriateness of such instruction.

> Between "understanding" because another person seeks to impress upon us an explanation of a thing by speech, and "understanding" the thing of ourselves, there is an immeasurable distance; the two are comparable to the impression made in soft wax, which will subsequently be effaced and replaced by other impressions, and the form chiselled in the marble by an artist [22, p. 215].

The belief that knowledge is derived through our senses and does not pre-exist in us in the way Plato argues, contains some important underlying assumptions for teaching. For instance, in order for the statement of a teacher, "Elephants live in jungles" to make sense to a child, the child already must have mental images of elephants and jungles; the words *elephants* and *jungles* must activate these images, and finally the appropriate arrangement of elephants in jungles must occur in imagery as the result of the activation of the images by their verbal counterparts. In other words, in order for appropriate learning to take place, the following conditions must be met: 1) The appropriate visual images already must exist in the child; 2) The mental link between the words and their corresponding visual images already must exist; 3) The words of the teacher must elicit the appropriate images in the child (the child could have the appropriate images and word-to-image units, and yet, at the particular moment, the teacher's words still might not elicit the appropriate images because the child is attending to some other feature in his/her talk); 4) Finally, the teacher's words must produce the appropriate grouping or regrouping of the mental images elicited by her words.

This analysis should make it clear what a difficult feat it is to teach through words alone, to try to instill through words alone true understanding—an understanding beyond the mere words themselves.

There are three individuals who have recognized the inadequacy of this predominantly verbal education and who have caused variations of the typical teaching practices in our century: Rudolf Steiner, Maria Montessori, and Jean Piaget. Their philosophies of how intelligence and knowledge grow differ widely from each other. Nevertheless, the translations of their philosophies into actual educational practices reveal that they each stress the importance of real experience with objects and events. This real experience, we postulate, will foster the apprehension of the world through the senses, particularly the visual sense, and thereby will allow the development of corresponding mental images, upon which the mind can then operate.

Rudolf Steiner (1861-1925)

The Waldorf Schools are a rather dramatic alternative to modern classroom instruction. The first Waldorf School was opened in Stuttgart, Germany, in 1919, by Rudolf Steiner for children of workers in the Waldorf Astoria Factory.

Today the Waldorf schools are worldwide. In Germany, the schools have been so successful that the German government is providing funds for their continuation and for analysis of their methodology.

Steiner's views on education and recommended teaching strategies are found in publications of various lecture series he gave in Europe during the early 1920s [23-25] (publications are posthumous). He recommended a number of basic principles for instruction: Whenever possible the teacher should develop all intellectual knowledge from real life, from things the child can see. Instruction should always begin with something visible, and thinking should never be separated from visual experience.

He believed the visual system to be central to the child's thinking and way of learning. "The child during the first seven years is really completely and wholly an eye" [25, p. 30]. To understand is to have a mental picture of that which we understand: "If we have had a mental picture of something, we say we have grasped it" [23, p. 34].

Thus, he devised a "*pictorial method*" of education in which all thinking should be developed in a pictorial, imaginative way [24, p. 140]. "What is necessary is that through artistic means we give the child in picture form perceptions, ideas, and feelings, which are capable of growing and changing." The teacher should create "*thought-pictures*" [25, p. 78] which are to grow with the child and to which the teacher can come back in the future to extend thought further. This pictorial knowledge is to become the foundation for abstractions on a purely intellectual level of thought.

Because of the importance of the picture thought in meaningful knowledge acquisition, Steiner gives sculpture and drawing a prominent place in teaching all subject matters.

Based upon this philosophy of teaching through pictures and building knowledge from daily experience, Steiner has described ways in which writing, reading, language, arithmetic, physics, geography, and so forth should be taught.

We will briefly describe some of the educational practices suggested by Steiner to show how he has realized his pictorial-thought method of instruction and how mental imagery might develop in such an instructional environment.

Steiner recommends teaching writing before reading, in order to make printed material and reading more meaningful to the child. Writing is first taught through pictures. For instance, to teach how to write the letter *M*, the children first might be asked to draw or paint a mouth. The upper lip is then accentuated to make it look like an *M*, which is also the first sound and letter in *mouth*

. In this manner, writing of letters is developed out of pictures, and the pictures originate directly in the children's lives.

Foreign-language instruction, central to Waldorf education, also relies heavily on the pictorial method and on imagery. Rather than teaching the new lexicon by pairing the new labels with labels in the mother tongue, it is taught by directly labeling the actual objects or pictures. Not only can the objects themselves be depicted in pictures but also characteristics of objects. For instance, one of us who learned French from a teacher who used the pictorial method to great advantage, was taught the meaning of the word *demi-tour* by the teacher drawing

a pig first facing in one direction, ; then he wiped off the head and the tail and drew them in reverse positions so that the pig faced the other

way, . We all immediately understood what *demi-tour* meant and remember it thirty years later!

For teaching arithmetic operations, Steiner advocates starting with the whole, because this is how we perceive things around us: First you see the forest as a whole and only when you come nearer, do you see it consists of single trees. Children, he claims, first perceive the whole, and then they start to analyze the whole. For instance, to teach addition, he starts with a heap of apples which the children count. Then, he distributes the apples among the children. The resulting little heaps are again counted. If the initial heap contained fifteen apples and there are three children, we might find that one child received five apples, another four, and another six. At this point, the teacher can show how this finding is represented: $15 = 5 + 4 + 6$. Another example beginning with the whole is: We have seven apples, and give four apples to Johnny, how many are left for Kathy? (Again the objects are directly in front of the children and the children count how many are left for Kathy). The finding is represented beginning with the whole: $7 = 4 + 3$. It becomes obvious that in this method of beginning with the whole, addition and subtraction are taught simultaneously, their only difference being a matter of perspective.

Steiner also has given quite explicit directions on how to approach instruction in the sciences. For instance, in geometry to teach the theorem of Pythagoras, he advocates the use of cutouts of the geometric figures and that the students actually lay out the proof with the cutouts. In physics, he suggests teaching the principle of heat by beginning with lighting a match, observing how the match burns, describing the flame, and perceiving the different colors and relating them to differences in heat.

Steiner's approach to instruction relies heavily on student observation, on pictures, and on concrete, imagery-evoking words. Such instruction, one would agree with Steiner, should increase the likelihood that images become an essential component of complex thought. To study systematically the effects of such instruction on imagery, creativity, and problem solving is an important research task for the future.

Maria Montessori (1907–1952)

Maria Montessori's success in teaching retarded children and the slum children of Rome remains impressive [26]. She was a physician by training, the first woman to receive a medical degree from an Italian university. As an intern in psychiatry, she became interested in the education of the mentally retarded and developed instructional materials for them. In her subsequent work with normal children from slums, she expanded and refined her educational methods. A brief review of Montessori's educational philosophy and a description of her educational methods will show that she, like Steiner, emphasized experiences which provide much opportunity for the development of mental imagery.

Montessori was dedicated to science and hoped to make education a scientific enterprise. She advocated a "scientific pedagogy," and science to her meant systematic observation. This conception she adopted from Wundt: "All methods of experimental psychology may be reduced to one; namely, carefully recorded observation of the subject" [21, p. 72].

Observation, the resulting images, and their systematic organization were for her also the essence of intelligence. She believed that the critical action of intelligence lay in the observation of the environment and in the subsequent selection of features that could serve as a basis for ordering and classifying: "Intelligence is a function of the capacity for receiving impressions from the environment, elaborating images." It "abstracts the dominant characteristics of things and thus succeeds in associating their images and keeping them in the foreground of consciousness" [21, p. 212].

The senses, Montessori believed, could be trained to become sharper and to organize the information obtained from the environment along systematic and meaningful dimensions. Thus, central to Montessori education is the training of the senses: "The *education of the senses* must be of the greatest *pedagogical* interest" [21, p. 215]. The manner in which the senses are to be educated flows from her philosophy on how knowledge is acquired—a philosophy that is amazingly similar to Piaget's. Mere transmission of knowledge is an antiquated conception of education: "Education is not something which the teacher does, but . . . it is a natural process which develops spontaneously in the human being. It is not acquired by listening to words, but by virtue of experiences in which the child acts on his environment" [27, p. 8]. Her method for educating the senses can be summed up by her motto: "Things are the best teacher."

In line with this philosophy is her *prepared environment*. It is the cornerstone of her instructional method. The prepared environment consists of objects and materials with which the children interact and through which they are to increase the speed and acuity of their senses. It is these materials which constitute the didactic system. The teacher merely plays a guiding role.

Her materials have a very important feature. They are self-correcting by eliciting visual-comparison processes. For instance, a child is arranging a set of cubes in descending order and chooses a wrong cube. He/She soon will become aware of the error through his/her sense of vision, by noticing the visual irregularities. Montessori writes about this self-correcting feature of her materials: "Learning is more effective if the child can see for himself whether his answer is correct. He can look at the outcome while the word is evanescent and makes the spoken answer difficult for inductive purposes."

The activities for the education of the senses begin with those that require very basic sense discriminations and move on to those which demand more and more complexly organized perceptions and mental images. Thus, in the first activities the child learns size discriminations by fitting objects into cutouts or by arranging objects according to their sizes. Initially the child performs the activities by trial and error, but then, through visual comparison processes, he/she learns to differentiate the size of the objects *purely by sight alone*. When he/she is able to arrange the objects without any errors, it is clear that he/she has learned to differentiate the objects visually and that his/her visual representations of the dimensions of the objects have become refined.

The activities for the refinement of basic sense discrimination are followed by activities for development of form perception. These activities, which use a rich variety of geometric forms, become progressively more complex in two ways: 1) the differentiation of the forms becomes more difficult; 2) the representations of the forms become more abstract, going from very thick wooden forms, to thin plane figures, to line drawings. Thus, the beginning exercise is with strongly contrasting wooden forms which are to be placed into their corresponding cutouts. The child traces with the index finger the contour of the shape as well as the contour of the cutout. This activity is to develop the association between the muscular-tactile sense and vision. In the last stages of this training, the child has to differentiate very complex, abstract line drawings.

These activities can all be made to require even more visual representational processing by adding a memory factor. For instance, the child may be asked to construct the form at a place different from where the necessary materials are located. Therefore, he/she must predict and remember which piece is required for the next step and which piece to choose from the array.

Reading instruction emphasizes the development of letter images and printed-word images. The child is introduced to letters by large letters made from sandpaper. The teacher presents the child with two letters at a time, saying the sounds of each. While the child looks at the letter, he/she moves his/her finger over the letter. "Touching the letters and looking at them at the same time, fixes the image more quickly" [21, p. 266]. Corresponding to each letter there is a picture representing the object whose name begins with the letter. These pictures serve to fix the letter sound to the object depicted, for example, the sound *a* to the picture of an apple.

In a later phase, the child constructs words by carefully saying a word and picking the letters corresponding to each sound. After construction of the word, the child reads it. Finally, he/she sorts the letters back to their sections. This activity associates sound in both directions, from sound to image and from image to sound: In selecting the graphic symbol that makes the sound, the association from sound to image is strengthened; while in reading the word constructed, the association from image to sound is strengthened. Through all these exercises "the child, on hearing the word, or on thinking of a word . . . *will see* with his mind's eye all the letters necessary to compose the word, arrange themselves" [21, p. 285].

Arithmetic operations are taught with the help of spatial arrangements of objects and with the help of rods of different lengths, increasing in one-decimeter increments from one decimeter to ten decimeters. The children learn to identify and name each rod in accordance with its length. Thus, the one-decimeter rod is the number *one* rod, the two-decimeter rod, the number *two* rod and so on. To assist in their visual identification, the rods also are marked with stripes one decimeter wide. One of the first exercises in addition is to put the rods one decimeter through nine decimeters long together in pairs to make rods the same length as the ten-decimeter rod. Thus, by trial and error, using visual cues as a guide, the child learns that number *one* rod and number *nine* rod make a number *ten* rod; a number *eight* rod and a number *two* rod make a number *ten* rod, etc.

In this concrete fashion all the arithmetic operations and algebraic equations are taught. The operations are not simply learned by rote but come to have meaning, because they can be represented in the mind with the images of the number rods from which they initially were derived.

Montessori believed that the direct training of the senses would develop thought, would develop intelligence. She implied that such training would create organized images upon which thought could operate. In other words, implicit in her writings is the notion that direct training of the senses actually may be direct training in mental imagery. By encouraging finer and finer observations and discriminations, with less and less trial and error, and more and more reliance on visual judgment alone, these activities develop visual representational processes. Through such training, the visual representations of the objects and of their attributes might become 1) more differentiated, 2) more firmly imprinted (carved in stone rather than scratched in wax) and therefore more reliable, 3) more readily activated by sensory input (i.e., minimal input which previous to the training did not activate visual representations now does activate them), and 4) more readily accessed by, or available to, thinking processes.

The Montessori activities also seem to promote more complex visual thought processes. The children are constantly judging, comparing, and selecting items according to some visual attribute. One might expect that eventually the child would internalize these visual thinking activities and become skilled in performing such thinking not only with the actual stimuli themselves but also with their generalized images. With practice, the child would require less information from the immediate environment to perform these mental operations and rely more on visual representations.

Finally, Montessori believed that such experiences might facilitate better attention to and observation of the environment in general and not only of those attributes emphasized. This general greater attention to attributes of objects might yield a large stock of mental images which would become available to thought.

Jean Piaget (1896-1980)

Piaget, unlike Steiner and Montessori, was not directly interested in education but rather in how the child went about acquiring knowledge. His contribution to education is therefore indirect, through adaptations of his observations and of his theories by educators. Since Piaget's writings are voluminous, rather complex, and open to various interpretations, these adaptations into concrete educational practice vary widely from each other.

A brief discussion of Piaget's cognitive-development theory will help to clarify his views concerning the function of imagery and the role imagery might have in education. Piaget argued that knowledge growth is a function of internal mechanisms which adapt and transform external information [28]. In the infant, these internal mechanisms are sensorimotor processes that coordinate sensory and motor activity. Repeated coordinating activity results in sensorimotor schemes, in systematic arrangement of sensorimotor representations. These sensorimotor schemes constitute the building blocks for further knowledge, and for further complex coordinations and schemes. The increasingly complex organization of mental thought structures is reflected in observable changes in the child's interaction with the environment, in the manner he/she solves problems, particularly logical problems: As the child's internal knowledge structures develop, he/she becomes less and less dependent upon environmental appearances and relies more and more on logical deductions. In present-day information-processing language, one could say that as the child develops cognitively, he/she moves from a totally data-driven state to a predominantly concept-driven state.

There are definite milestones in this cognitive development; each change in the cognitive process is necessary to the following one. Several early sensorimotor stages follow each other in quick succession. An important change during this early period is the acquisition of representational capacities, or memory. One of these representational capacities is imagery. Around the ages six or seven, the concrete operational stage of thought begins. The presence of concrete operations in thought is reflected in a child's ability to conserve on Piaget's well-known conservation tasks. For instance, the child is shown two identical beakers containing an equal amount of water. Subsequently, the content of one of the two beakers is poured into a container of different dimensions, let us say a tall thin glass. A child who is in possession of the concrete operations will not be fooled by the inequality of the water levels but will know that the amounts of liquid in the two containers is still identical. The final stage of logical thought begins at age eleven or twelve, when the child becomes capable of logical hypothetical deductions and able to perform operations not only upon the objects themselves, but between classes, relationships, etc. of objects.

What role does Piaget give mental imagery in this scheme of thought development? When the infant begins to develop representational thought, mental imagery emerges as one of the symbolic functions together with language. For Piaget, mental images are not mere photocopies of the external world but internal representations resulting from internalized imitations of the movements of the eyes [29]. Therefore images are not identical to perceptions but resemble perceptions in that the imitation involved "actively copies the perceptual data, and may even elicit sensations in the same way as an imagined movement elicits muscular contractions" [30, p. 69].

Piaget distinguishes two types of images: reproductive images, "which are limited to evoking sights that have been perceived previously," and anticipatory images "which envisage movements or transformations as well as their results, although the subject has not previously observed them" [30, p. 71]. For instance, we can predict that when equal amounts of water are poured into a thin test tube and into a bowl, the water level in the test tube will be much higher than in the bowl. We can anticipate and envision this outcome even though we may never have made such a comparison.

Piaget found that the mental images of the young, preoperative child typically are static and merely reproduce what has been seen [29, 31]. Only after the age of 7, do his/her images become truly anticipatory and are no longer based merely on reproductions.

According to Piaget, it is operational thought which produces this change in the type of mental image, and it is not anticipatory imagery which produces operational thought. For instance, if a child does not conserve, he claims that no amount of perceptual information at that point will bring the child to conserve. It is only the operational thought which allows the emergence of the image (as the result) of transformations yet unknown. Therefore, he views imagery as a symbolic instrument and an auxiliary instrument, which is not an element of thought itself but simply an aid to the process of thought. "After the age of seven or eight, the image becomes anticipatory and so better able to serve as a base for the operations. This progress is not the result of an internal or autonomous modification of the images, however, but rather the intervention of external factors due to the development of the operations" [30, p. 79]. In short, Piaget believes that imagery is at most a necessary condition in the development of operational thought but definitely not a sufficient condition.

At first glance, Piaget does not seem to give mental imagery a very important role in learning. However, closer inspection of his conception of mental imagery and of learning in general, reveals that he actually ascribes to mental imagery a very important function in cognitive development. Although he maintains that mental imagery is not sufficient for the development of operational thought, he does admit that it is a necessary condition: "Even if representation of the liquid levels is not a sufficient condition for operational compensation, it is nevertheless sooner or later necessary, and will act as an indispensable auxiliary" [29, p. 264].

Thus, mental imagery itself cannot be operational thought, but it is an essential tool of operational thought. Without mental images to represent features of the environment, the corresponding sensorimotor schemes could not develop, could not yield the symbols upon which thought must operate.

An expansion of the previous example will reveal the implications of Piaget's concept about the interaction between imagery and thought. In predicting the different levels of liquids in the bowl and the test tube, based upon the knowledge that the height of the liquid is a function of the width of the container, we perform the following logical operation: The test tube is much narrower than the bowl, therefore, the water must go higher in the test tube. This mental operation then determines our anticipatory imagery about the water levels. Yet, if we had not had previous experiences with differently shaped containers and different content levels (or with events that yielded similar experiences) and if we had no representations of these experiences, no images, we could not have derived (at least not on our own) the essential knowledge structure of the relationship between height and width of the container and the height of the liquid.

Piaget's conception of the growth of knowledge also implies a central role for imagery in learning. Piaget maintained that the child's active interaction with the environment is critical for cognitive growth, that all knowledge is constructed, is reinvented by the individual himself/herself.

> The fundamental relationship that constitutes all knowledge is not, therefore, a mere "association" between objects, for this notion neglects the active role of the subject, but rather the "assimilation" of objects to the schemes of that subject [32, p. 24].

The impetus for cognitive growth results from the observation of one's own actions and the actions of others. It results from the observation of the effects of these actions upon the environment and from the reflection upon these observations [33].

This emphasis on the child's interaction with the environment, on the child's systematic observation of the result of his/her actions, and on the reflection upon the outcome of these actions, are features in Piaget's theory that, if they were contained in an educational program, would encourage the acquisition of a rich store of reproductive or static mental images, and the use of these images in problem solving, in more abstract thought.

How such experiences might be realized in an educational setting is shown in a program for preschoolers developed by Sigel and his colleagues [34, 35]. The program contains many art and construction activities, which Sigel calls visible thinking activities.

We ourselves have found that systematic art instruction in forming clay promotes creativity as well as the acquisition of concrete operations [36]. We have speculated that imagery is a plausible mediator [37]. In creating a picture, a sculpture, or in constructing a building, the child must have a visual representation, an image of the object he/she is making. He/She must continuously compare his/her construction with the image. He/She constantly must be able to anticipate the kind of changes necessary in the construction to achieve the desired outcome. The actual performance of such construction tasks confronts the child with unknowns about the actual appearance of familiar objects. For example, a car, yes, it has four wheels, but where exactly are the wheels placed on the bottom of the car? Such construction experiences prompt the child to check out the environment further, and to reflect upon these observations. In sum, such activities appear to be ideal for nurturing both reproductive and anticipatory imagery.

Educational programs influenced by Piaget exist more commonly for the younger child [38, 39]. The programs for older students, which have a Piagetian basis are usually innovative science programs [40, 41]. Here again, the emphasis is typically on the interaction of the individual with the environment. The students are prompted to formulate hypotheses, and to conduct experiments or to carry out whatever manipulations necessary to confirm or revise their hypotheses.

Issues Arising From Steiner, Montessori, and Piaget

The path to knowledge is real experience and not experience presented through didactic instructions of a teacher. Upon this point all three, Steiner, Montessori, and Piaget, agree. The educational practices they advocate and that are implied in their theories, all emphasize experience with the environment. They thereby provide the necessary conditions for the development of rich mental imagery.

In contrast to this fundamental consensus, there is no agreement amongst them on more complex questions such as, What is the nature of the mental images essential to cognitive growth? How can the acquisition of imagery be promoted? How does imagery actually function in thought, in problem solving, or in gaining understanding of abstract events? We shall discuss some of these disagreements, since we believe their resolution is fundamental to research on imagery in education.

What Kind of Imagery? As we had noted in the introduction, the term mental imagery is vague, and it has had many different meanings throughout the ages. It seems virtually impossible to define mental imagery more concretely. Yet, some reflection will show that Steiner, Montessori, and Piaget differ in their conception of imagery in tangible and describable ways. One can draw up an operational definition of imagery for each of the three, based upon the educational practices they consider important. For Montessori, the central issue is the refinement and organization of imagery derived from basic sensory perception of physical attributes of objects (attributes such as size, form, and color). It is development along these dimensions that she believed necessary for classification and for higher-level conceptual abstraction.

Piaget gives the most tangible definition of imagery and even has described ways of assessing the use of imagery by asking the child to draw outcomes of transformations. It will be remembered that he distinguishes between two types of imagery which differ with respect to their nature and their functions: 1) representational imagery, the visual representation of static objects (not necessarily representation of their attributes, as is the case with Montessori), and 2) anticipatory imagery which envisions changes and transformations of objects and their attributes. Piaget believes that the two types of imagery are discontinuous developmentally. Even though representational imagery occurs earlier than anticipatory imagery, the latter does not emerge out of the former. Representational imagery is of great importance because it is a tool of thought development, an essential feature for a child's acquisition of logical thought structures. It is out of these logical thought structures that anticipatory imagery emerges and can, in turn, become a tool for even more complex abstract logical thought.

Steiner emphasizes the content of the images: For him the duty of education is to develop the images of nature, and to use these nature images to bring about an understanding of modern-day abstractions and inventions—the association of the unknown, the abstract, with images from life. He gives importance not only to static images, but also to images of living organisms interacting with each other and with the elements of nature. It seems that initially the images are of a representational kind; the teacher evokes images of actual objects and also uses actual objects, or pictures of objects for instruction. However, very soon these representational images are used in a transformational manner. The teaching of alphabet letters through gradual modification of representations of real objects into abstract symbols illustrates this transformational use; for example,

the drawing of a fish is altered into an f and an upper lip is changed into an M. Thus, in contrast to Piaget's position, the representational images and anticipatory images are not totally separate entities, rather the representational images come to have a transformational function.

Facilitation of Imagery: Role of the Teacher. Both Piaget and Montessori renounce the importance of the teacher in promoting intellectual growth. In fact, they even consider that the teacher-student interactions can obstruct the learning process under certain conditions. Montessori's motto will be remembered: "Things are the best teachers."

Steiner's position on this point is in sharp contrast. The teacher is a pivotal factor in the educational process; his/her behavior becomes a model for the children to internalize. The personal bond between teacher and student is so important that the teacher is to remain with the class from kindergarten until the child leaves school. The teacher is the key to the selection of thought pictures appropriate to the children. He/She ensures that these original thought pictures are reintroduced whenever necessary for making abstractions understood.

It is obvious that the child has to do the actual learning by himself/herself. Furthermore, if a child is to learn from the instructions of the teacher, the teacher and child must focus on the same event and from the same perspective; it is impossible to ensure such a situation. Should the child focus on something different, the learning intended by the teacher may not take place, or worse, the child may misunderstand, may actually learn something wrong.

It is nevertheless also obvious that each child does not reinvent the wheel but that much of his/her knowledge is acquired from members of his/her society. These opposing views of the role of the teacher must somehow be integrated, must be resolved. This is particularly necessary with respect to the presently very popular position of Vygotsky, who proposes that the joint performance of tasks by mother and child, or teacher and child is the major vehicle for learning.

Facilitation of Imagery: Role of a Prepared Environment. Our three authors differ again on the importance they ascribe to a prepared environment for facilitating learning. For Montessori, the prepared environment is fundamental to the establishment of systematic, organized mental images. Specific materials are necessary for the development of the appropriate perceptual differentiations and their related visual representations. The success of education is based upon choosing the right kind of stimuli (toys) for the children to interact with.

Piaget, in contrast, does not believe that the nature of the cognitive structures changes nor that the rate at which these structures are acquired is appreciably affected as a function of the learning environment (at least not within normal ranges of environmental fluctuations). In other words, the nature of reproductive imagery and the nature and derivation of anticipatory imagery are not perceptibly altered by environmental circumstances, nor can the acquisition of imagery be speeded up through alterations in the environment. It is noteworthy, however, that the Piagetian educational programs in the United States and in England do betray considerable preoccupation with the arrangement of the environment. Moreover, the studies on learning by Inhelder, Sinclair, and Bovet provide us with some guidelines with repsect to the kind of environment that would enhance cognitive growth [33].

Steiner takes an intermediate position here. The teacher should use materials based upon the children's experiences and from nature in order to develop meaningful thought pictures, or images, upon which the abstractions can be pegged. The teacher, though, is given much latitude in choosing the specific materials. He/she develops many instructional items on his/her own. The "canning" of the educational materials, as in Montessori classrooms, would be counter to the Waldorf school philosophy.

How Does Imagery Function in Thought? As yet, there is no comprehensive and no precise description of how imagery might function in different kinds of thought: in problem solving, in gaining deeper understanding of phenomena, or in creativity. Each of our authors seems to have looked at somewhat different parts of the puzzle of imagery in thought. Perhaps we need a model or a metaphor that captures the different roles of imagery more comprehensively and describes the specific processes more concretely. Maybe we need a better "image" of imagery than those which have been used until now. In the final part of this paper, we will propose a metaphor that may fulfill this function.

IMPLICATIONS FOR RESEARCH

During the last fifteen years, beginning with the Symposium on Imagery in Children's Learning [42], there has been a sharp upswing in the number of studies on mental imagery. Does our historical survey of the concept of mental imagery have any message for present research in mental imagery and education?

Our historical account identifies two different educational functions of imagery: 1) the use of imagery to represent in the mind information grasped through our senses, particularly the visual sense; 2) the use of imagery in problem solving, in understanding unobservable relationships among observable events, and in creative thought. The distinction between the two is very important, but it is frequently not made. The first function of imagery, which is called representational imagery in Piagetian terms, reflects a conceptualization of the manner in which factual knowledge is stored in specific concrete images. The second function, which is called anticipatory or transformational imagery in Piagetian terms, requires manipulation of images of a more abstract nature. It reflects the role imagery plays in active memory enhancement, in acquiring a clear and full understanding of the nature, character, or functioning of phenomena. In short, it refers to the role imagery plays in higher cognitive processes.

Recent research has dealt mainly with the representational function, with imagery as an encoding process of visual information [14, 43, 44]. The second function of imagery been studied mainly with respect to the simplest type of memory aid — the use of imagery to enhance paired-associate learning [43, 45, 46]. The more complex role of imagery in memory, as in the method of *loci* and in Luria's patient, and the role of imagery in gaining full understanding of the environment, in acquiring knowledge that is useful in dealing with the physical world, has not yet been studied thoroughly.

Educators, though, must come to understand the second, more elusive function of imagery. They must do more than emphasize the visual representation of information; they must go beyond using imagery merely as a helpful mnemonic device. Researchers in the ivory tower and researchers in the schools must try to unlock how mental imagery functions in thought, in problem solving, in the prediction of possible outcomes of hypothetical actions. All our verbal understanding is useless, if we cannot at some point translate it into manipulations, actions, and constructions in the world around us. The ultimate test of whether understanding is useful, whether it is functional, is the application of that understanding to coping with the real world.

From Simonides to Aquinas, to Steiner, Montessori and Piaget, thinkers realized that abstract concepts cannot be taught through words alone, but rather that images are necessary for their full understanding. They recognized that imagery formed an integral part of problem solving and creativity.

Montessori, Piaget, and Steiner offer suggestions for research into this second function of imagery. Particularly relevant to the function of imagery in more complex thought are two interesting notions about imagery.

1. Montessori and Piaget stress the importance of interaction with the environment. The implication in their argument is that *imagery arising from active investigation of the environment will be a "better" kind of imagery* for attaining a full understanding and for problem solving than will be imagery elicited indirectly through words, or imagery elicited by passive observation of phenomena.

2. Piaget and Steiner present the notion of an image undergoing changes and transformations. This notion of the changing image is essential for understanding images in problem solving, in unlocking new knowledge. This feature of images has not been captured in the metaphors that typically have been used: the "picture in the head," the "wax imprint." These metaphors are static ones, focusing on the structural nature of imagery. The static connotations of the word "image," itself, obstruct our appreciation of the more complex kinds of images that are necessary for complex thought, namely images that clarify relationships, that capture movements, or that are composite generalizations of characteristics of similar but not identical objects. It is these types of images, or visual representations, that are important in problem solving, in bridging the gap between the known and the unknown, in mediating the transfer of characteristics from the familiar to the unfamiliar. What is needed are metaphors that capture these functions of imagery in higher cognitive processes.

For instance, the function of imagery in Einstein's discovery was the creation of a familiar analogue of the abstract, elusive phenomenon to be understood. In creating an analogue with which we are familiar and which is similar in certain essential ways to the invisible, or vague phenomenon, we build ourselves a bridge from the known to the unknown.

To help us further understand mental imagery, we propose the *lock and key* metaphor introduced by Sheperd [1]: The image of the known phenomenon acts as a key to the unknown. The key fits, if the image captures essential characteristics of the unknown phenomenon and thereby unlocks a door to further understanding of the unknown phenomeon. The lock and key metaphor is an appropriate metaphor for mental imagery, if the images created by the metaphor capture the characteristics of the functions of imagery in thought. The key will fit the lock, if the image of locks and keys extends our grasp of imagery, letting us search for the relevant characteristics.

Let us explore how this image of a lock and key might help us to understand imagery. The analogy we are proposing is that images are to problem solving as keys are to locks: The images are the keys, the problems to be understood are the locks. Such an analogy immediately lets us see the importance of rich and differentiated images. The more images we have, the more keys we have with which to unlock problems, to unlock new understanding. Some keys will not fit at all, some keys will fit in the keyhole but will not turn. Still other keys will unlock only an antechamber, or perhaps even the wrong door. And then there is one key that unlocks the door to a room which leads us to greater understanding.

Let us carry this image of lock and key one step further: The more differentiated our observations, the more differentiated will be our images, and the more differentiated will be the teeth of the keys we have. As infants, we start out with blank keys and over time the keys come to have more and more teeth. The doors of early understanding have locks which require keys of little differentiation in their teeth arrangement. The more complex and abstract the phenomena become, the more complex are their locks, and the more sharply differentiated must be the keys. Perhaps, the images derived from active observation of the environment will yield finer and sharper teeth in our keys than the images derived from words or passive observation.

The task of the teacher is to help the pupil to acquire many keys, with differentiated teeth, and to classify the keys according to certain features. Perhaps Montessori pointed the way with her sensory education. It is interesting to note here that a recent review of preschool programs suggests that for boys, 1 year of Montessori preschool experience has positive effects on school performance five to seven years later [47].

The teacher must learn which images will help the child attain full understanding of complex phenomena, which images contain the essential features for unlocking a certain kind of knowledge. Steiner's pictorial method of instruction, which uses images from nature and from everyday life, may be a good place for study to begin.

Finally, the teacher also must help the pupil to fit the key to the lock, to produce images that will relate to the phenomena which is to be understood. The pupil must learn to control and to manipulate his/her visual images. Individuals who can control and manipulate their images are able to apply their images successfully in problem solving; whereas, individuals who have only static images, albeit of great vividness, cannot [48].

In applying the characteristics of locks and keys to imagery and problem solving, we have modeled one way in which imagery may function in problem solving, namely, through the application of characteristics of the known to the unknown.

Our review of imagery in education has revealed several functions for images in mental activities. The function most interesting, yet most neglected until now, is the role of imagery in complex thought: its role in the understanding of phenomena, in creativity, and in problem solving.

REFERENCES

1. R. N. Shepard, The Mental Image, *American Psychologist*, *33*, pp. 125-137, 1978.
2. R. R. Holt, Imagery: The Return of the Ostracized, *American Psychologist*, *19*, pp. 254-264, 1964.
3. F. Attneave, How Do You Know?, *American Psychologist*, *29*, pp. 493-499, 1974.
4. Plato, Theaetetus, *Plato's Theory of Knowledge*, F. M. Cornford (trans.), Bobbs-Merrill Co., Inc., New York, New York, 1957.
5. A. E. Taylor, *The Mind of Plato*, University of Michigan Press, Ann Arbor, Michigan, 1922.
6. Aristotle, *De Anima: In the Version of William of Moerbeke and the Commentary of St. Thomas Aquinas*, K. Foster and S. Humphries (trans.), Yale University Press, New Haven, Connecticut, 1951.
7. Aristotle, *On the Soul, Parvia Naturalia, on Breath*, W. S. Heet (trans.), Harvard University Press, Cambridge, Massachusetts, 1936.
8. *Rhetorica ad Herennium*, H. Caplan (trans.), Harvard University Press, Cambridge, Massachusetts, 1944.
9. M. T. Cicero, *De Oratore*, H. Rackham (trans.), Harvard University Press, Cambridge, Massachusetts, 1948.
10. M. F. Quintilian, *Institutio Oratoria*, H. E. Butler (trans.), G. P. Putnam's Sons, New York, New York, 1921.
11. A. R. Luria, *The Mind of a Mnemonist*, Basic Books, Inc., New York, New York, 1968.
12. F. A. Yates, *The Art of Memory*, Routledge and Kegan Paul, London, England, 1966.
13. S. M. Kosslyn, S. Pinker, G. E. Smith, and S. P. Schwartz, On the Demystification of Mental Imagery, *The Behavioral and Brain Sciences*, *2*, pp. 535-581, 1979.
14. S. M. Kosslyn, *Image and Mind*, Harvard University Press, Cambridge, Massachusetts, 1980.
15. W. J. Stahl, R. Johnson, and E. L. Burge, *Martianus Capella and the Seven Liberal Arts*, Vols. 2 and 3, Columbia University, New York, New York, 1971.
16. A. Magnus, De Bono, in *Opera Omnia*, H. Kuhle, C. Feckes, B. Geyer, and W. Kubel (eds.), Monasterii Westafalorum in Aedibus Aschendorff, Vol. 28, 1951.
17. T. Aquinas, *Summa Theologica*, D. J. Sullivan (trans.), Encyclopaedia Brittanica, Chicago, Illinois, 1952.
18. M. C. Wittrock, The Generative Processes of Memory, in *The Human Brain*, M. C. Wittrock (ed.), Prentice-Hall, Inc., Englewood Cliffs, New Jersey, 1977.
19. W. J. Ong, *Ramus: Method and the Decay of Dialogue*, Harvard University Press, Cambridge, Massachusetts, 1958.
20. H. Mehan, *Learning Lessons*, Harvard University Press, Cambridge, Massachusetts, 1979.

21. M. Montessori, *The Montessori Method*, A. E. George (trans.), (Original work published 1912), Robert Bentley, Inc., Cambridge, Massachusetts, 1965.

22. M. Montessori, *Spontaneous Activity in Education*, F. Simmonds (trans.), (Original work published 1917), Schocken Books, Inc., New York, New York, 1965.

23. R. Steiner, *The Roots of Education*, H. Fox (trans.), Rudolf Steiner Press, London, England, 1968.

24. R. Steiner, *The Modern Art of Education*, J. Darrell (trans.), Rudolf Steiner Press, London, England, 3rd edition, 2nd impression, 1972.

25. R. Steiner, *The Kingdom of Childhood*, H. Fox (trans.), Rudolf Steiner Press, London, England, 2nd impression, 1st English publication 1964, 1974.

26. L. B. Miller and R. P. Bizzell, The Long-Term Effects of Four Preschool Programs: Sixth, Seventh and Eighth Grades, *Child Development*, *54*, pp. 727-741, 1983.

27. M. Montessori, *The Absorbent Mind*, Holt, Rinehart and Winston, New York, New York, 1967.

28. J. Piaget, *L'épistémologie génétique*, Presses Universitaires de France, Paris, France, 1972.

29. J. Piaget and B. Inhelder, *Mental Imagery in the Child: A Study of the Development of Imaginal Representation*, P. A. Chilton (trans.), Basic Books, New York, New York, 1971.

30. J. Piaget and B. Inhelder, *The Psychology of the Child*, Basic Books, New York, New York, 1969.

31. B. Inhelder, Operational Thought and Symbolic Imagery, *Monographs of the Society for Research in Child Development*, *30*, pp. 5-18, 1965.

32. J. Piaget, The Psychogenesis of Knowledge and its Epistemological Significance, *Language and Learning: The Debate between Jean Piaget and Noam Chomsky*, Harvard University Press, Cambridge, Massachusetts, pp. 23-34, 1980.

33. B. Inhelder, H. Sinclair, and M. Bovet, *Learning and the Development of Cognition*, Harvard University Press, Cambridge, Massachusetts, 1974.

34. I. E. Sigel, A. Secrist, and G. Forman, Psychoeducational Intervention Beginning at Age Two: Reflections and Outcomes, in *Compensatory Education for Children, Ages Two to Eight: Recent Studies of Educational Intervention*, J. C. Stanley (ed.), John Hopkins University Press, Baltimore, Maryland, 1973.

35. C. Copple, I. E. Sigel, and R. Saunders, *Educating the Young Thinker: Classroom Strategies for Cognitive Growth*, D. Van Nostrand Company, New York, New York, 1979.

36. G. E. Speidel and A. L. Pickens, Art, Mental Imagery and Cognition, in *The Potential of Fantasy and Imagination*, A. A. Sheikh and J. T. Shaffer (eds.), Brandon House, Inc., New York, New York, pp. 199-213, 1979.

37. G. E. Speidel, Developing Creative Thinking Through Clay Forming Activities, *Educational Perspectives*, in press.

38. M. Almy, The Impact of Piaget on Early Childhood Education, in *The Impact of Piagetian Theory*, F. B. Murray (ed.), University Park Press, Baltimore, Maryland, pp. 159-189, 1979.

39. K. Lovell, Intellectual Growth and the School Curriculum, in *The Impact of Piagetian Theory*, F. B. Murray (ed.), University Park Press, Baltimore, Maryland, pp. 191-207, 1979.

40. J. W. McKinnon, The College Student and Formal Operations, in *Research, Teaching, and Learning with the Piaget Model*, J. W. Renner, D. G. Stafford, A. E. Lawson, J. W. McKinnon, F. E. Friot, and D. Kellogg (eds.), University of Oklahoma Press, Norman, Oklahoma, pp. 110-129, 1976.

41. F. E. Friot, Curriculum Experiences and Movement from Concrete-Operational Thought, in *Research, Teaching and Learning with the Piaget Model*, J. W. Renner, D. G. Stafford, A. E. Lawson, J. W. McKinnon, F. E. Friot, and D. Kellogg (eds.), University of Oklahoma Press, Norman, Oklahoma, pp. 79-89, 1976.

42. H. W. Reese, Imagery in Children's Learning: A Symposium, *Psychological Bulletin, 73*, pp. 383-421, 1970.

43. A. Paivio, *Imagery and Verbal Processes*, Holt, Rinehard and Winston, New York, New York, 1971.

44. S. Pinker, Mental Imagery and the Third Dimension, *Journal of Experimental Psychology, 109*, pp. 354-371, 1980.

45. A. Paivio, Neomentalism, *Canadian Journal of Psychology, 29*:4, pp. 263-291, 1975.

46. W. D. Rohwer, Images and Pictures in Children's Learning, *Psychological Bulletin, 73*, pp. 393-403, 1970.

47. L. B. Miller and R. P. Bizzell, The Long-Term Effects of Four Preschool Programs: Sixth, Seventh and Eighth Grades, *Child Development, 54*, pp. 727-741, 1983.

48. M. E. Troy, *The Function of Imagery as a Mediator in Relational Learning*, Unpublished Doctoral Dissertation, University of Hawaii, 1983.

CHAPTER 2

Imaginative Play: Its Implication for the Process of Education

DIANA SHMUKLER

The present century is marked by an appreciation of childhood, and contemporary investigators are genuinely seeking to understand the child's developing intellect with a view to guiding it. Intelligence as a concept has been found lacking in explaining how the child deals with new situations. On the other hand, creativity is an elusive notion which does not lend itself readily to assessment or definition. In the search for understanding the child's intellect, if we observe how young children express themselves naturally and react to new experience, we see an activity which does not appear to be immediately goal directed and which adults call play. Imaginative play in the young child appears to be an overt expression of aspects of creativity in that it "makes something out of nothing."

As we watch preschoolers creating scenes and characters out of thin air, swinging on a swing making the accompanying sounds of a jet plane, gently putting a doll to bed with soothing sounds, we cannot but be slightly overcome and awed by the sense of being deeply in touch with the developing child's emotional and conceptual world. Imaginative play in young children is readily observed and appears to be a manifestation and expression of the human tendency to create, transcend the immediate, and be aware of the possible.

Imaginative play has been of longstanding interest to psychologists, researchers, educators, and parents. Despite different emphases, followers of the major schools of psychology agree that it serves important developmental goals. Yet imaginative play continues to pose a number of problems for academic psychology. A major difficulty is one of suitable definition. Inherent in the problem of definition, lie other questions such as its nature, function, and purpose. Thus an integrated approach to understanding imaginative play, necessitates a look at the various perspectives from which it has been described.

The earliest descriptions of play in man arose from an evolutionary or biological orientation. According to this view, as a species progresses up the phylogenetic scale, the young engage in longer, more frequent, and more complex sequences of play. Play is seen as practice, in a safe environment (where survival risks are lowered), of evolutionarily important skills and behavior. The freedom to experiment and explore in relative safety is considered an important aspect of the definition of play, and thus imaginative play is firmly rooted in man's survival mechanisms.

The major contributions to a psychological understanding of play, particularly symbolic play, came from the clinical perspective emphasizing its affective role on the one hand and the cognitive developmental role, which stresses intellectual growth, on the other.

As psychoanalytically oriented clinicians began working directly with emotionally disturbed children, a number of important facts about play soon became apparent. First, it was used as a medium of communication, since a young child is often unable to articulate his/her feelings or the nature of the problem. It is the natural tendency of play to express what is uppermost or pressing. In this sense then, symbolic play, like free association and catharsis, reveals the emotional and intellectual status of the child. Of further significance was the insight that the play process itself provides the therapy and is thus autotherapeutic [1-3].

From the analytic perspective, play was seen as drive reducing and hence pleasurable to both normal and disturbed children. Although the clinical perspective is recognized as offering an important explanation of the emotional role that play has in development, it suffers from the criticisms that can be levelled at the more general theory of drive reduction and homeostatis [4, 5]. White and others have shown that we must adopt a broader view of motivation [5]. Exploration, curiosity, and the need for competence and mastery are part of our inherent nature, have evolutionary significance, and often supercede more fundamental biological needs such as hunger, sleep, or safety. The ego analysts, in particular, have developed theories of play which stress the competence and mastery aspects [6].

The cognitive theorists, who studied the growing intellectual awareness of the child, recognized that play was serving major intellectual goals [7-11]. Piaget's monumental contribution rests firmly on careful observation of children, often in natural settings. Inevitably he addressed the question of the nature of such a commonly occurring behavior as play. He integrates play into his more general theory, and in so doing he discusses it from a stage perspective. The play stages follow the more general stages of development. The first stage is marked by mastery or sensory-motor play. Symbolic play follows, arising at the same time as the semiotic or symbolizing function, and in fact is seen as part of this more general capacity. During the final play stage, children prefer games with consensually agreed-upon rules. Piaget places play at the assimilation end of the assimilation-accommodation cycle and stresses its link with the creative process. Piaget has been criticized for disregarding the affective features and not giving play a more central role in intellectual growth; for, he regards it as less important to the construction of cognitive schema than accommodation [9-11]. By contrast, Vygotsky emphasizes the intellectual achievement of using an object in a pretend sense, to stand in place of or as a pivot for a concrete object; thus, he gives play a key position in intellectual development [2].

The most recent approaches to play rest on a cognitive-affective integration and signal a more general trend in psychology. They rest on the belief that we cannot afford to focus on one aspect to the exclusion of the other. Therefore, we need a model which allows for a true integration of both cognitive and affective development.

Singer is a leading exponent of a cognitive-affective view, and he provides a conceptual framework for such an integration [13-16]. His empirical research opened the way for the flourishing interest and investigations of the last decade, and this led to a greater appreciation of the importance of imaginative play to developmental psychology, in general, and of its clinical and educational possibilities, in particular.

It seems that Singer's approach, based on a broad, integrative theoretical understanding and a sound methodology, is well suited to dealing with the complexity and practical implications of the question addressed in this review.

A COGNITIVE-AFFECTIVE INTEGRATION: SINGER'S APPROACH TO IMAGINATIVE PLAY

In integrating cognition with affect, Singer addressed the major criticisms levelled at previous approaches [13]. His integration, however, goes beyond a mere combination; for, he provides a model which shows how cognition and affect are interlinked and function together. He sees Tomkins' theory of affect as both the most general and the most specific for describing play phenomena [17]. Whereas the classic psychoanalysts ascribe motivation to drive, Tomkins views affect, one of the organism's basic systems, as a more useful alternative. Man's emotions are related to the rate and complexity of his information-processing function. Incoming material is compared with the material in long-term storage, and this is used as feedback about the discrepancy between the present state and the stored information. In this way, the affect system is activated so that it is both motivational and cue producing. Affective behavior is seen as determined by the rate and persistence of cognitive input directly at the level of the neuronal firing process. Three fundamental instances are considered: when information comes in too fast for adequate processing, the resultant emotion is anxiety; if incoming information is too persistent and repetitive, it leads to frustration; and when it comes neither too fast nor too slowly but is readily assimilated, the experience is pleasurable with affects varying from arousal, to interest, to satisfaction, and to joy. The stress on the rate of input allows us to talk about assimilation of material into established schema at a rate which can match previously learned material. When the child has control over the rate and complexity of the incoming material, he/she can develop a novel stimulating environment, recycle and integrate material into existing schema in tune with his/her limited and developing cognitive schemata. All this is accompanied by the alternating affects of surprise, interest, joy, and liveliness.

This model then highlights the control and mastery aspects emphasized by Erikson [6], Sutton-Smith [9] and White [5]: the assimilation to existing schema of new material [8] and the pleasurable positive affect [1, 3]. It goes further than a cathartic model, by suggesting that mood can be altered by the play and fantasy process. The cognitive model is extended by relating information processing to affect and bringing in the motives of autonomy and competence as fundamental developmental goals. Singer views imaginative play as a fundamental potential available to every child. He considers it to be a cognitive skill that enables the child to explore both his/her internal and external environment and that allows for the processing and reprocessing of material until it is fully assimilated. In this model, the brain is seen as endlessly processing and reprocessing material, with a set towards attending to it, rather than as functioning as a static computer.

Singer's definition of imaginative play is probably one of the most comprehensive ones to date, resting on his integrated conceptual framework.

> It is a form of exploration, a controlled examination of novelty and a gradual assimilation of that novelty that is accompanied by the alternating affects of interest, surprise and joy. But the exploration is not of the physical environment but of a stimulus field created by the child's as yet insufficiently assimilated experiences and fantasies or memories of adult interactions or communications [15, pp. 33, 34].

An Approach to the Study of Imaginative Play: Methodology

"One of the messages of this book is that we had better get on with the work of formal research in addition to theorizing" [13, p. 42].

The empirical work of the last decade has focused on isolating the adaptive features, cross-cultural and subgroup differences, intervention strategies, and the implications of this research for clinical, educational, and developmental settings. The publication of *The Child's World of Make-Believe* [13] a decade ago, which rests on the view that "man's inner products are available for scientific study [18, p. 26], marked a new era in the scientific approach to the study of children's imaginative play. Imaginative play is a form of readily observable overt behavior, which lends itself to high observer and rater agreement in regard to occurrence, frequency, and intensity. The basic method rests on direct observations of children's spontaneous play and subsequent ratings, which have been shown to be consistently reliable. In conjunction with observation of levels of play, Singer uses a simple interview technique, which involves asking children directly about their play behavior. One of the questions concerns imaginary friends, whose presence in early childhood has been linked to creativity in adolescence and adulthood [19-21]. The Imaginative Play Predisposition Inventory (IPPI) has been shown both to be reliable and to distinguish children who are high on overt imaginative-play behavior from children who are low [13].

ADAPTIVE FEATURES OF IMAGINATIVE PLAY: BENEFITS TO THE DEVELOPING CHILD

"Make believe behavior of children is an important facet of development, socialization and cognitive growth" [15, p. 67].

The studies of the correlates and benefits of imaginative-play predisposition are extensively reviewed by Singer [13-15]. What follows below are the main features with particular focus on the importance of imaginative play to the educational process. Fantasy[1] is viewed as a skill that can be used in a variety of ways: to plan; to anticipate; to amuse ourselves, and to maximize our human potential.

Imaginative Play and Affect

In line with the theoretical position adopted above, imaginative play is seen as a means of coping with redundant stimulation and a way of controlling emotion. Imaginative play is likely to generate positive affect because the child controls the rate and persistence of inputs and is able to deal with internal material in his/her own time. The empirical evidence that exists concerning the relationships between imaginative activity and affect suggests that by using fantasy skills to turn to a novel stimulus field, the child can reduce or escape from the effects of an unpleasant external environment and so indirectly control affect. Fantasy is seen as a means of changing mood rather than reducing drive, as in a cathartic model (see [22] and discussion below).

The positive emotions of interest, joy, liveliness, and excitement seem to be a result of processing and of the control the child can exercise. These positive and motivating features contain the key to the autolectic and autotherapeutic aspects of play. The use of imaginative sequences in interactions with young children is likely to increase their level of joy, happiness, and positive experience and is an important aspect of this approach. Simply making children happier at school has intrinsic value. Empirical studies consistently show positive relationships between high levels of imaginative play and positive affect [13, 14, 25, 26]. The observations on disadvantaged children are particularly important, as the benefits include changing apathy and lack of motivation to positive goal-directed behavior [26-28].

---

[1] Imaginative play, symbolic play, make-believe play will be used synonymously in this review. Fantasy and daydreaming are seen as related processes where the differences are developmental rather than in underlying structure or function [13, 23, 24].

Fantasy and Aggression. There is empirical evidence to show that children who engage in a variety of imaginative play are less likely to show aggressive behavior. Significant relationships have been found between high fantasy levels and low overt aggression [13, 29, 30]. But how this happens is the subject of much theroetical controversy.

Freud believed that fantasied aggression discharges quantities of energy and thus reduces the pressure of the aggressive drive. In a well-known study supporting this position, Feshbach showed that after exposure to frustration, subjects given the opportunity to write stories were less aggressive than those who had had no fantasy outlet [31]. Similar supporting research is provided by Spivak and Levine, for example, who showed that imaginative adolescents were less likely to be discipline problems [32]. As noted above, the clinicians generally explain the therapeutic effects in terms of catharsis.

However the bulk of evidence is in conflict with this hypothesis: It appears that fantasy opportunities increase the expression of aggression in an elicitory way or through disinhibition [33-36].

Biblow offers an interesting reconciliation of these views and highlights the possible effect of imaginative play [37]. Using Feshbach's experimental approach, he split a group of children into those who were high on imaginative predisposition and those who were low, and subjected them to a frustrating situation. Half the children in each group were given a fantasy opportunity immediately afterwards and half were not. The introduction of fantasy predisposition as an additional variable enabled Biblow to show that there is a significant difference in response between high- and low-fantasy children. High-fantasy children use fantasy to lower aggression, whereas low-fantasy children use fantasy as a model to increase expressed aggression. Therefore it seems that the role fantasy plays in the expression of aggression is complex, and it depends, among other things, on the child's predisposition to fantasy. A further significance of this study lies in its demonstration of how contrasting models can be tested.

According to the cognitive-affective position, fantasy affords the child the opportunity to change mood and thus to reduce the expression of aggression. Singer and Singer's recent research is directed towards understanding the impact of television viewing and ameliorating the effects of viewing violence in young children. The use of imaginative-play training as an intervention with parents and children, is based on the rationale that increasing fantasy skills will offer an alternative to acting out behavior and reduce the overt expression of aggression [38].

Reality vs. Fantasy: The Question of Mental Health

"Imagination may be one of the greatest untapped resources in the amelioration of pathology or in developing socially constructive orientations in all children" [15, p. 68].

It is popularly held that a high level of fantasy may be detrimental to mental health; for, it can encourage children to withdraw and cause confusion between reality and fantasy. But on the contrary, the evidence points to the fact that imaginative predisposition enables a child to deal more clearly with reality. A study by Tucker, for example, showed that more imaginative children had better recall of stories, were more accurate, and less prone to distortion [39]. Saltz and Johnson showed that children trained in imaginative play are better at detecting absurdities and show an increased ability to distinguish reality from fantasy [40, 41]. The child lacking a well-developed inner life, in fact, seems more susceptible to acting-out and poor impulse control. Singer puts this more strongly by stating: "The risks of an underdeveloped fantasy life may include delinquency, violence, overeating and the use of dangerous drugs" [42, p. 32].

The constructive possibilites of imaginative play in the normal socialization process suggest that imaginative play would be important for troubled youngsters [43]. On the other hand, the seriously disturbed youngster may be incapable of normal play. A number of studies suggest that severely disturbed children have difficulty in playing and that imaginative children are more accessible to a therapist [44]. Gould points out that the failure to develop the capacity for play can in fact be taken as a sign of serious pathology, as it blocks the normal route for working through problems [45]. A program of imaginative-play training of only brief duration with severely disturbed hospitalized children led to improved expression of feelings and increased imaginative ability [44]. Psychotherapists often try to recreate or capture the circumstances of early childhood [46, 47]. Imagination and imagery lead to vivid access to the emotional experience and often to a vivid recreation of unlabeled memories. Thus imaginative ability can be seen as an important asset at any stage of development in dealing with psychological trauma.

Imaginative Play and Creativity

"What is now proved was once only imagin'd." *William Blake*

Creativity, a term overused and misused in the popular cry for more creative solutions to the pressing problems of the late 20th century, for more creative scientists, teachers, students and politicians, is elusive, but it may become clarified through the study of play.

Throughout the literature, a theoretical connection is made between the two. Freud in "Creative Writers and Daydreaming" makes it explicit by definition [48]. Piaget also suggests that play is the source of creative imagination [8]. This connection is stressed by many others [7, 9, 11, 12, 23, 49, 50].

The term creativity means many different things to different people, and like imaginative play, it lacks clarity of definition. For this reason, when we turn to empirical studies, it makes more sense to regard creativity as an aspect of the general capacity for divergent production and then to relate aspects of cognitive skills to divergent functioning. In this way, too, imaginative play and creativity are connected implicitly by definition.

The empirical connection however is less clear than the theroetical and definitional ones. In general, research shows that "high-fantasy" children are equipped with many of the cognitive skills which contribute to the creative process.

Lieberman carried out one of the few direct studies [41, 52]. Basically she investigates the question whether the quality of a child's play provides clues to his/her divergent-thinking abilities. Playfulness, conceptualized as physical, social and cognitive spontaneity, manifest joy, and sense of humor, was found to be related, through structured tests, to ideational fluency, spontaneous flexibility, and originality. Intelligence may have been a contaminating factor, since older, brighter children were rated as being more playful and more creative.

Another study, which throws light on this question from a different perspective, is that of Dansky and Silverman [53] who showed that an increased opportunity to play with objects leads to increases in associative fluency in relation to these objects. Similarly, Sutton-Smith [9] showed that preschoolers give more alternate uses (a classic way of measuring divergent thinking, e.g. see [54]) to familiar than to unfamiliar toys.

Indirect evidence comes from Smilansky's extensive research with disadvantaged children [28]. She showed that sociodramatic play influences the creative, intellectual, and social skills of the child. The particular factors of creativity included creating new combinations out of experience, the acquisition of flexibility, a sense of creativity, the capacity to control personal responses, the increased capacity for the development of abstract thought by learning to substitute an image for overt action and then coding a verbal system for both action and image, and finally a heightened capacity for generalization.

In an interesting study, linking exploration with inventiveness and play, Hutt showed how initial exploration develops into full-blown play, and further that the more inventive, exploratory children have higher ratings of originality [55].

A number of investigations provide correlative evidence. Gottlieb, in examining the effects of modeling on fantasy production, concluded that children high in imaginative predisposition wrote more complex, well-developed stories of a divergent character [56]. Singer's studies confirm the creativity and imagination found in stories by imaginative children [13]. Research with creative adolescents and students indicates that many report having had imaginary friends[2] and having done much daydreaming in early childhood [19-21].

From a factor analytic approach to the assessment of imaginative play, Shmukler developed a model of elements of creativity based on three factors [50]. The first, an inner component of imaginative production, was shown to be

---

[2] Reports of imaginary friends are often used in research as indications of imaginative-play predisposition.

closely related to originality. The other two, identified as expressive imagination and social competence, were linked to mastery and competence, giving empirical credence to these notions of Erikson and White [5, 6].

In a further longitudinal investigation, Shmukler addressed the topic of imaginative-play predisposition [57]. Preschoolers, whose play behavior had been observed and rated, were reassessed in third grade. The earlier assessments of imaginative-play predisposition were found to be predictive and strongly related to third-grade expression of imagination and creativity, as well as to reading, comprehension, independence, and maturity. Similar results were obtained from another longitudinal study with a larger and more heterogenous sample [58].

Although there appears to be theoretical evidence and some empirical support for the notion that early predisposition towards imaginative play is linked to the capacity for divergent production, more definitive and longitudinal investigations are needed to show that it forms the basis of what is known as creative behavior.

Imaginative Play and Waiting Behavior: (Frustration Tolerance)

Young children often find themselves in situations which are potentially boring and frustrating to them. An important attribute, particularly in a school context, is frustration tolerance, for example, the ability to be seated and still and to exercise control over impulsive responses.

In one of his earliest experiments in this area, Singer demonstrated that high-fantasy children were able to better delay gratification, sit still, and contain themselves through the use of imagination and fantasy [13, 24]. Singer asked children between the ages of six and nine to pretend that they were confined in a space capsule. The imaginative subjects with skills at waiting were observed to be talking to themselves and using internal sources to occupy themselves in the potentially frustrating situation. These children, by avoiding boredom, also avoid irritation, and becoming a nuisance or discipline problem to the authorities.

The Semiotic Function: Relationship between Imagination-Play Predisposition and Language. The development of imaginative behavior has been linked to the capacity for symbolization [8, 13, 59]. It seems reasonable to believe that both imagery and language develop at the same time and are part of the more general semiotic function. The relationship is not likely to be a simple one, however, but part of a more complex feedback system [15].

Studies of the origins of pretending link early forms of pretending to language development [59, 60] and propose that the earliest forms occur at the time of the more general symbolizing capacity.

In Piagetian framework, the onset of pretend play, late in the sensory motor period, coincides with other milestones of cognitive development. Drawing together early language and symbolic play, Nicholich makes the point that both systems employ a representational component. Both involve the function of communication and of sharing objects with others [61]. Children use play and language to experiment with representational equivalence and acceptable symbolic transformations. Also both systems show substantial growth in the second year. Therefore, much correlational evidence exists of a general relationship between symbolic play and language production and comprehension in their earliest forms [59, 60] and in the later preschool and primary-school periods [13, 14, 40, 57].

Piaget suggests that symbolic activity expressed in play is useful in acquiring language, and also that the stimulation of one system should lead to an improvement of the other as a result of changes in underlying structure. Pretend vocabulary in the beginning is limited to a few gestures and a small number of single-element themes and grows, as does language, during the second year to complex combinations and elaborate themes.

The Singers conclude that at the preschool age, language and pretending form part of a complex feedback process. In an effort to express the imaginative possibilities in play, the child will draw on previous knowledge of words and word structures. The child not only practices vocabulary, but also increases his/her ability to distinguish verbally between things. The data suggest that the effects are transactional rather than causal [16, 38]. Further evidence of play and language links is outlined in the intervention studies below.

Imagery. The importance of imagery to cognitive development in particular and to psychological theory more generally is covered in good reviews (e.g., [62-65]) and in other chapters of this book. Therefore, it suffices to point out that imagery is seen as a basic form of information processing associated with storage and memory. Bruner takes a developmental approach and gives precedence to early iconic or pictorial processing [7]. Recent research has suggested that verbalization is necessary for the full development of imagery. Although imagery and imaginative play have not been specifically linked, it is implicit that imaginative play depends very much on internally generated images and on a capacity for their manipulation and organization. Some experimental evidence shows that children who report having imaginary companions are high on imagery and divergent production [66].

CONDITIONS CONDUCIVE TO THE DEVELOPMENT OF IMAGINATIVE PLAY

Early home environment, parental attitudes and practices long have been regarded by psychologists as major factors in child development. The developmental characteristics of language, concept formation, and symbolic functions are among those usually shown to be empirically related to early environmental conditions. Imaginative-play predisposition, characterized by the use of symbols, is therefore likely to fall into this category. However, little direct empirical evidence singling out salient features exists, and indirect evidence is drawn from research on creativity.

The Development of Imaginative Play

Although imaginative play can be considered a skill available to most children, optimal conditions for its development include a particular home environment and a set of early circumstances. Of primary importance to its development seems to be caring by a consistent, loving parent (parent figure) who provides security and allows the child to start building up tolerance of the parent's absence without overwhelming anxiety. According to the clinical perspective, best represented by classic psychoanalytic and object relations theory, as the infant develops the ability to "hallucinate" (form an image of) the breast, he/she will tolerate parental absence more easily [3, 67, 68]. This imaginative ability alleviates the rising anxiety. If the mother is overly protective, no opportunity arises for the infant to develop this resource. When the mother is unreliable, depressed, or abusive, there is little security or safety even in her presence. Fantasy may be the only possible way to deal with the reality, but the lack of a secure outer reality, severely stunts the child's emotional growth in another way [3].

A fascinating series of studies examines the origin of pretending in another way and views the very earliest evidence of imaginative ability from a developmental perspective [59, 60]. As described above, the onset occurs in the late sensory-motor stage and coincides with the more general development of the symbolizing capacity. The earliest appearance is the functional use of schema outside their normal context, that is, shifting from the nonpretend use of an object to the pretend use, for instance, drinking from a pretend cup, followed by pretend eating and sleeping. The child then moves to feeding someone else (usually mother) and then a doll. Fein describes this shifting sequence during which the child needs anchor support, as moving from analogue to digital processing [59]. Finally, by eighteen months, the child is free of many of the features of the immediate environment. Once the digital-process stage is reached, play becomes less and less object-centered and comprises more and more the enactment of scenarios. From this stage it becomes increasingly social and cooperative.

By three to four, the child is able to transcend space and time, and optimal development now depends on warm, concerned parents who spend time with their children but also leave them to their own devices. Imaginative play often reflects assimilated raw material of the adult world not clearly understood by the child. Tolerant, sensitive parents who support their children's immaturity and encourage expression and who are not threatened by regression and uncertainty, encourage growth and the development of expressive resources.

Characteristics of Parent-Child Interaction

Since little direct evidence exists, what follows has been extrapolated from the research on the home backgrounds of creative people. A number of years ago, Weisberg and Springer postulated that a certain set of home circumstances may not only sustain creativity but actually create it [69]. They suggested that the relationship between parent and child should be unpossessive, although not unaffectionate, and conducive to self-reliance and independence [70, 71]. This hypothesis fits well with the description above.

A study aimed directly at determining some parental characteristics important for imaginative expression by the child, was carried out by Dennis [72]. The main findings showed that mothers who were less restrictive and engaged in play and fathers who did not discourage imaginative action enhance this ability in children.

Shmukler was stimulated by the lack of much empirical evidence on this interesting question to investigate the effects of the mother-child relationship on children's imaginative-play predisposition [73]. Observations of mothers and children in an unstructured play situation showed that imaginative interaction between mother and child and giving the child room or "psychological" space in play were among the most significant factors related to the child's imaginative ability. Once the mother had structured the situation and provided some input in the form of ideas, play suggestions, and stories, what seemed to be important was her ability to move back or avoid interfering with the child's play sequence. In this way, play could develop in the child's control and in the service of the child's needs. This observational study therefore confirmed the notion that a balance between involvement and fostering of independence seems to provide conducive conditions for the development of imaginative resources.

Characteristics of Other Adults

Research on parents shows that nonintrusive, flexible, nondirective attitudes combined with involvement, caring, and taking into account a modeling effect, seem to be the optimal attitudes of parents to facilitate imaginative expression [26, 73]. One of the few empirical studies on the direct influence of adult intervenors on children's play shows that emotional involvement on the part of facilitators combined with lack of restrictiveness are the most effective in encouraging make-believe play. Adults with experience or training in child care were more effective than untrained facilitators [74]. Gershowitz recommends that involvement in early stages should be followed by a gradual decrease in adult-directed activity to best foster imaginative expression. This recommendation is in direct agreement with Shmukler's findings described above [73].

Role of Other Children

Piaget suggests that other children form an important source of cognitive input and stimulation in childhood. Much research, particularly on social development, altruism, and empathy, conducted in the last few years confirms this notion [75]. In a cross-cultural investigation which compared imaginative play in Israeli and in South African children, Udwin and Shmukler suggest that the higher levels of imagination in middle-class Israeli children are due to the greater significance of the peer group for these children [26]. A careful experiment designed to examine the effects of play tutoring (see below) by Smith, Dalgleish, and Herzmark [76] showed that social skills and participation may be the biggest single benefit of imaginative-play intervention (training). Another play training experiment, conducted by Naveh [77] with disadvantaged white South African children highlights the positive effect an "imaginative leader" (a child who is more imaginative than the rest) has on a group of low imaginative children. Such a child serves both as a model and as a source of stimulation.

SUBGROUP DIFFERENCES: CROSS-CULTURAL RESEARCH: SOCIOECONOMIC FACTORS

Introduction

It is generally accepted that situational factors, which include home backgrounds, cultural factors, and socio-economic status, play a crucial role in the development of imaginative expression. Many studies, in fact, point to deficits in all kinds of cognitive skills, in particular in language and academic abilities, in lower-class children [78-80]. Further, many investigators proceed on the assumption that children fail to learn certain modes of play due to broad environmental factors.

As early as 1920, Gulick observed an absence of play among the lower classes [81]. Subsequent studies supported that lack of space, material, and perhaps most significant of all, "know-how" led to deficits in play ability [26, 61, 80, 81]. Studies of disadvantaged children by Smilansky showed virtual absence of play among them [28]. Others confirmed her observations [29, 49]. In contrast, Eifferman argued that disadvantaged children do play pretend games but at later ages [83]. Other cross-cultural evidence shows that imaginative-play fantasy is practically nonexistent in some societies (in some Russian and East African groups [84-86]) and rich and varied in others (New Zealand and Okinagowan [86, 87]).

Cross-cultural studies on disadvantaged children do not usually include middle-class children for comparison [76, 88, 89]. In view of the contradictory evidence, it seems unlikely that the deleterious effects of poverty or disadvantage are uniform on children of different cultural groups. A closer analysis is required to tease out the exact factors which have a determining influence.

Overcrowding and lack of privacy seems to be important. Children who report having imaginary friends often are only children or children in a family where there are big gaps between siblings [13, 29, 92]. Although Singer stresses physical space and privacy as important factors in the development of imagination, it seems that "psychological space," the freedom to develop idiosyncratic expression unhampered by criticism or the need to conform, is equally important [29, 73]. This would include the endorsement or validation of fantasy as a legitimate activity by parents. Lower-class parents are often insensitive to and do not understand the value of protected play opportunity.

Materials

Udwin and Shmukler conclude that it is not the lack of stimulation *per se* in the disadvantaged environment, but the failure of parents to help children integrate the plethora of stimuli confronting them in the course of everyday life that seems to be the critical feature [26]. On the other hand, play materials provide a valuable adjunct for children, and in modern Western society they are being produced on an unprecedented scale. The use of toys, educational toys, and now computers by middle-class parents for stimulating the child's development, make lower-class children even more disadvantaged by comparison.

Another line of investigation has examined the effects of the structure of toys on imaginative play. Pulaski showed that toys with less structure provide more opportunity for imaginative expression [25]. Gilmore [91] and Hutt [55] stress the appeal that novel objects have for children.

Media

Fantasy material, such as stories, plays, films, radio, and television, must all influence imaginative expression and form an important source of ideas. Bettelheim emphasizes the emotional value of fairy stories for children [92]. His hypothesis, resting on a psychoanalytic foundation, is that fairy tales symbolically represent the major conflicts of early childhood as universal themes, such as incest, sibling rivalry, separation and loss of parents. They help the child understand and cope with these unconscious themes through symbolization and by presenting solutions.

What effects television has on the developing child in general and on imaginative ability in particular, remains speculative and the source of much controversy. Most researchers, parents, and educators express concern about the amount of violence that growing children view [93-95]. Another major concern is the passivity aspect of viewing large amounts of television; it is a passive medium allowing for vicarious fantasy or play. Further, it competes heavily with alternative uses of a child's time and attention.

On the ther hand, it is possible that this medium opens doors to the culturally disadvantaged by exposing them to stories, scenes from other lands, and a variety of stimulation which would ordinarily be unavailable to them. In fact, Singer and Singer [16, 38] recently concluded that we do not have enough evidence, either positive or negative, that television may be providing a new and alternative form of consciousness for growing children. Television viewing is replacing play, a valuable resource available to children. In view of this, Singer and Singer are examining the effects of educational and intervention programs designed for parents and teachers aimed at enhancing imaginative-play possibilities and thus perhaps ameliorating some of the negative effects. Television is a medium of great power and great limitations, and how we, as parents, teachers, and concerned members of society, use it ultimately determines its effects.

PLAY TUTORING: INTERVENTION STUDIES

Given the considerable benefits that accrue to imaginative children, a line of empirical investigation has been pursued which seems both promising and fits in with the other intervention attempts for disadvantaged and deprived children begun in the 1960s. A prototype of such studies was Smilansky's [28] attempt to use sociodramatic techniques with disadvantaged children to help them adjust to school and improve socialization and cognitive deficits.

The theoretical rationale for these studies, rooted in social-learning theory, stresses the importance of modeling and imitation particularly in the young. The adult intervenor operates as an elicitory or disinhibitory agent rather than as a model for direct imitation [13, 33, 34, 49, 96]. All studies make the following assumptions implicitly or explicitly [15, 49, 58]: Imaginative play is important to the development of social and intellectual ability; it can be learned; it is often underdeveloped in children.

Most of the studies follow the pattern of using adult models, who present dramatic situations, plots, and role-taking situations with dolls [27], pipe cleaner figures [29], through thematic fantasy play [40], play tutoring [49, 89], structured versus unstructured story situations [77].

The overall findings of these studies are clear. Imaginative-play ability increases as a result of training, usually with concomitant rises in emotional, cognitive, and social correlates associated with imaginative play. Specifically, the benefits found as a result of play tutoring include originality, imagination, conservation of social role, concentration, complexity of play, verbalization, group constructs and cooperation, perceptual, cognitive, and affective perspective taking which includes increases in scores on WPSSI, IPAT, PPVT, conservation of mass and liquid, and mathematical readiness [27, 29, 40, 41, 45, 80, 89, 97-99].

A number of criticisms however have been leveled at these studies. Schwartzmann argues: "Specifically 'training' the 'poor' 'urban disadvantaged' etc. in make-believe or sociodramatic play is questionable although many investigators, Smilansky, Sutton-Smith, Singer would seem to argue to the contrary" [100, p. 315].

She bases her criticisms on cross-cultural and anthropological evidence, arguing that we impose a Western middle-class perspective and value system, when we describe children as "imaginative disadvantaged"; she prefers to view them as culturally different rather than deficient [101].

A serious criticism of these studies comes from Smith and co-workers [76, 89] who question the interpretation of the empirical evidence. They direct their criticisms at the controls used in most of the play intervention studies and suggest that the majority of the effects found could be caused by the stimulation of warm involved adults rather than by the sociodramatic training *per se*. Few of the above studies report adequate control of the factors which may have been just as instrumental to the effects, such as active adult involvement, including the quantity and quality of verbal stimulation which naturally is part of play tutoring.

Thus Smith and Syddall [76] designed a carefully controlled study, where play and training were compared to skills training, with amount of adult interaction and involvement carefully matched. They concluded that adult-guided activity may account for most effects. Although fantasy skills are valuable for preschoolers, particularly for those from disadvantaged background, play training is not the only way of intervention. However, play tutoring did differentially enhance peer interaction and social competence; whereas, skills tutoring or other staff structured activities tended to cut down on this aspect. When intervention techniques are matched, then, the major advantage occurs in the social realm. However fantasy skills training has the advantage of being easy and economical to implement, and, a factor not to be overlooked, children really enjoy participating. Play training allows for the sensitive structure of activities, and for adults to participate in a stimulating and encouraging way with young children. Smith largely disregards the affective benefits of play training. Nonetheless his critique warns us to examine empirical evidence critically and to be aware of how design pitfalls contaminate our conclusions. Smith does not reject the value of play training, *per se*, particularly for the economically disadvantaged. In conclusion then, play training must be seen as useful, with important educational implications, although perhaps it is not the only way of obtaining the widespread benefits claimed for it.

EDUCATIONAL IMPLICATIONS

It remains then to draw the above together and highlight the implications for the educational process. The approach to education adopted here is a broad humanistic one. A critique of modern educational practice or a description of the goals of education is beyond the scope of the present review. Briefly stated, the model of successful learning which arises from Piaget's interactive view of cognitive development is adopted. A traditional classroom, which can be regarded as an artificial and relatively inefficient learning environment invented by modern society to teach basic skills such as reading, writing, and mathematics, does not necessarily provide the optimal setting for learning.

In considering the place imaginative play has in the process of education, it is interesting to note that play is a process. Its useful attributes for the developing child lie in the process of playing. Therapy occurs through the process, and Piaget stresses how the process of the child's interaction leads to the development of new cognitive schema.

The focus of this discussion is on early education, as imaginative play is widely recognized as peaking in the preschool and early school years. Imagery, drama, and creativity are discussed in other sections of the book.

Already by the 1890s, the work of Froebel [102] and Pestalozzi [103], pioneers in developing educational theory, had been translated into English, and they discussed the importance of play in early childhood. They maintained that dramatic play enriched the child's power of imagination and advanced learning, and they went further and were among the first to recommend the systematic use of play in childrearing and education. Another important early contributor to educational theory, Dewey [104], stressed the importance of children's active investigation as a means of learning from the environment. Play was regarded as the starting point which led to the child's reasoning, discovery, and thought. The popular American interpretation of Dewey's theories led to an emphasis on the provision of an enriched and spacious environment [28]. The adult role was seen as being largely one of nonintervention.

Contemporary investigators stress imaginative play's constructive implications and its part in the normal socialization process. Given the central role in development of imaginative play, there is a danger that certain skills and attitudes will be impeded if this ability is underdeveloped. The studies quoted above indicate that skill in imaginative play does not develop automatically and that play training is effective and also brings concomitant advantages in its wake.

Play training is an advance on previous noninteraction and therapeutic approaches in a number of significant ways: a) The role of both cognitive and affective processes is emphasized; b) Imaginative-play training aims at synthesizing and integrating cognitive, affective, and social skills; c) The active involvement on the part of the adult facilitator and the teaching of skills and techniques is stressed.

Specific Implications for Teachers

It has been shown that specific skills and techniques can be effectively taught and the impact is broad. Social-learning theory underpins the role of the teacher as model. The adult model functions in an elicitory and disinhibitory way rather than as someone to be directly imitated, although the "as if" stance is an important characteristic of the model [9, 13]. The modeling effect seems to be more influential with low-fantasy children and have less impact on older children [37, 56]. Direct involvement and encouragement seems to be important, and the intervenor functions as a source of information and as a source of support for trying-out behavior. The child needs help with expression and encouragement to strive for full elaboration. By focusing on process rather than content, teachers can concern themselves with skills rather than subconscious contents or release of emotion. The importance of the teacher standing back and giving the child freedom of expression also has been explained above.

Techniques

Many assume that toys and other play materials are excellent stimuli and sufficient in themselves to stimulate children into more elaborate and complex play sequences. This assumption has been shown to be invalid, and direct forms of intervention are necessary. On the other hand, the supply of raw material is important as a starting point. Stories, fairy tales, and other play themes are commonly used in intervention studies (see above); also Singer and Singer [105] have compiled a set of techniques and exercises for use by parents and teachers. Further suggestions are provided by de Mille [106] and Jones [107], for example. However there is overall agreement that the teacher and his/her attitude are more important to the success of a program than the particular techniques used.

Which Children

The preschool period seems to be most important for the enhancement of imaginative play. These are the years crucial to language, concept formation, imagination, creativity, development of awareness of self and others [8, 13, 28]. Group intervention at a preschool level is economical, efficient, and advances particularly social skills and cooperation and decentration in the Piagetian sense. There is a general consensus that imaginative-play training is particularly useful for disadvantaged and emotionally disturbed children. Kohlberg [108] and Feitelson and Ross [49], among others, argue that programs should concentrate on core tasks rather than on specific learning disabilities: Particularly with disadvantaged groups, help with organizing information into meaningful concepts would be a broader basis and more effective than small task programs. Disadvantaged children suffer most from the lack of mediated learning experience [11, 109], from the inadequacy of adult intervention which is needed to provide the skills necessary for conceptual integration. Imaginative play, by its very nature, demands that the child use his/her potential to combine scattered experiences in flexible ways. Thus, play tutoring helps the child convert and organize a multitude of experiences and stimuli into organized conceptual schemes. Aimless wandering in the school yard is unproductive, but encouragement to play converts the child into an independent and happy participant of a preschool program.

In conclusion then, imaginative play helps a child to achieve a balance between inner and outer experience; to develop a reservoir of personal resourcefulness, liveliness, creativity, and self-esteem; to indulge his/her curiosity and the drive to explore; and to exercise his/her capacity for organization. Imaginative play should receive priority in a preschool program and be recognized as a powerful adjunct to early educational, preventive, remedial, and clinical programs for young children.

REFERENCES

1. A. Freud, *The Ego and the Mechanisms of Defense*, Hogarth, London, 1937.
2. M. Klein, The Psychoanalytic Play Technique, *American Journal of Orthopsychiatry, 25*, pp. 223-237, 1955.
3. D. W. Winnicott, *Playing and Reality*, Pelican Books, England, 1974.

4. D. E. Berlyne, Laughter, Humor and Play, in *The Handbook of Social Psychology*, Vol. 3 (2nd edition), G. Lindzey and E. Aronson (eds.), Addison-Wesley, Reading, Massachusetts, pp. 795-852, 1969.

5. R. W. White, Motivation Reconsidered: The Concept of Competence, *Psychological Review*, *66*, pp. 297-333, 1959.

6. E. H. Erikson, *Childhood and Society*, Pelican Books, England, 1950.

7. J. S. Bruner, Nature and Uses of Immaturity, *American Psychologist*, *27*, pp. 678-708, 1972.

8. J. Piaget, *Play, Dreams and Imitation in Childhood*, W. W. Norton, New York, 1962.

9. B. Sutton-Smith, The Role of Play in Cognitive Development, *Young Children*, *6*, pp. 202-214, 1967.

10. B. Sutton-Smith, Piaget, Play and Cognition Revisited, in *The Relationship between Social and Cognitive Development*, W. Overton (ed.), Erlbaum, New York, 1980.

11. M. Almy, Spontaneous Play: An Avenue for Intellectual Development, in *Early Childhood Education Rediscovered*, J. L. Frost (ed.), Holt, Rinehart and Winston, New York, 1968.

12. L. S. Vygotsky, Play and Its Role in the Mental Development of the Child, in *Play: Its Role in Development and Evolution*, J. S. Bruner, A. Jolly and K. Sylva (eds.), Penguin Books, England, 1976, reprinted from *Soviet Psychology*, *12*:6, pp. 62-76, 1966.

13. J. L. Singer, *The Child's World of Make-Believe*, Academic Press, New York, 1973.

14. J. L. Singer, Imagination and Make-Believe Play in Early Childhood: Some Educational Implications, *Journal of Mental Imagery*, *1*, pp. 127-144, 1977.

15. J. L. Singer and D. G. Singer, Imaginative Play and Pretending in Early Childhood: Some Experimental Approaches, in *Child Personality and Psychopathology*, Vol. 3, A. Davids (ed.), Wiley, New York, 1976.

16. J. L. Singer and D. G. Singer, Imaginative Play in Preschoolers: Some Research and Theoretical Implications, paper presented at the 10th Annual Interdisciplinary Conference on Piagetian Theory and the Helping Professions, UAP, University of Southern California, Los Angeles, January, 1981.

17. S. S. Tomkins, *Affect, Imagery and Consciousness*, Vols. I and II, Springer, New York, 1962-1963.

18. J. L. Singer, The Importance of Daydreaming, *Psychology Today*, *1*:11, April 26, 1968.

19. A. Anastasi and C. E. Schaefer, Biographical Correlates of Artistic and Literary Creativity in Adolescent Girls, *Journal of Applied Psychology*, *53*:4, pp. 267-273, 1969.

20. R. Helson, Childhood Interest Clusters Related to Creativity in Women, *Journal of Consulting Psychology*, *29*:4, pp. 352-361, 1965.

21. C. E. Schaefer and A. Anastasi, A Biographical Inventory for Identifying Creativity in Adolescent Boys, *Journal of Applied Psychology*, *52*:1, pp. 42-48, 1968.

22. S. Feshbach, The Drive-Reducing Function of Fantasy Behavior, *Journal of Abnormal and Social Psychology*, *50*, pp. 3-11, 1955.

23. E. Klinger, Development of Imaginative Behavior: Implications of Play for A Theory of Fantasy, *Psychological Bulletin, 72*:4, pp. 277-298, 1969.

24. J. L. Singer, Imagination and Waiting Ability in Young Children, *Journal of Personality, 29*, pp. 396-413, 1961.

25. M. A. S. Pulaski, Toys and Imaginative Play, in *The Child's World of Make-Believe*, J. Singer (ed.), Academic Press, New York, 1973.

26. O. Udwin and D. Shmukler, The Influence of Sociocultural, Economic and Home Background Factors on Children's Ability to Engage in Imaginative Play, *Developmental Psychology, 17*:1, pp. 66-72, 1981.

27. H. R. Marshall and S. C. Hahn, Experimental Modification of Dramatic Play, *Journal of Personality and Social Psychology, 5*:1, pp. 119-122, 1967.

28. S. Smilansky, *The Effects of Socio-dramatic Play on Disadvantaged Preschool Children*, Wiley, New York, 1968.

29. J. T. Freyberg, Increasing the Imaginative Play of Urban Disadvantaged Kindergarten Children Through Systematic Training, in *The Child's World of Make-Believe*, J. Singer (ed.), Academic Press, New York, 1973.

30. J. L. Singer, The Constructive Potential of Imagery and Fantasy Process: Implications for Child Development, Psychotherapy, and Personal Growth, in *Interpersonal Psychoanalysis*, E. G. Witenberg (ed.), J. Wiley, New York, 1978.

31. S. Feshbach, The Catharsis Hypothesis and Some Consequences of Interaction with Aggressive and Neutral Play Objects, *Journal of Personality, 24*, 449-462, 1956.

32. G. Spivak and M. Levine, Self Regulation and Acting Out in Normal Adolescents, progress report for National Institute of Mental Health Grant M-4531, Devoon Pennsylvania Devereaux Foundation, 1964, *cited in The Child's World of Make-Believe*, J. L. Singer (ed.), Academic Press, New York, 1973.

33. A. Bandura, D. Ross and S. A. Ross, Transmission of Aggression Through Imitation of Aggressive Models, *Journal of Abnormal and Social Psychology, 63*, pp. 575-582, 1961.

34. A. Bandura, D. Ross and S. A. Ross, Imitation of Film-mediated Aggressive Models, *Journal of Abnormal and Social Psychology, 66*, pp. 3-11, 1963.

35. L. Berkowitz and E. Rawlings, Effects of Film Violence on Inhibitions Against Subsequent Aggression, *Journal of Abnormal and Social Psychology, 66*, pp. 405-412, 1963.

36. P. Mussen and E. Rutherford, Effects of Aggressive Cartoons on Children's Aggressive Play, *Journal of Abnormal and Social Psychology, 62*, pp. 461-464, 1961.

37. E. Biblow, Imaginative Play and the Control of Aggressive Behavior, in *The Child's World of Make-Believe*, J. Singer (ed.), Academic Press, New York, 1973.

38. J. L. Singer and D. G. Singer, *Television, Imagination and Aggression: A Study of Preschoolers*, Erlbaum, Hillsdale, New Jersey, 1980.

39. J. Tucker, The Role of Fantasy in Cognitive-Affective Functioning: Does Reality Make A Difference in Remembering?, unpublished doctoral dissertation, Teachers' College, Columbia University, 1975.

40. E. Saltz and J. Johnson, Training for Thematic-Fantasy Play in Culturally Disadvantaged Children: Preliminary Results, *Journal of Educational Psychology, 66*:4, pp. 623-630, 1974.
41. E. Saltz, D. Dixon and J. Johnson, Training Disadvantaged Preschoolers on Various Fantasy Activities: Effects on Cognitive Functioning and Impulse Control, *Child Development, 48*, pp. 367-380, 1977.
42. J. L. Singer, Fantasy: The Foundation of Serenity, *Psychology Today*, pp. 32-37, July 1976.
43. R. E. Hartley, L. K. Frank and R. M. Goldenson, *Understanding Children's Play*, Columbia University Press, New York, 1952.
44. L. Nahme-Huang, D. G. Singer, J. L. Singer and A. Wheaton, Imaginative Play Training and Perceptual-motor Interventions with Emotionally-disturbed Hospitalized Children, *American Journal of Orthopsychiatry, 47*:2, pp. 238-249, 1977.
45. R. Gould, *Child Studies Through Fantasy*, Quadrangle Books, New York, 1972.
46. K. S. Pope and J. L. Singer, *The Stream of Consciousness. Scientific Investigations into the Flow of Human Experience*, Wiley and Sons, New York, 1978.
47. J. L. Singer and K. S. Pope, *The Power of Human Imagination. New Methods in Psychotherapy*, Plenum Press, New York and London, 1978.
48. S. Freud, Creative Writers and Day-dreaming, 1908, in *The Complete Psychological Works of Sigmund Freud* (translated by James Strackey in collaboration with Anna Freud), Vol. IX (1906-1908): Jensen's 'Gradiva' and other works, Hogarth, London, 1959.
49. D. Feitelson and G. S. Ross, The Neglected Factor—Play, *Human Development, 16*, pp. 202-223, 1973.
50. D. Shmukler, A Factor Analytic Model of Elements of Creativity in Preschool Children, *Genetic Psychology Monographs, 105*, pp. 25-39, 1982.
51. J. N. Lieberman, Playfulness and Divergent Thinking: An Investigation of Their Relationship at the Kindergarten Level, *Journal of Genetic Psychology, 107*, pp. 219-224, 1965.
52. J. N. Lieberman, *Playfulness: Its Relationship to Imagination and Creativity*, Academic Press, New York, 1977.
53. J. L. Dansky and I. W. Silverman, Effects of Play on Associative Fluency in Preschool-Aged Children, *Developmental Psychology, 9*:1, pp. 38-43, 1973.
54. E. P. Torrance, *Guiding Creative Talent*, University of Minnesota Press, Minneapolis, 1963.
55. C. Hutt, Exploration and Play in Children, in *Child's Play*, R. E. Herron and B. Sutton-Smith (eds.), Wiley, New York, 1971, originally published in *Symposium of Zoological Society of London, 18*, pp. 61-81, 1966.
56. S. Gottlieb, Modeling Effects Upon Fantasy, in *The Child's World of Make-Believe*, J. Singer (ed.), Academic Press, New York, 1973.
57. D. Shmukler, Preschool Imaginative Play Predisposition and Its Relationship to Subsequent Third Grade Assessment, *Imagination, Cognition and Personality, 2*:3, pp. 231-240, 1982-1983.

58. D. Shmukler and I. Naveh, Modification of Imaginative Play in Preschool Children Through the Intervention of An Adult Model, *South African Journal of Psychology*, *10*, pp. 99-103, 1980.

59. G. G. Fein, A Transformational Analysis of Pretending, *Developmental Psychology*, *11*:3, pp. 291-296, 1975.

60. L. M. Nicolich, Beyond Sensorimotor Intelligence: Assessment of Symbolic Maturity Through Analysis of Pretend Play, *Merrill-Palmer Quarterly*, *23*:2, pp. 89-99, 1977.

61. J. Dunn and C. Wooding, Play in the Home and Its Implications for Learning, in *Biology of Play*, B. Tizard and D. Harvey (eds.), Spastico International Medical Publication, London, 1977.

62. R. R. Holt, Imagery: The Return of the Ostracized, *American Psychologist*, pp. 254-264, 1964.

63. A. Paivio, On the Functional Significance of Imagery, *Psychological Bulletin*, *73*:6, pp. 385-392, 1970.

64. W. D. Rohwer Jr., Images and Pictures in Children's Learning: Research Results and Educational Implications, *Psychological Bulletin*, *73*:6, pp. 393-403, 1970.

65. S. J. Segal, *Imagery: Current Cognitive Approaches*, Academic Press, New York, 1971.

66. H. Litt, Imagery in Children's Thinking, unpublished doctoral dissertation, Liverpool University, Liverpool, England, 1973.

67. S. Freud, *Beyond the Pleasure Principle*, International Universities Press, London, 1922.

68. H. Hartmann, *Ego Psychology and the Problem of Adaptation*, International Universities Press, New York, 1958.

69. P. A. Weisberg and K. J. Springer, Environmental Factors in Creative Function, *Archives of General Psychiatry*, *5*, pp. 64-74, 1961.

70. J. E. Drevdahl, Some Developmental and Environmental Factors in Creativity, in *Widening Horizons in Creativity*, C. W. Taylor (ed.), Wiley, New York, 1964.

71. D. W. Mackinnon, The Nature and Nurture of Creative Talent, *American Psychologist*, pp. 484-495, 1962.

72. L. B. Dennis, Individual and Familial Correlates of Children's Fantasy Play, unpublished doctoral dissertation submitted to the University of Florida, 1976.

73. D. Shmukler, Mother-Child Interaction and Its Relationship to the Predisposition to Imaginative Play, *Genetic Psychology Monographs*, *104*, pp. 215-235, 1981.

74. M. Gershowitz, Fantasy Behavior and Clinic-Referred Children in Play Encounters with College Undergraduates, unpublished doctoral dissertation *cited* in J. L. Singer and D. G. Singer, Imaginative Play and Pretending in Early Childhood: Some Experimental Approaches, in *Child Personality and Psychopathology*, A. David (ed.), Wiley and Sons, New York, 1976.

75. P. A. Cowan, *Piaget: With Feeling*, Holt, Rinehart and Winston, New York, 1978.

76. P. K. Smith, M. Dagleish and G. Herzmark, A Comparison of The Effects of Fantasy Play Tutoring and Skills Tutoring in Nursery Classes, *International Journal of Behavioral Development*, 4, pp. 42-1441, 1981.

77. I. Naveh, Enhancement of Imaginative Play in Pre-school Children, unpublished master's thesis submitted to University of the Witwatersrand, Johannesburg, 1983.

78. J. L. Frost, *Early Childhood Education Rediscovered*, Holt, Rinehart and Winston, New York, 1968.

79. B. R. McCandless, *Children: Behavior and Development*, Holt, Rinehart and Winston, New York, 1967.

80. C. E. Rosen, The Effects of Sociodramatic Play on Problem-solving Behavior among Culturally Disadvantaged Preschool Children, *Child Development*, 45, pp. 920-927, 1974.

81. L. Gulick, *A Philosophy of Play*, Wiley, New York, 1920.

82. P. Griffing, Sociodramatic Play among Young Black Children, *Theory into Practice*, 13, pp. 257-264, 1974.

83. R. R. Eifermann, Social Play in Childhood, in *Child's Play*, R. E. Herron and B. Sutton-Smith (eds.), Wiley, New York, 1971.

84. F. N. Ebbeck, Learning from Play in Other Cultures, in *Revisiting Early Childhood Education*, J. L. Frost (ed.), Holt, Rinehart and Winston, New York, 1973.

85. D. El'Konin, Symbolics and Its Functions in the Play of Children, in *Child's Play*, R. E. Herron and B. Sutton-Smith (eds.), J. Wiley and Sons, New York, 1971.

86. B. B. Whiting (ed.), *Six Cultures: Studies of Child-rearing*, Wiley, New York, 1963.

87. M. V. Seagoe, A Comparison of Children's Play in Six Modern Cultures, *Journal of School Psychology*, 9, pp. 61-72, 1971.

88. P. K. Smith, Play and Its Role in Education, *Educational Analysis*, 2:1, pp. 15-24, 1980.

89. P. K. Smith and S. Syddall, Play and Non-play Tutoring in Pre-school Children: Is It Play or Tutoring Which Matters?, *British Journal of Educational Psychology*, 48, pp. 315-325, 1978.

90. M. Manosevitz, N. M. Prentice and F. Wilson, Individual and Family Correlates of Imaginary Companions in Preschool Children, *Developmental Psychology*, 8, pp. 72-79, 1973.

91. J. B. Gilmore, Play: A Special Behavior, in *Current Research in Motivation*, R. N. Haber (ed.), Holt, Rinehart and Winston, New York, 1966.

92. B. Bettelheim, *The Uses of Enchantment: The Meaning and Importance of Fairy Tales*, Thames and Hudson, London, 1976.

93. G. Gerbner and L. Gross, Living with Television: The Violence Profile, *Journal of Communication*, 26, pp. 173-199, 1976.

94. G. S. Lesser, *Children and Television*, Random House, New York, 1974.

95. D. G. Singer, Television and Imaginative Play, *Journal of Mental Imagery*, 2, pp. 145-164, 1978.

96. A. Bandura, *Psychological Modeling*, Aldine-Atherton, New York, 1971.

97. S. M. Burns and C. J. Brainard, Effects of Constructive and Dramatic Play on Perspective Taking in Very Young Children, *Developmental Psychology*, *15*, pp. 512-521, 1979.

98. R. Fink, The Role of Imaginative Play in Cognitive Development, in *Piagetian Theory and the Helping Professions*, M. K. Paulsen, J. F. Magary and G. I. Lubin (eds.), University of Southern California Press, Los Angeles, 1976.

99. S. Lovinger, Sociodramatic Play and Language Development in Preschool Disadvantaged Children, *Psychology in the Schools*, *11*, pp. 313-320, 1974.

100. H. B. Schwartzman, The Anthropological Study of Children's Play, *Annual Review of Anthropology*, *5*, pp. 289-328, 1976.

101. M. Cole and J. S. Bruner, Preliminaries to a Theory of Cultural Differences, in *Early Childhood Education*, J. Gordon (ed.), University of Chicago Press, Chicago, 1972.

102. F. Froebel, *Pedagogics of the Kindergarten*, (J. Janis trans.), Appleton, New York, 1895.

103. J. H. Pestalozzi, *How Gertrude Teaches Her Children: An Attempt to Help Mothers Teach Their Own Children*, (L. E. Holland and F. C. Turner trans.), Bardecky, New York, 1898.

104. J. Dewey, *Art As Experience*, Minton, New York, 1934.

105. D. G. Singer and J. L. Singer, *Partners in Play*, Harper and Row, New York, 1977.

106. R. de Mille, *Put Your Mother on the Ceiling: Children's Imagination Games*, The Viking Press, New York, 1976.

107. R. M. Jones, *Fantasy and Feeling in Education*, New York University Press, New York, 1968.

108. L. Kohlberg, Early Education: A Cognitive-Developmental View, *Child Development*, *39*, pp. 1013-1062, 1968.

109. R. Feuerstein, Y. Rand, M. B. Hoffman and R. Miller, *Instrumental Enrichment*, University Park Press, Baltimore, Maryland, 1979.

CHAPTER 3

Educational Applications of Mnemonic Pictures: Possibilities Beyond Your Wildest Imagination

JOEL R. LEVIN

What's new in educational mnemonics? Lots—as I hope to convince you before we are done. But first let me take a few lines to delineate the domain of present concern. Mnemonic techniques, devices, or strategies refer to systematic procedures for improving one's memory for something. And, in the context of this chapter, *educational* mnemonics are even more restrictive in scope. They encompass mnemonic techniques that are applied to school-learning tasks and content. Inasmuch as this volume is concerned with imagery applications, the educational mnemonics that I will describe will be pictorial (rather than verbal) in nature. Finally, I will focus primarily on the application of mnemonic techniques by children, rather than by adults (for recent reviews of the latter, see [1-3]).

In the first part of the chapter, I will review the distinguishing characteristics of mnemonic pictures in a school-learning context. In so doing, mnemonic pictures will be contrasted with pictures of the more traditional "nonmnemonic" variety. Once the groundwork for mnemonic pictures has been laid, some specific research examples will be presented—taken from different curricular domains—that document both the potency and potential of mnemonic pictures. The educational potential of mnemonic pictures will continue to be discussed in the final section, where "possibilities beyond your wildest imagination" will be considered.

MNEMONIC VERSUS NONMNEMONIC PICTURES

Let us begin with a distinction that I view as critical for the present discussion. Pictures can take many different forms and serve a variety of different needs and "functions" [4]. Thus, whereas a commercial publisher of children's

* The work represented here was funded by a grant from the National Institute of Education through the Wisconsin Center for Education Research. Preparation of the manuscript was facilitated by a Romnes Faculty Fellowship awarded by the Graduate School of the University of Wisconsin.

books may wish to include illustrations in order to make a book more attractive and marketable, an educator interested in the instructional value of pictures would include them to make the substantive content more interesting, comprehensible, or memorable. It is important to note that even with a *general* instructional objective in mind, one can specify a variety of *specific* instructional objectives. Indeed, different instructional objectives should be regarded as the rule rather than the exception.

Take, for example, a science lesson that contains novel concepts and factual material. What exactly does a teacher wish a student to take away from such a lesson? Should the student be able to recite the facts contained therein? Should he/she be able to understand the underlying concepts and the interrelationships among them? Or should he/she be able to demonstrate this understanding by constructing appropriate inferences in a novel situation or by conducting an original experiment based on the lesson? It is only after one or more of these specific instructional objectives is articulated that an educator can prescribe the kind of text "adjuncts" [5] that are most directly relevant to achieving that objective.

In the present context, the text adjuncts of interest are pictures. Based on a perusal of empirical research studies in the areas of science and social studies learning, I think that it can safely be concluded that the major functions served by pictures in those domains are essentially *organizational* and *interpretational* [4]. Organizational pictures include maps, graphs, and taxonomic arrangements, whose primary purpose is to display concepts and relationships succinctly (i.e., to augment or replace lengthy—and frequently not-as-precise—verbal descriptions). The "one picture is worth a thousand words" adage seems to be appropriately associated with many of these organizational pictures [6, 7]. Interpretational pictures are represented by those whose ostensible purpose is one of clarifying difficult-to-comprehend textual concepts and relationships. For example, the function of a pictorial flowchart used to illuminate the components of the nitrogen cycle is primarily interpretational [8]. The same can be said when concrete illustrations [9], or pictorial analogies [10] are provided with the aim of clarifying otherwise abstract textual concepts. I have argued elsewhere [11] that pictures of this kind should be regarded as "comprehension directed," inasmuch as their major function is to increase the meaningfulness of the material that is subsequently encoded by the student.

In contrast to the kind of pictures just discussed, mnemonic or *transformational* pictures are those whose major function is one of facilitating students' memory for factual prose information. Being "memory directed," mnemonic pictures are assumed to produce direct memorial benefits; whereas, whatever memorial benefits accrue to the other (nonmnemonic) pictures are assumed to be byproducts of the primary functions that such pictures serve. The memorial benefits ascribed to mnemonic pictures are firmly grounded in both theory and supporting empirical data. On the theoretical side, the storage and retrieval processes associated with mnemonic pictures can be articulated, which makes the direct connection between such pictures and improved memory readily apparent [12-14]. And on the empirical side, there is now a plethora of data that are consistent both with predictions derived from these theoretical coding and decoding operations, and with the assertion that mnemonic pictures are by far the most consistently potent facilitators of factual information recall [3, 15].

A few concrete examples derived from recent discussions should help to illustrate these distinctions [11, 14]. The first of my examples is based on Meyer's *parakeet* passage, which describes the evolution of the parakeet's more than sixty-six color varieties that are listed by the Budgerigar Society today [16]. One of the sentences of the passage reads as follows: "The first living parakeets were brought to Europe from Australia by John Gould, a naturalist, in 1840." I asked a commercial artist (Robert Cavey, to whom I am grateful) to construct a "conventional" textbook illustration that might accompany this information. The result is presented as Figure 1.

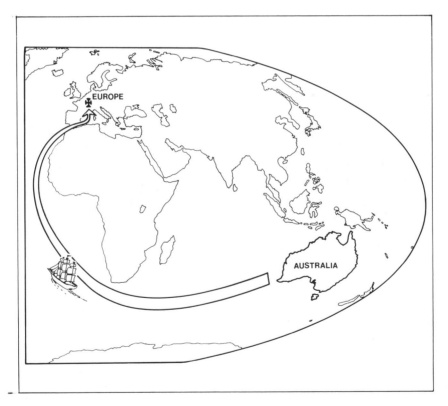

Figure 1. Organizational (nonmnemonic) picture for prose learning.

Note that the particular illustration constructed is of the organizational/map genre. In this context, it gives the reader a concrete representation of the geographic parameters of the text content, as well as a hypothetical connecting route traveled by Gould, from Australia to Europe. The pictorial map enables the reader to assimilate rapidly the novel text information. As such, it can be argued that the picture provides an efficient framework for organizing and comprehending the incoming passage content. But such a picture would not be expected to facilitate students' recall of the specific information associated with these events—in particular, the naturalist's name (John Gould) and the critical year (1840). Even adding the character of John Gould and the printed date of 1840 to the illustration would not be expected to be helpful, in that additions of that kind would not provide a direct link with the to-be-remembered information [17, 18]. If recall of the specific name and date information were deemed important to the objectives of the lesson, then a mnemonic approach is clearly indicated, a sample of which is offered as Figure 2.

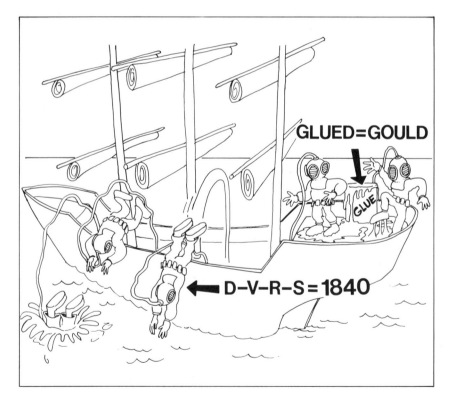

Figure 2. Transformational (mnemonic) picture for prose learning.

The picture shows some deep sea divers on a ship; two have their feet glued to the deck of the ship. The fact that the feet are glued is significant, for the word *glued* is acoustically linked to the to-be-recalled name *Gould*. A similar link has been established between the word *divers* and the date *1840*, although one's ability to benefit from this link presupposes familiarity with a popular mnemonic system wherein the digits 0 through 9 are recoded as consonant sounds [19]. According to this system, the number 1 is recoded as a "t" or a "d" sound; the number 8 is recoded as an "f" or a "v" sound; the number 4 is recoded as an "r" sound; and the number 0 is recoded as an "s" or a "z" sound. Selecting from these possibilities to construct a word (excluding vowels) to represent the date 1840, one could produce *divers* = d-v-r-s. The elements of this picture capitalize on three critical mnemonic components—recoding, relating, and retrieving— recently referred to as the "three R's" of associative mnemonic techniques [17]. In each case, the *recoded* element in the picture (glued and divers) provides a direct *retrieval* path back to the appropriate associated information (Gould and 1840), via the semantic *relationship* afforded by the pictorial context (the ship, to represent the Australia-Europe voyage). [Note that in this particular illustration, Australia and Europe are not mnemonically represented, even though it would certainly be possible to add such information if desired [18, 20].

Other examples of the mnemonic/nonmnemonic picture distinction may be found in the vocabulary-learning studies of Pressley and Levin [21] and Levin, *et al.* [22], in the prose-learning studies of Shriberg, Levin, McCormick, and Pressley [23] and Levin *et al.* [18], and in the president-learning studies of Levin, McCormick, and Dretzke [24] and Levin *et al.* [25]. But perhaps the most convincing demonstration of the distinction comes from a study by Levin, McCormick, Miller, Berry, and Pressley [26].

In that study, fourth-grade students were required to learn the meanings of several unfamiliar English vocabulary items (e.g., *surplus, vagabond, persuade, refuge*). The pictorial mnemonic technique devised for that purpose was an extension of the "keyword method," popularized by Richard Atkinson [12]. With the keyword method, the unfamiliar vocabulary word (e.g., *surplus*) is first recoded as a more familiar concrete "keyword" (e.g., *syrup*). This keyword is then semantically related to the meaning of the vocabulary item, which for *surplus* was given as *having some left over, having more than was needed*. In the keyword (mnemonic) illustration condition, students were shown a picture in which two children were conversing about a surplus of syrup in front of a cupboard that was loaded with syrup (see Figure 3). In the nonmnemonic-illustration condition, exactly the same scenario and dialogue were constructed, with the single exception that the surplus of syrup (an acoustically similar stimulus and keyword) was replaced by a surplus of *ketchup* (an acoustically unrelated stimulus and keyword)—see Figure 4.

Whereas mnemonic illustrations substantially facilitated students' recall of the vocabulary items' definitions relative to a no-picture control condition,

Figure 3. Mnemonic picture for vocabulary learning.
(From Levin et al., 1982; reprinted by permission.)

nonmnemonic illustrations produced not even a hint of facilitated performance. In short, the direct link between the keyword and the vocabulary word that mediated definition recall in the mnemonic-picture condition was absent in the nonmnemonic-picture condition. Because the nonmnemonic pictures provided were not directly relevant to the definition-retrieval process, no performance advantage was associated with studying such pictures.

Thus, based on both theory and data, the mnemonic- versus nonmnemonic-picture distinction is an important one: The former leads to enhanced memory for factual information and the latter does not. In the section that follows, I will draw from specific research examples in which mnemonic pictures have substantially facilitated students' memory for factual information.

Figure 4. Nonmnemonic picture for vocabulary learning.
(From Levin et al., 1982; reprinted by permission.)

EDUCATIONAL APPLICATIONS OF PICTORIAL MNEMONICS

Foreign-Vocabulary Learning

The mnemonic technique that has been investigated extensively with respect to educational applications is the keyword method and extensions thereof [3]. Although components of the method have been well-known and well-used throughout the centuries [27], only in recent years did the method and its components come under controlled scrutiny [12]. Initial applications of this mnemonic technique were made in the context of the learning of foreign-language vocabulary by adults [28, 29]. For example, to remember that the Spanish vocabulary word *carta* means *(postal) letter*, a subject would first recode the unfamiliar Spanish word *carta* into the concrete, familiar English word *cart* (the keyword). Then, a semantic relationship between a cart and a letter would be pictured, such as a cart transporting a letter. Given successful recoding and relating, retrieval of the definition from the vocabulary item is a straightforward process: The Spanish word *carta* elicits *cart*, which in turn elicits the picture of a cart and a letter. In this context, the keyword method has proven itself to be extremely potent: Users of the method outperform control subjects by a wide margin.

Children's Learning of Foreign Vocabulary. The first experimental studies showed that college students and other adult learners could effectively apply a pictorial mnemonic technique to acquire a foreign-language vocabulary.

But would the technique also be effective for younger learners (namely, elementary-school children)? That was the question addressed by Michael Pressley in his doctoral research [30]. As part of that research, Pressley devised a keyword condition that provided more concrete support than had been provided in the earlier adult studies. In particular, whereas the adults had to generate their relational images between keywords and definitions internally, Pressley's children were given actual illustrations that specified these relationships. Children at two grade levels were tested: Fifth graders were given an 18-item list of Spanish nouns to learn, and second graders were given a 12-item list. Compared to students in two control conditions, mnemonic subjects recalled substantially more vocabulary definitions (fifth grade: means of 64% correct and 34% correct for mnemonic and control, respectively; second grade: 68% and 29%). Thus, at both grade levels, the mnemonic advantage was about 2 to 1.

Subsequent research with children permits the conclusions that: 1) mnemonic illustrations can improve the foreign-vocabulary learning of even three-year-olds [31]; 2) it is not until the upper elementary grades that children can successfully apply the original self-generated imagery version of the keyword method [21], even though an alternative self-generated sentence version of the method *can* be applied by younger elementary-school children [32]; 3) the keyword method can be adapted to accommodate vocabulary other than concrete nouns [33]; and 4) the keyword method has proven effective not just when administered to students individually, but also when implemented in either small or classroom-sized groups of elementary school children [34]. Additional mnemonic vocabulary instruction issues have been explored with adult subjects. Many of these are covered in the review articles of Pressley *et al.* [3] and of Paivio [2], and will not be repeated here.

Children's Learning of New Vocabulary

In recent years, we have found that pictorial mnemonic techniques are very effective for teaching children the meanings of new vocabulary of the kind they would encounter in books or in their daily lives. For example, in the study by Levin *et al.* [26], fourth graders were taught the meanings of words such as *harvest, orbit, quaint, sentiment,* and *intend.* And in the study by Levin *et al.* [22], fourth- and fifth-grade students were taught the meanings of words associated with sports and hobbies (e.g., *angler, equestrian, camaraderie, accolades*) and with store purchases (e.g., *exorbitant, nominal, flatware, haberdashery*). Note that in both studies, the vocabulary words selected did not especially lend themselves to mnemonic instruction in that they neither consisted exclusively of concrete nouns nor contained easily derived and picturable keywords. Yet, in each study, it was possible to construct mnemonic illustrations that directly related the vocabulary item to its meaning via a keyword (as in the *surplus* example described earlier). Such mnemonic illustrations produced a sizeable advantage in children's recall of the vocabulary items' definitions. In Levin *et al.*'s [26] second experiment, mnemonic-picture subjects outperformed both nonmnemonic-picture and no-picture control subjects by about 60 percent; and in the Levin *et al.* [22] study, the facilitation relative to two popular semantic-based treatments (semantic mapping and contextual analysis) amounted to about 50 percent.

Vocabulary Comprehension. In addition to improving students' memory for definitions *per se*, benefits of mnemonic vocabulary instruction also have appeared on measures thought to require some degree of vocabulary comprehension. These measures typically are administered to students following exposure to the new vocabulary words and their meanings, and they have included sentence construction using the vocabulary words, judgments of the appropriateness of the vocabulary words in sentence contexts, "cloze" tasks where students are required to select appropriate vocabulary words to be inserted in sentence blanks, and other contextually bound tasks. (For additional discussion of vocabulary comprehension tasks and their validity see [15,35].) The finding of mnemonic facilitation of vocabulary comprehension was initially reported with college students [36] and it has since been replicated [37]. In addition, similar findings were obtained by Aurentz with high school seniors [38]. The study by Levin *et al.* [22] with elementary school children is the one that will be described here.

In that study, twelve new vocabulary items (six from one semantic category, and six from another) were taught to fourth and fifth graders from two different elementary schools. One of these schools had attained a mean achievement level that was considerably above the national norms, and the other school's mean achievement level was somewhat below the national norms. Students were assigned randomly to one of three experimental conditions: mnemonic pictures, where contextual keyword illustrations representing the new vocabulary words were provided (as in the previous *surplus* example); semantic mapping, where the new vocabulary words were related both to one another and to other familiar concepts, via a structured "map" and experimenter-guided instruction [39]; and contextual analysis, where students received instruction in inferring the meanings of new vocabulary words on the basis of semantic and syntactic contextual clues that appeared in paragraphs [39]. Both definition-recall and comprehension measures of vocabulary learning were taken, with the latter including appropriateness judgments of sentences and sentence completions.

As was mentioned in the preceding section, mnemonic pictures led to a higher level of definition recall in comparison to that obtained in either the semantic-mapping or contextual-analysis condition. This was true in both the higher- and the lower-achieving samples (higher: means of 70%, 49%, and 47% correct in the mnemonic, semantic-mapping, and contextual-analysis conditions, respectively; lower: means of 69%, 49%, and 44%). In addition, however, in the higher-achieving sample, mnemonic subjects performed significantly better than contextual-analysis subjects on the comprehension tests (one administered the day after instruction, and a parallel form administered a week later). On the initial comprehension measures, the performance means were 79 percent and 64 percent correct for mnemonic and contextual-analysis subjects, respectively; and on the delayed comprehension measures, the corresponding means were 78 percent and 63 percent. (The comprehension performance of the higher-achieving sample's semantic-mapping subjects was intermediate to those in the two other conditions, not differing reliably from either.)

The important point to be extracted from these data is that in contrast to what many suggest is a shortcoming of mnemonic strategies—namely, that they *inhibit comprehension* [15, 40]—in this study there was some evidence of mnemonic *facilitation* with respect to vocabulary comprehension. When combined with the documented positive effects of mnemonic instruction on high school and college students' vocabulary usage (mentioned earlier), it is clear that the mnemonic critics' claims of "rote memory at the expense of comprehension" are empirically indefensible.

Children's Memory for Science and Social Studies Facts

Pictorial mnemonic techniques also have been adapted to facilitate students' memory for science and social studies facts. Jones and Hall found that junior high school students could be taught the imagery version of the keyword method in the context of remembering definitions of medical terminology, as well as famous people and their inventions [41]. Pressley and Dennis-Rounds similarly taught the method to both secondary and elementary school students in the context of associating cities and their products [42]. Mnemonic illustrations have been devised to teach junior high school students the order in which U.S. presidents served [24, 25]; and to teach elementary-school children the U.S. capital cities [43, 44]. A recent dissertation study will serve as an example of the impressive benefits that can be expected of pictorial mnemonic strategies in the social studies and science domain.

Margo Mastropieri taught "learning-disabled" ninth graders the scientific hardness levels associated with fourteen minerals (ranging from 1 = bauxite to 10 = diamond) [45]. Adopting the Levin *et al.* [24] combined pictorial mnemonic strategy for learning the order of U.S. presidents, Mastropieri provided mnemonic subjects with interactive illustrations that included keywords for the minerals and rhyming "pegwords" for their associated numerical hardness levels (1 = bun, 2 = shoe, 3 = tree, . . . 10 = hen). For example, the keyword for *bauxite* was *box*, and the pegword for its associated hardness level of *1* was *bun*. The interactive illustration for bauxite depicted a box full of buns. The learning of mnemonic subjects was contrasted with both no-strategy control subjects and subjects who were taught the minerals and their hardness levels according to a method of "direct questioning" that has been advocated for students with learning disabilities. It was found that the average percentage of correct recalls produced by mnemonic subjects (75%) was more than twice as great as that produced by subjects in the two other conditions (28% and 36% for direct questioning and no-strategy control subjects, respectively), with no reliable difference between the latter two. Follow-up research by Mastropieri, Scruggs, and Levin revealed strikingly similar mnemonic effects both with children two years younger who were not classified as "learning disabled" and with educable mental retardates [46, 47].

Learning to Read

In a recent discussion [17], I speculated about the kind of illustrations that should be ideal for enabling children to master beginning reading and pre-reading skills (i.e., identifying letters and associating letters with their sounds). In particular, such "mnemonic" illustrations would have to include the recoding and retrieval components mentioned earlier. I asserted that illustrations lacking these components would not be nearly as effective memory enhancers as those that did contain them. Preliminary data from a study by Morris appear to be consistent with this assertion [48], and the data from a recent study by Ehri, Deffner, and Wilce provide even stronger support for it [49].

In Experiment 1 of their study, Ehri *et al.* presented lower middle-class first graders with a list of five lower-case letters, which had been selected on the basis of their names and sounds being unfamiliar to the children. Children were taught the letter sounds using one of two types of accompanying illustrations. Nonmnemonic illustrations displayed an object whose initial sound corresponded to the desired letter (e.g., a flower for *f*, as in the left portion of Figure 5). Mnemonic

Nonmnemonic Flower   *Mnemonic Flower*

Figure 5. Nonmnemonic picture (left) and mnemonic picture (right) for letter-sound learning. (From Ehri *et al.*, in press; reprinted by permission.)

illustrations displayed the same objects, but with one important exception: Each object was drawn so that the associated letter's *shape* was a salient aspect of the picture. For example, for the letter *f*, the flower was drawn in such a way that the vertical "|" appeared as the stem, the horizontal "−" as leaves, and the upper "hook" as the drooping petals (see the right portion of Figure 5). The rationale for developing such physically related pictures was simply that the sight of the letter (e.g., f) should readily elicit the associated picture (the f-resembling flower), from which could be extracted the appropriate sound (/f/).

Six days of instruction were provided for children in the two conditions, followed the next day by a test of letter-sound recall. On the average, children in the mnemonic picture condition were able to produce about twice as many correct letter sounds in comparison to students in the nonmnemonic-picture condition, 74 percent vs. 36 percent. Such results convincingly extend the previously made distinction between mnemonic and nonmnemonic pictures to the pre-reading skill domain of letter-sound acquisition. Appropriately designed "mnemonic" illustrations would be expected to facilitate children's letter and word identifications as well (see [17] for additional discussion).

Reading to Learn

Pictorial mnemonic techniques also have been successfully applied to the prose learning of junior high school students. In such tasks, science and social studies factual information has been embedded in short passages, and students have been required to recall that information following passage presentation. In most of the studies to date, the prose passages have been read to the students by an experimenter, while the students followed along silently. In the dozen or so experiments that now have been conducted in this domain [18, 20, 23, 50], one conclusion is resoundingly clear: Pictorial mnemonic encoding of the to-be-associated factual information substantially facilitates subsequent retrieval of that information. This is true whether the target information is concrete or relatively abstract, whether there are few or many facts to be recalled, whether the mnemonic pictures consist of actual illustrations or student-generated images, and whether performance is gauged in terms of an initial test administered immediately following passage presentation or in terms of a retest administered a few days later. Until very recently, however, an educationally important question that remained unanswered was: Will similar mnemonic facilitation be produced if students are required to read such factual prose passages on their own (rather than along with an experimenter)? This was a major question addressed by Ellen Peters in her doctoral dissertation [51].

Peters selected eighth-grade students with above- and below-average reading comprehension skills (based on standardized-test assessment). On the average, these students were reading approximately two years above and two years below grade level, respectively. Students were randomly assigned to mnemonic and no-strategy control conditions, where they read twelve short passages describing the purported accomplishments of fictitious people. The names selected (e.g., Charlene Fidler, William King, Julia Gardner) were those developed by Shriberg *et al*. [2, 3] . Mnemonic subjects were alerted that each of the surnames could be easily transformed into a picturable person (e.g., Fidler = a fiddler; King = a king; Gardner = a gardener), and that they should picture each person interacting with his/her described accomplishment. Control subjects were simply told to try their best to remember the accomplishments associated with the people about whom they were reading.

At both reading levels, mnemonic subjects outperformed controls by a wide margin on an immediate test of name/accomplishment recall. The mean percentages of correct accomplishments recalled in the above-average reading group were 74 percent and 46 percent for mnemonic and control subjects, respectively; in the below-average reading group, these figures were 63 percent and 21 percent. A similar pattern of results was obtained on a retest given a week later. It is interesting to note that the magnitude of the mnemonic effect across reading levels (about 100% facilitation) is almost identical to the size of the effect that had emerged in the previous mnemonic prose-learning studies where students were not required to read the passages themselves. In addition, it can be seen from these data that providing *below-average* readers with a mnemonic strategy on this task allowed them to perform at a level (63%) that was at least as high as that of *above-average* readers in the no-strategy control condition (46%). Thus, there can be little doubt that the previously obtained mnemonic facilitation reported in this context generalizes to a pure reading situation, for students with both above-average and below-average reading skills.

NEW APPLICATIONS, NEXT DIRECTIONS

In the final section of this chapter, I will mention what I view as some critical questions about educational mnemonic pictures that still need to be addressed. These questions span the range from an educational psychologist's research agenda for the next several years to a classroom teacher's need for effective curriculum materials and learning strategies that can be delivered to today's and tomorrow's students.

Limits and Limitations of Mnemonic Pictures

Whenever one is forced to consider the "real-world" applicability—and, I might add, acceptability—of mnemonic pictures, one is faced with finding the delicate balance between what might be regarded as their *limits* on the one hand, and their *limitations* on the other.

Limits. In my scheme of things, the limits of mnemonic-picture application are defined only by the limits of the applier's creative imagination. An extreme (though yet-to-be-refuted) assertion is that *pictorial mnemonic techniques can be successfully adapted to any curriculum content whose mastery depends on the retrieval of factual associations.* In all such situations, the mnemonic technique provides the critical direct retrieval path leading from the "asked" to the "asked for" information.

From the initial mnemonic research involving associations between a stimulus and a response [19, 52, 53] come some interesting extensions that serve to augment such techniques' versatility and potential value for school learning. We began with the well-documented success of the mnemonic keyword method in the context of vocabulary learning, where an association is formed between a recoded stimulus (a proxy for the unfamiliar vocabulary item) and a response (the meaning) [12]. Dual keyword approaches permit associations between a recoded stimulus and a recoded response, as in learning the capital cities of the United States [44]. Combinations of two or more mnemonic systems (such as keyword, pegword, and loci) can be profitably applied to the acquisition of *ordered* associations, as in learning the numbers of U.S. presidents [24] or minerals [45]. Moreover, and perhaps most importantly, mnemonic techniques permit the efficient storage and retrieval of the constituent facts and concepts embedded in expository-prose passages [23, 51]. Such facts need not consist of single entities [25, 50], nor need they represent concrete (directly visualized) concepts [20].

Yet, I believe that the true limits of pictorial mnemonic techniques in the educational domain have yet to be tested. Can mnemonic strategies, either by themselves or in combination with strategies based on other theoretical perspectives, facilitate the integration of large chunks of curriculum content? Consider, for example, the combined mnemonic system that junior high school students applied to the task of associating U.S. presidents and their numbers. Can additional pictorial mnemonics be incorporated into those already representing the presidents' numbers, in order to improve students' subsequent coding of biographical information about the presidents? This mnemonic "add on" question was answered in the affirmative in a recent doctoral study [54].

The question of mnemonic/nonmnemonic strategy combinations can best be illustrated in the context of expository prose learning. As I have argued previously [11], to date mnemonic-strategy applications have focused on the factual details associated with the text's "microstructure," and these have proven highly effective. But is it possible to combine mnemonic strategies with prose-processing strategies that are known to provide useful organizations and interpretations of the text's theme or "macrostructure?" In terms of our earlier *parakeet* example, the organizational Australia/Europe map (Figure 1) combined with the transformational Gould/1840 illustration (Figure 2) may be just the ticket needed to optimize, respectively, students' initial comprehension of the passage's theme and their subsequent recall of the passage's details. The educational potential of combined mnemonic and nonmnemonic strategies of this kind is currently being investigated in our laboratory.

Limitations. While the limits of pictorial mnemonic techniques are being explored, the potential limitations of these techniques also should be assessed. By "limitations," I am referring to both the neutral and negative consequences that can be expected from students' use of mnemonic strategies. It is foolhardy to expect mnemonic strategies to be all things for all people (i.e., to regard mnemonic strategies as a panacea for attaining all curriculum-related objectives). As has been already stated, mnemonic strategies are basically memory directed and, thus, curriculum objectives that do not include memory-demanding activity as a principal ingredient would not be expected to be mnemonic-strategy beneficiaries.

In this sense, then, the converse of the assertion made under the above "limits" discussion would be that *pictorial mnemonic techniques should not facilitate the acquisition of curriculum content whose mastery does not depend on the retrieval of factual associations.* For example, curriculum objectives related to mathematical and scientific reasoning, critical thinking, creative writing, good penmanship, or the performance of athletics, the arts, and industrial arts would not be expected to benefit—at least, in any obvious fashion—from the application of mnemonic strategies. At the same time, however, two points should be made clear: First, as Higbee has effectively argued [40], even if mnemonic strategies do not enhance students' attainment of such curriculum objectives, this should not be read as a *fault* or *condemnation* of mnemonic strategies. After all, can anyone name *any one* strategy that is capable of facilitating every kind of performance? Mnemonic strategies typically are not designed with the just-stated curriculum objectives in mind. This is not to say that if mnemonic-strategy attempts were made here, they would prove successful; but neither can it be said that creative, relevant mnemonic-strategy attempts would prove unsuccessful either.

A second point that needs to be made in this context is extremely important. Note that I opened this section on "limitations" by referring to *potential* limitations. The reason for this is simple: On more than one occasion, a mnemonic strategy has been applied to a task with the expectation that facilitating one aspect of task performance would be accompanied by a debilitating effect on some other aspect of task performance. For example, one argument has it that even though mnemonic vocabulary instruction may enhance definition recall, it will be devastating to vocabulary comprehension. As was discussed earlier in this chapter, however, the empirical data bearing on this argument permit not just discounting this argument, but even coming full circle with it; for it now appears that mnemonic-strategy use may well *facilitate* certain aspects of vocabulary comprehension. Many other instances of intuitively appealing, yet empirically disconfirmed, mnemonic-strategy outcomes are easy to document [55]. Thus, when it comes to speculating about the consequences of mnemonic-strategy use, one quickly learns to expect the unexpected!

Mnemonic Pictures and Student Differences

If only one feature of mnemonic pictures had to be recommended from an educational standpoint, it likely would be that they benefit all kinds of students. We have recently devoted a good deal of space providing evidence to support the statement that mnemonic-picture effects are generalizable across students with varying characteristics (e.g., across students differing considerably in age, intelligence, academic skill, and cultural background) [15]. To be sure, different *adaptations* of mnemonic techniques may be required for different kinds of students (e.g., in comparison to older students, younger students may require strategies with more concrete structure and support) [56]. But the important point is that it is possible to devise such mnemonic adaptations that will be of substantial benefit to most (if not all) students.

Five recently completed studies clearly support claims of mnemonic-strategy generalizability:

1. In one of these, it was found that "academically precocious" junior high school students were able to take maximum advantage of mnemonic illustrations when learning the numbers of U.S. presidents [25].
2. The recall of both above- and below-average readers was greatly facilitated by mnemonic imagery instructions in Peters's expository prose-learning study [51].
3. Both lower- and higher-achieving elementary-school students profited from mnemonic illustrations in the Levin *et al.* [22] vocabulary-learning study.
4. Mastropieri *et al.* [57] found marked improvement in the vocabulary acquisition of learning-disabled students who were provided with mnemonic illustrations.
5. Mastropieri found the same thing with learning-disabled students in her mineral hardness task [45]; and in a follow-up study by Mastropieri *et al.* [47], educable mental retardates also benefited from mnemonic illustrations.

The empirical fact that students who would otherwise be labeled "slow learners" or "poor students" can perform at an impressively high level when given mnemonic instruction should convince educators of the potential of receiving some very real educational payoffs from mnemonic approaches. Similarly, the existing data should silence the oft-heard argument that "good" students will not be helped by—or may even suffer from—use of mnemonic techniques [25, 58].

Mnemonic Strategy Training

Most of the optimistic recommendations in this chapter follow from research in which specially constructed mnemonic pictures are provided to students. That is, the mnemonic strategies have consisted of *imposed* (experimenter-provided) illustrations rather than *induced* (subject-generated) imagery [59]. The imposed approach certainly can be defended on the grounds that it is more globally effective with children—especially when the specific task and materials require the utilization of relatively complex transformational strategies. Accordingly, the present author has advocated the development, empirical validation, and classroom dissemination of mnemonic curriculum materials [14]. At the same time, however, there are at least three compelling reasons why greater effort should be devoted to the induced mnemonic-strategy approach: First, good mnemonic illustrations are costly to produce. Second, the same single mnemonic illustration may not be meaningful or appropriate for all students. Third, and perhaps most importantly, one cannot depend on mnemonic illustrations "being there;" as a matter of fact, they will not be there in most real-world situations. For all of these reasons, it makes good "dollars and sense" to provide students with systematic instruction in knowing why, how, and when to generate facilitative mnemonic images on their own.

Knowing Why: Mnemonic-Strategy Metacognitions. Accepting the argument that connects knowledge about a particular memory strategy's operation with the likelihood that strategy will be either spontaneously adopted or spontaneously abandoned [60-62], some researchers have begun to explore the importance of students' metacognitions with respect to mnemonic strategy deployment [63-67].

The results of the recent Pressley *et al.* study [66] make one observation abundantly clear: Before students come to believe in a mnemonic strategy's effectiveness, they must personally experience success in using that strategy. Thus, it is not sufficient simply to say to a student, "Let me tell you about a new way of learning something. . . ." Rather, the student must receive direct instruction in, practice with, and positive consequences from the strategy in order to increase the probability that he/she later will employ that strategy when given the choice. The degree of explicitness of such "metacognitive experiences" [62] varies with age: Greater explicitness is required for children than for adults [66]. Additional research is needed to determine the nature and sequence of specific metacognitive experiences that will ensure the most effective mnemonic-strategy training.

Knowing How: Mnemonic-Strategy Acquisition and Maintenance. How can we best instruct students to generate good mnemonic pictures (i.e., pictures whose recoded and related components are retrievable)? What research there is on this topic suggests that after some instruction, older children and adults can capably employ mnemonic strategies on their own, but younger children and less able students experience difficulty [3]. It must be pointed out, however, that this conclusion is based on the execution of a comparatively simple mnemonic strategy (i.e., the keyword method, as applied to learning the meanings of concrete nouns). With more complex strategies (e.g., number/name mnemonics for learning the presidents, and combined mnemonic/nonmnemonic approaches to expository-prose learning), it is reasonable to expect that even more sophisticated learners will experience some strategy-execution difficulties.

Similar questions of mnemonic-strategy deployment arise when time passes between initial instruction in the strategy's use and a subsequent opportunity to use it. A few days or a week following instruction, will students remember how to employ the strategy effectively, if reminded of it? Or, if not reminded, will students even remember that a previously learned strategy would be useful (i.e., will they exhibit metacognitive awareness)? Such issues of long-term maintenance have not been extensively investigated in this domain, even though issues of long-term retention (of previously learned content) now have been explored [20, 22, 38, 44, 50, 51]. The few studies that have focused on mnemonic-strategy maintenance, however, have offered very encouraging results [41, 68]. In particular, students who have received mnemonic-strategy instruction *do* spontaneously employ the strategies effectively on postinstructional maintenance tasks.

Knowing When: Mnemonic-Strategy Transfer. An issue closely related to (yet an additional step away from) the strategy maintenance issue is that of strategy generalization or transfer. The question here concerns whether, in the absence of explicit prompting, a student is able to adapt a mnemonic strategy that was initially applied to one task domain to a different task domain. The "knowing when" aspect of mnemonic-strategy transfer refers to the student's ability to discern the specific components and requisites of the transfer task that would make strategy adaptations either appropriate or inappropriate. For example, keyword-method transfer possibilities should seem more appropriate when one is going from a vocabulary-learning task to a names-and-accomplishments task then when one is going from a vocabulary-learning task to a digit-span or a pursuit rotor task.

Based on work that has already been done in this area [41, 42, 69] the prospects for obtaining some degree of mnemonic-strategy transfer seem promising. Yet, as with the other strategy topics discussed here, age and related cognitive-developmental indicators may constitute important moderates of transfer success. In the Pressley and Dennis-Rounds study, for instance, elementary-school children did not spontaneously transfer the keyword method from a cities-and-their-products task to a Latin-vocabulary task, whereas high-school students did. Only when the elementary-school children were provided with a general strategy-transfer "hint," did they exhibit successful transfer. However, O'Sullivan and Pressley further found that such hints are not necessary as long as the initial strategy training includes adequate metacognitive information about the strategy. Thus, once again, effective transfer cannot be divorced from the possession and deployment of relevant metacognitions on the part of the student [70].

Classroom Implementation of Mnemonic Pictures

We finally get to what most of us would agree is the "bottom line" regarding the use of pictorial mnemonic techniques: Even though they have consistently proven their worth under controlled experimental conditions, will they do similarly in actual classroom-learning situations? Although no definitive answer to this question can be given at this time, I will nonetheless attempt to address it briefly in this concluding section. I will do so on three fronts, as represented by *can, should,* and *will* subquestions: Can (Should) (Will) pictorial mnemonic techniques be implemented in the classroom?

Can Mnemonic Techniques Be Implemented in the Classroom? Something that often is tied in with the "classroom implementation" issue is what might be called the "group administration" issue. That is, the positive mnemonic effects that have been produced repeatedly when strategies are administered *individually* to subjects do not always materialize when the strategies are administered to subjects *in groups*. There certainly are enough citable instances of group-administered mnemonic-strategy successes for us to conclude that it is possible to adapt mnemonic techniques to group-administration procedures [20, 34, 38, 46, 47, 50]. Yet, some notable failures [34, 71] have been regarded as the Achilles' heel of classroom mnemonic applications [72].

I believe that criticism of mnemonic techniques strictly on the grounds of their failing to satisfy a group-administration criterion is unwarranted for a couple of reasons. In the first place, and as was noted above, the basic premise is not entirely correct. Several experiments now have been conducted where group-administered mnemonic strategies *have* proven facilitative. Second, and of major significance, the terms "group administration" and "classroom implementation" are not synonymous. Failure with the former in no way precludes success with the latter. One can conceive of many classroom-learning instances where individualized instructional approaches are adopted (via teachers, teacher aides, tutors, or the computer). If mnemonic techniques prove to be beneficial under any of these conditions, then, *regardless of their group-administration potential*, they still would have classroom-implementation potential. That is, determining whether or not mnemonic strategies can lend themselves to *classroom implementation* requires only that such strategies be evaluated in an actual school-learning context rather than in a laboratory-learning context. Systematic research satisfying this criterion has not yet been conducted, and it must be before conclusions about the classroom potential of mnemonic strategies are reached. At the same time, unsuccessful laboratory-based research attempts to teach mnemonic strategies in groups cannot be construed as the nail in the classroom-implementation coffin.

Should Mnemonic Techniques Be Implemented in the Classroom? This is a philosophical question that is bound to generate a good deal of emotion. Obviously, I think they should. But equally obviously—as I have emphasized here and previously—I believe that mnemonic strategies should not be taught *exclusively*. Rather, they should be considered carefully in conjunction with a teacher's specific instructional objectives. In some cases (in particular, when memory for factual content is the primary objective), a mnemonic-strategy approach will be not only appropriate but optimal. When other objectives are primary, alternative instructional strategies will be appropriate and optimal.

To exclude mnemonic strategies from the classroom because of their perceived "limitations" [40] is, I believe, as indefensible as teaching them exclusively. In the first place, their "memory" promise has been indicated in multitudinous empirical demonstrations throughout the past decade. And as has been illustrated throughout this chapter, such demonstrations have encompassed not just simple vocabulary learning, but also learning in a wide variety of curriculum content domains. It appears that we have barely scratched the surface with respect to potentially beneficial mnemonic applications in the classroom. Moreover, and of utmost importance to educators, the memorial benefits associated with mnemonic techniques have not been obtained at the expense of other valued performance measures. That is, it certainly cannot be argued on the basis of existing data that mnemonic strategies inhibit comprehension, problem-solving, critical thinking, and the like. Mnemonic critics may want to *believe* that that is the case; however, at least to date, such beliefs are empirically unfounded.

Will Mnemonic Techniques Be Implemented in the Classroom? Michael Pressley and I recently concluded that a series of interrelated events must occur before mnemonic techniques will find their way into tomorrow's classrooms (see [15]). Briefly stated, mnemonic techniques must both prove their effectiveness (as in the previous "Can" question) and overcome prevailing biases against them (as in the previous "Should" question). Whether or not such events will occur is anybody's guess. It is gratifying to discover, however, that mnemonic approaches are being given serious consideration by school practitioners and decision-makers. For example, our mnemonic states-and-capitals materials [73] are being requested for use by teachers; various mnemonic and prereading materials have been incorporated into ongoing classroom instruction [74] ; and mnemonic vocabulary and comprehension units are currently capturing the attention of curriculum materials developers [75, 76] .

I started out this chapter by claiming that mnemonic pictures offered new and exciting possibilities for facilitating classroom learning. It is hoped that these possibilities will continue to be explored, and that rational classroom-implementation decisions will follow from the results of such explorations.

REFERENCES

1. F. S. Bellezza, Mnemonic-Device Instruction with Adults, in *Cognitive Strategy Research: Psychological Foundations*, M. Pressley and J. R. Levin (eds.), Springer-Verlag, New York, 1983.
2. A. Paivio, Strategies in Language Learning, in *Cognitive Strategy Research: Educational Applications*, M. Pressley and J. R. Levin (eds.), Springer-Verlag, New York, 1983.
3. M. Pressley, J. R. Levin, and H. D. Delaney, The Mnemonic Keyword Method, *Review of Educational Research, 52*, pp. 61-91, 1982.
4. J. R. Levin, On Functions of Pictures in Prose, in *Neuropsychological and Cognitive Processes in Reading*, F. J. Pirozzolo and M. C. Wittrock (eds.), Academic Press, New York, 1981.
5. L. T. Frase, *A Heuristic Model for Research on Prose Learning*, paper presented at the annual meeting of the American Educational Research Association, New York, February 1971.

6. R. S. Dean and R. W. Kulhavy, The Influence of Spatial Organization in Prose Learning, *Journal of Educational Psychology, 73*, pp. 57-64, 1981.

7. W. G. Holliday, The Effects of Verbal and Adjunct Pictorial-Verbal Information in Science Instruction, *Journal of Research in Science Teaching, 12*, pp. 77-83, 1975.

8. W. Winn, *Processing and Interpreting Spatial Information in Graphic Materials*, paper presented at the annual meeting of the American Educational Research Association, Montreal, April 1983.

9. M. S. Dillingofski, *The Effects of Imposed and Induced Visual Imagery Strategies on Ninth Grade Difference-Poor Readers' Literal Comprehension of Concrete and Abstract Prose*, unpublished doctoral dissertation, Department of Curriculum and Instruction, University of Wisconsin, Madison, 1980.

10. J. M. Royer and G. W. Cable, Illustrations, Analogies, and Facilitative Transfer in Prose Learning, *Journal of Educational Psychology, 68*, pp. 205–209, 1976.

11. J. R. Levin, Pictures as Prose-Learning Devices, in *Discourse Processing*, A. Flammer and W. Kintsch (eds.), North-Holland, Amsterdam, 1982.

12. R. C. Atkinson, Mnemotechnics in Second-Language Learning, *American Psychologist, 30*, pp. 821-828, 1975.

13. F. S. Bellezza, Mnemonic Devices: Classification, Characteristics, and Criteria, *Review of Educational Research, 51*, pp. 247-275, 1981.

14. J. R. Levin, The Mnemonic '80s: Keywords in the Classroom, *Educational Psychologist, 16*, pp. 65-82, 1981.

15. J. R. Levin and M. Pressley, Mnemonic Vocabulary Instruction: What's Fact, What's Fiction, in *Individual Differences in Cognition* Vol. 2, R. F. Dillon and R. R. Schmeck (eds.), Academic Press, New York, in press.

16. B. J. F. Meyer, *The Organization of Prose and Its Effects on Memory*, North-Holland, Amsterdam, 1975.

17. J. R. Levin, Pictorial Strategies for School Learning: Practical Illustrations, in *Cognitive Strategy Research: Educational Applications*, M. Pressley and J. R. Levin (eds.), Springer-Verlag, New York, 1983.

18. J. R. Levin, L. K. Shriberg, and J. K. Berry, A Concrete Strategy for Remembering Abstract Prose, *American Educational Research Journal, 20*, pp. 277–290, 1983.

19. A. Paivio, *Imagery and Verbal Processes*, Holt and Co., New York, 1971.

20. L. K. Shriberg, *Comparison of Two Mnemonic Encoding Strategies in Children's Recognition and Recall of Abstract Prose Information*, unpublished doctoral dissertation, Department of Curriculum and Instruction, University of Wisconsin, Madison, 1982.

21. M. Pressley and J. R. Levin, Developmental Constraints Associated with Children's Use of the Keyword Method of Foreign Vocabulary Learning, *Journal of Experimental Child Psychology, 26*, pp. 359-372, 1978.

22. J. R. Levin, D. D. Johnson, S. D. Pittelman, B. L. Hayes, K. M. Levin, L. K. Shriberg, and S. Toms-Bronowski, A Comparison of Semantic- and Mnemonic-Based Vocabulary-Learning Strategies, *Reading Psychology, 5*, pp. 1–15, 1984.

23. L. K. Shriberg, J. R. Levin, C. B. McCormick, and M. Pressley, Learning about "Famous" People via the Keyword Method, *Journal of Educational Psychology*, *74*, pp. 238-247, 1982.

24. J. R. Levin, C. B. McCormick, and B. J. Dretzke, A Combined Pictorial Mnemonic Strategy for Ordered Information, *Educational Communication and Technology Journal*, *29*, pp. 219-225, 1981.

25. J. R. Levin, B. J. Dretzke, C. B. McCormick, T. E. Scruggs, J. E. McGivern, and M. A. Mastropieri, Learning via Mnemonic Pictures: Analysis of the Presidential Process, *Educational Communication and Technology Journal*, *31*, pp. 161-173, 1983.

26. J. R. Levin, C. B. McCormick, G. E. Miller, J. K. Berry, and M. Pressley, Mnemonic versus Nonmnemonic Vocabulary-Learning Strategies for Children, *American Educational Research Journal*, *19*, pp. 121-136, 1982.

27. F. A. Yates, *The Art of Memory*, Routledge and Kegan Paul, London, 1966.

28. R. C. Atkinson and M. R. Raugh, An Application of the Mnemonic Keyword Method to the Acquisition of a Russian Vocabulary, *Journal of Experimental Psychology: Human Learning and Memory*, *104*, pp. 126-133, 1975.

29. C. E. Ott, D. C. Butler, R. S. Blake, and J. P. Ball, The Effect of Interactive-Image Elaboration on the Acquisition of Foreign Language Vocabulary, *Language Learning*, *23*, pp. 197-206, 1973.

30. M. Pressley, Children's Use of the Keyword Method to Learn Simple Spanish Vocabulary Words, *Journal of Educational Psychology*, *69*, pp. 465-472, 1977.

31. M. Pressley, J. Samuel, M. M. Hershey, S. L. Bishop, and D. Dickinson, Use of A Mnemonic Technique to Teach Young Children Foreign Language Vocabulary, *Contemporary Educational Psychology*, *6*, pp. 110-116, 1981.

32. M. Pressley, J. R. Levin, and C. B. McCormick, Young Children's Learning of Foreign Language Vocabulary: A Sentence Variation of the Keyword Method, *Contemporary Educational Psychology*, *5*, pp. 22-29, 1980.

33. G. E. Miller, J. R. Levin, and M. Pressley, An Adaptation of the Keyword Method to Children's Learning of Foreign Verbs, *Journal of Mental Imagery*, *4*, pp. 57-61, 1980.

34. J. R. Levin, M. Pressley, C. B. McCormick, G. E. Miller and L. K. Shriberg, Assessing the Classroom Potential of the Keyword Method, *Journal of Educational Psychology*, *71*, pp. 583-594, 1979.

35. J. M. Royer and D. J. Cunningham, On the Theory and Measurement of Reading Comprehension, *Contemporary Educational Psychology*, *6*, pp. 187-216, 1981.

36. M. Pressley, J. R. Levin, and G. E. Miller, How Does the Keyword Method Affect Vocabulary Comprehension and Usage? *Reading Research Quarterly*, *16*, pp. 213-226, 1981.

37. J. R. Levin, B. J. Dretzke, M. Pressley, and J. E. McGivern, In Search of the Keyword Method/Vocabulary Comprehension Link, *Contemporary Educational Psychology*, in press.

38. J. Aurentz, *Self-Instruction and the Keyword Method: Effects Upon Vocabulary Usage*, unpublished manuscript, Department of Educational Research, Development, and Foundations, Florida State University, Tallahassee, 1982.

39. D. D. Johnson and P. D. Pearson, *Teaching Reading Vocabulary*, Holt and Co., New York, 1978.

40. K. L. Higbee, Some Pseudo-Limitations of Mnemonics, in *Practical Aspects of Memory*, M. M. Gruneberg, P. E. Morris, and R. N. Sykes (eds.), Academic Press, New York, 1978.

41. B. F. Jones and J. W. Hall, School Applications of the Mnemonic Keyword Method as a Study Strategy by Eighth Graders, *Journal of Educational Psychology*, *74*, pp. 230-237, 1982.

42. M. Pressley and J. Dennis-Rounds, Transfer of A Mnemonic Keyword Strategy at Two Age Levels, *Journal of Educational Psychology*, *72*, pp. 575-582, 1980.

43. J. R. Levin, J. K. Berry, G. E. Miller, and N. P. Bartell, More on How (And How Not) To Remember the States And Their Capitals, *Elementary School Journal*, *82*, pp. 379-388, 1982.

44. J. R. Levin, L. K. Shriberg, G. E. Miller, C. B. McCormick, and B. B. Levin, The Keyword Method in the Classroom: How To Remember the States and Their Capitals, *Elementary School Journal*, *80*, pp. 185-191, 1980.

45. M. A. Mastropieri, *Mnemonic Strategies with Learning-Disabled Students*, unpublished doctoral dissertation, Department of Special Education, Arizona State University, Tempe, 1983.

46. M. A. Mastropieri, T. E. Scruggs, and J. R. Levin, Mnemonic Strategy Instruction with Learning Disabled Adolescents, *Journal of Learning Disabilities*, in press.

47. _____, Direct Instruction vs. Mnemonic Instruction: Relative Benefits for Exceptional Learners, *Journal of Special Education*, in press.

48. E. B. Coleman, *Analysis of Imagery for a Reading Technology*, Research proposal, 1974.

49. L. C. Ehri, N. D. Deffner, and L. S. Wilce, Pictorial Mnemonics for Phonics, *Journal of Educational Psychology*, in press.

50. C. B. McCormick and J. R. Levin, A Comparison of Different Prose-Learning Variations of the Mnemonic Keyword Method, *American Educational Research Journal*, *21*, pp. 379–398, 1984.

51. E. E. Peters, *Effect of a Transformational Imagery Strategy on Poor and Good Comprehenders' Recall of Concrete Prose*, unpublished doctoral dissertation, Department of Special Education, Arizona State University, Tempe, 1983.

52. G. H. Bower, Mental Imagery and Associative Learning, in *Cognition in Learning and Memory*, L. Gregg (ed.), John Wiley and Sons, New York, 1972.

53. W. D. Rohwer, Jr., Elaboration and Learning in Childhood and Adolescence, in *Advances in Child Development and Behavior* (Vol. 8), H. W. Reese (ed.), Academic Press, New York, 1973.

54. B. J. Dretzke, *Building Factual Knowledge About the U.S. Presidents Via Pictorial Mnemonic Strategies*, unpublished doctoral dissertation, Department of Educational Psychology, University of Wisconsin, Madison, 1984.

55. J. R. Levin and M. Pressley, Understanding Mnemonic Imagery Effects: A Dozen "Obvious" Outcomes, in *Mental Imagery and Learning*, M. L. Fleming and D. W. Hutton (eds.), Educational Technology Publications, Englewood Cliffs, N.J., 1983.

56. J. E. McGivern and J. R. Levin, The Keyword Method and Children's Vocabulary Learning: An Interaction with Vocabulary Knowledge, *Contemporary Educational Psychology, 8*, pp. 46-54, 1983.

57. M. A. Mastropieri, T. E. Scruggs, J. R. Levin, J. Gaffney, and B. McLoone, Mnemonic Vocabulary Instruction with Learning Disabled Students, *Learning Disability Quarterly*, in press.

58. M. Pressley, J. R. Levin, G. V. Nakamura, D. J. Hope, J. G. Bispo, and A. R. Toye, The Keyword Method of Foreign Vocabulary Learning: An Investigation of its Generalizability, *Journal of Applied Psychology, 65*, pp. 635-642, 1980.

59. J. R. Levin, When Is a Picture Worth a Thousand Words?, in *Issues in Imagery and Learning: Four Papers* (Theoretical Paper No. 36). Wisconsin Research and Development Center for Cognitive Learning, Madison, 1972.

60. J. G. Borkowski and F. P. Buchel, Learning and Memory Strategies in the Mentally Retarded, in *Cognitive Strategy Research: Psychological Foundations*, M. Pressley and R. Levin (eds.), Springer-Verlag, New York, 1983.

61. A. L. Brown, Knowing When, Where, and How to Remember: A Problem of Metacognition, in *Advances in Instructional Psychology*, R. Glaser (ed.), Erlbaum, Hillsdale, New Jersey, 1978.

62. J. H. Flavell, Cognitive Monitoring, in *Children's Oral Communication Skills*, W. P. Dickson (ed.), Academic Press, New York, 1981.

63. M. G. Lodico, E. S. Ghatala, J. R. Levin, M. Pressley, and J. A. Bell, The Effects of Strategy-Monitoring Training on Children's Selection of Effective Memory Strategies, *Journal of Experimental Child Psychology, 35*, pp. 263-277, 1983.

64. J. E. McGivern, J. R. Levin, E. S. Ghatala, and M. Pressley, *Developmental Differences in the Vicarious Acquisition of an Effective Learning Strategy*, paper presented at the annual meeting of the American Educational Research Association, Montreal, April 1983.

65. E. D. Moynahan, Assessment and Selection of Paired Associate Strategies: A Developmental Study, *Journal of Experimental Child Psychology, 26*, pp. 257-266, 1978.

66. M. Pressley, J. R. Levin, and E. S. Ghatala, Memory-Strategy Monitoring in Adults and Children, *Journal of Verbal Learning and Verbal Behavior, 23*, pp. 270-288, 1984.

67. J. J. Shaughnessy, Memory Monitoring Accuracy and Modification of Rehearsal Strategies, *Journal of Verbal Learning and Verbal Behavior, 20*, pp. 216-230, 1981.

68. W. D. Rohwer, Jr. and J. Litrownik, Age and Individual Differences in the Learning of a Memorization Procedure, *Journal of Educational Psychology*, in press.

69. J. T. O'Sullivan and M. Pressley, Completeness of Instruction and Strategy Transfer, *Journal of Experimental Child Psychology*, in press.

70. M. Pressley, J. G. Borkowski, and J. T. O'Sullivan, Children's Metamemory and the Teaching of Memory Strategies, in *Metacognition, Cognition and Human Performance*, D. L. Forrest-Pressley, G. E. MacKinnon, and T. G. Waller (eds.), Academic Press, San Diego, in press.

71. J. W. Hall, K. P. Wilson, and R. J. Patterson, Mnemotechnics: Some Limitations of the Mnemonic Keyword Method for the Study of Foreign Language Vocabulary, *Journal of Educational Psychology*, *73*, pp. 345-357, 1981.

72. J. M. O'Malley, R. P. Russo, and A. U. Chamot, *A Review of the Literature on Learning Strategies in the Acquisition of English as a Second Language: The Potential for Research Applications*, InterAmerica Technical Report DREMS 83-01, Rosslyn, Virginia, 1983.

73. J. R. Levin and L. K. Shriberg, *U.S. States and Capitals*, Wisconsin Center for Education Research, Madison, 1982.

74. H. Nicholson and M. Putnam, *Putnik: Phonics of Today* (3rd edition), PUTNIK, St. Paul, 1975.

75. A. S. Escoe, Personal communication, June 1983.

76. B. F. Jones, Personal communication, June 1983.

CHAPTER 4

The 4Rs: Readin', 'riting, 'rithmetic, and the Right Hemisphere. A Review of the Application of the Brain Laterality Model to Education

ROBERT G. LEY
AND MELVIN KAUSHANSKY

In recent years, public-school education has been under attack. It has been criticized for being "lopsided" and "asymmetric" [1], "left-brained" [2], and perhaps even "no-brained." Fault has been found with curricula, instructional methods, teachers, and administrators for "discriminat(ing) against the right hemisphere" [1, p. 29] and for "prejudice against the analogic, intuitive, wholistic functions of the right mind" [3, p. 24]. Such criticisms have evolved from claims about the differential information-processing styles of the brain's two cerebral hemispheres.

A simplistic view of cerebral asymmetry holds that the left hemisphere has a specialization for speech and language; whereas, the right hemisphere is relatively specialized for nonverbal functions, such as visual-spatial tasks, face or emotion recognition, and many musical and imagery abilities [4-6].

Since the mid-1970s, teacher-oriented journals have reported findings from the neurosciences and discussions of the implications of these experimental data for educational policy and practice [7]. The concept of "hemispheric specialization" or "brain lateralization," according to which, the left and right hemispheres of the cerebral cortex are functionally different, has much relevance for educators. Education journal articles, with titles of the following ilk have proliferated: "Right-brained kids in left-brain schools" [2], "Educating for both sides of the human mind" [8], and "Cerebral symmetry: An urgent concern for education" [9]. Books such as Williams' [1] *Teaching for the Two-sided Mind*, or Buzan's [11] *Use Both Sides of Your Brain* have enjoyed considerable popular and professional circulation. For example, Edwards' [12] *Drawing on the Right Side of the Brain* aims to improve the reader's artistic skills by tapping the creative potential and "drawing abilities of the right half of the brain," has sold hundreds of thousands of copies and was on the New York Times Best Seller's list for more than thirteen months.

Assumedly, on the basis of contemporary brain research, articles, books, and even workshops of this genre often advocate a radical reconceptualization of teaching practice so that it is more "brain-congruent." Educators have been exhorted to develop teaching strategies which are attuned to the right hemisphere's supposedly unique independent cognitive mode. Many authorities agree upon the use of visual imagery as a vehicle for stimulating "right-brain" learning and problem solving. Imagery-based techniques for achieving such an end include "affective teaching" [13], diagramming and modeling [14], "clustering" or brain-storming [15], and the direct deployment of "visual arts," such as basket weaving, woodwork, coloring, and crocheting [16].

The present chapter reviews the efforts to apply the brain laterality model to educational practice. In so doing, we seek to assess if the empirical data on hemispheric asymmetries has been applied correctly in the classroom. In other words, has the "translation" or information transfer between neuroscientist and school teacher been an accurate one? It is not our intention to suggest instructional techniques which capitalize on purported hemispheric functional differences [10, 11], but rather to evaluate the panoply of "right-brain" instructional methods and the "whole-brain" educational philosophies which have been advocated.

A PRIMER ON CEREBRAL LATERALITY

Before assessing the adequacy of left-brain/right-brain educational strategies, it is prudent to examine the neuropsychological evidence upon which these techniques allegedly are founded. Thus a summary of what is and is not known about the cerebral hemispheres seems appropriate. This review will provide a frame of reference against which the educator's application of the laterality model can be contrasted.

Various chroniclers of the history of cerebral localization are fond of citing neurologically relevant anecdotes and aphorisms from antiquity [17]. However, the musings of Greek and German poets withstanding, there is a contemporary consensus that the principal impetus for localizing specific brain functions was provided by the French physician, Broca. In 1861, Broca claimed that autopsy data demonstrated that left frontal lobe lesions resulted in loss or disturbance of speech (aphasias). Broca is further credited with being the first in the medical community to suggest that the asymmetry of the human brain was related to a speech center and hand preference [18].

Around the same time that Broca was conducting his clinical studies in France, John Hughlings Jackson, a British neurologist, was investigating the focal/motor seizure patterns of epileptics. Jackson proposed the concept of a "leading hemisphere," which was a theoretical precursor of the idea of cerebral dominance, the degree to which one hemisphere "dominates" a particular cognitive function. Jackson also coined the term "propositional hemisphere," referring to the speaking, writing, and mathematical functions of the left hemisphere [1]. Jackson believed that the posterior lobes of the right hemisphere subserved visual ideation, a postulate which anticipated contemporary evidence linking imagery and the right hemisphere [5]. Given Jackson's findings and the attribution of cognitive functions to each hemisphere, it is not surprising that the left hemisphere's "superiority" and the right hemisphere's relatively minor role had been clearly established by the turn of the century.

Since that time, the seminal research on hemispheric specialization has been conducted on three general groups of subjects: brain-lesioned or brain-injured patients, "split-brain" patients [19], and normal, neurologically intact individuals [4]. Each of these subject populations has offered a unique opportunity to investigate brain-behavior relationships. For example, the soldiers wounded in the Boer War, Balkan conflicts, and World War I were excellent subjects for neuropsychological study. Their "excellence" as research subjects was due to the likelihood that their missile wounds often were precisely localized in the cerebral cortex, and the resultant cognitive or behavioral disabilities could be readily observed. Additionally, the soldiers' posttraumatic functioning could be contrasted with their premorbid status which had been routinely established during military induction.

The brain lesion data from the war years indicated that, depending on the site, left-hemisphere lesions predominantly produce disturbances in language (aphasia), as well as inabilities to read (alexia) or calculate (acalculia). In contrast, right-hemisphere lesions yield visuospatial disorders, such as disturbances in facial- and emotional-expression recognition, and in form and color recognition. Visual imagery (and dreaming) also was found to be disrupted by right-hemisphere damage [5].

Data from the "split-brains" confirmed most of the clinical findings derived from studies of brain-lesioned patients. Split-brain surgery is a radical procedure in which the corpus callosum, the bundle of nerve fibers which connects the left and right hemispheres, is (partially) severed. In the 1960s, this surgery was performed on a small group of patients with intractable epilepsy, with the aim of confining seizure activity to a single hemispheric focus. The surgery was successful in delimiting seizures, but naturally the split-brain patients were without a communicative bridge or network between their two hemispheres.

The group of psychological effects resulting from the cutting of the cerebral commissures became known as the "callosal syndrome" [20]. Because of the contralateral ennervation of the human body (i.e., sensory stimuli on the left side of the body and space are projected to the right hemisphere; whereas, percepts on the right side are projected to the left hemisphere), once the left and right hemispheres were disengaged, sensory information in one hemisphere was cut off from processing, mediating, or expression by the other hemisphere. For example, let us say that the split-brain patient palpated an unseen common object, such as an apple. When the apple was held in the right hand, it could be named (via the verbal expressive functions of the left hemisphere); whereas, when it was held in the left hand, it could not be verbally identified (because of the restricted linguistic capacity of the right hemisphere).

In short, the initial systematic behavioral study of the split-brain patients confirmed the principal dichotomy of left hemisphere/verbal abilities and right hemisphere/visual, spatial abilities, although rudimentary evidence of right hemispheric emotion and imagery processing also emerged [20]. Additionally, around this same time, it was first suggested that each hemisphere deploys a different information-processing style [21]. The right hemisphere was characterized as a synthesizer, specialized for gestalt perception; whereas, the left hemisphere seemed to operate in a logical, analytic, computerlike fashion. These cognitive-style attributes, left/logical versus right/gestalt, would later become a most common nomenclature, and they foreshadowed the construal of educational policies and strategies in like terms.

Recently, the split-brain studies have been criticized for providing a nonrepresentative model for normal cortical functioning. It is felt that, because of the limited number of subjects examined, the lack of knowledge about the patients' premorbid abilities and the resultant possibility of functional reorganization occurring prior to surgical intervention, it is unsound to generalize to the normal brain [22]. Despite such criticism, the empirical yield of the split-brain studies is substantial and widely recognized: Sperry received the Nobel prize for science in 1982.

The metaphoric and figurative yield from the callosal syndrome also was considerable and had a profound impact on educators. While it has traditionally been rare for pioneering neuroscientists to write for a national magazine (e.g., *Saturday Review*) or a national teacher's journal, the principle researchers of the original group of commissurotomy patients did so. In these articles, Sperry [23] and Bogen [1] speculated about the dual nature of man's mind. The unique and independent cognitive functioning of each hemisphere was implied in numerous intriguing (and often amusing) anecdotes about the split-brain subjects' behavior, for example, by observations of a patient who attempted to pull down his pants with one hand and to pull them up with the other [24]. Sperry suggested that each cerebral hemisphere has "its own and private sensations, perceptions, concepts, its own impulses to act, with related volitional, cognitive and learning experiences" [25, p. 724].

Bogen, the neurosurgeon who originally examined the split-brain patients, wrote a series of highly influential articles, which frequently were quoted as a demonstration of "a neurosurgeon's view of creativity and a neglected right hemisphere" [26, 27]. These articles were to be oft-cited as justification for applying the brain laterality model to educational practice.

In these papers, Bogen reviewed the 100-year history of hemispheric specialization and delineated broad hemispheric characteristics. He also introduced the notion of the relative neglect of the right hemisphere and the potentially salutary effects of "greater consideration" of it. Hence, hemispheres were no longer to be considered major and minor, and the concept of cerebral dominance was largely discredited.

Bogen was particularly interested in creativity and hypothesized that the right hemisphere was instrumental for the creative process and that the corpus callosum could be construed as the mediator of interhemispheric creative problem solving. Bogen was especially adroit at culling delightful quotations, from diverse sources, which were relevant to his position [26, 27]. For example, on the creative experience, Bogen cites Reusch and Kees, "The writer depends necessarily upon invoking non-verbal images to verbal means," and Einstein, "The physical entities which seem to serve as elements in thought are certain signs and more or less clear images . . . [in] combinatory play." Bogen intimated that such "non-verbal images" and "combinatory play" were the province of the right hemisphere.

Despite the immense intuitive appeal of Bogen's formulations, many of his adherents seemingly failed to recognize the speculative nature of his position and the personal viewpoint implicit in it [7]. Sperry's [23] and Bogen's [1] popular press articles represented undeniably creative but perhaps fanciful extrapolations from the neuropsychological data base, rather than explications of it.

From the mid-1960s to the early 1970s, knowledge about the differential cognitive functions of the cerebral hemispheres increased exponentially. Clinical research on brain-damaged individuals continued unabated. Most significantly, however, a host of investigative strategies for studying hemispheric specialization were applied to both clinical and normal groups [4]. Three principal techniques have been used: dichotic listening, tachistoscopic visual half-field presentations, and electroencephalography (EEG). More recent, advanced methodological techniques include regional cerebral blood flow (rCBF), Positive Emission Tomography (PET), and Nuclear Magnetic Resonance (NMR). However, these latter three techniques are expensive and have correspondingly lower utilization rates. For example, it is estimated that there are perhaps not more than ten to fifteen PET scanners in North America, each one costing in excess of one million dollars.

The findings of these research endeavors with normal subjects, although by and large confirmatory of the executive speech and visuospatial functions of the left and right hemispheres, also revealed that the distribution of cognitive functions between hemispheres was not as simple, neat, and parsimonious as some laterality zealots had inferred. For example, the subject's age, sex, handedness, mood, cognitive and attentional styles, as well as the experimental methodology, were factors found to markedly influence perceptual asymmetries [4]. It also was discovered that the right hemisphere had some rudimentary language representation [28, 29] and that the left hemisphere was involved in rhythmic components in music [30]. A host of left/right hemispheric cognitive style dichotomies also were proposed. In addition to Levy-Agresti and Sperry's analytic/ holistic distinction [21], characterizations such as temporal/sequential processing [31], focal/diffuse [32], and serial/parallel [33] also were advanced.

Inside the laboratory and clinic, research on cerebral laterality proliferated; outside the scientific community the popularization of "left-brain/right-brain" differences reached faddish proportions. In both communities, there was seeming haste to narrow human performance into two modes; "dichotomania" prevailed. Since 1970, hemispheric differences in function have been mustered to explain divergent behaviors ranging from classroom seating [34] to tennis playing [35] to business management [36].

Before turning to the interpretation and application to the classroom of the extant knowledge of cerebral laterality (which began in earnest after 1974) [7], the prevalent beliefs in lay and scientific circles need identification. Many of the beliefs had evolved considerably and were quite discrepant from the data that had fostered them. Nonetheless, the beliefs and trends noted below had much popular currency and came to constitute the "laterality model" as it was understood and interpreted by educators. The components of the laterality model were the following:

1. In spite of the incongruities of the research findings, poor methodology, and in some cases, an unawareness of mitigating factors, such as sex, handedness, attention, etc., many researchers maintained a notion of information processing that was fully lateralized in one hemisphere or the other.
2. There seemed to be an urgency to replace the original verbal/visuospatial model with an all-inclusive dichotomy of analytic versus holistic cognitive styles [37].

The consequences of the above two trends were the following:

1. Concepts such as holistic/analytic or serial/parallel process were not receptive to operational definition. Such conceptual "looseness" may be of heuristic value, but these broad and general terms also could be manipulated to fit the researcher's needs (or data).
2. There was a strong tendency to use the disparate characteristics of hemispheric specialization to globally represent each hemisphere. This tendency resulted in the upgrading of a processing feature to a cognitive style, which ultimately became a *fixed* description of the *unique* and largely *independent* function of that hemisphere. Thus, although the right hemisphere was said to have holistic information-processing characteristics, this sole feature now came to describe the right hemisphere *in toto*. As Segalowitz has astutely noted [6], this assignation led to even wider-ranging extrapolations: holistic thinking thus became "emotional," "creative," and "intuitive."
3. As the humorist Robert Benchley has observed, there are two types of people: those who divide things into two groups and those who do not! As dichotomies were rapidly articulated, it became necessary to assign a hemisphere to one pole of the dichotomy in a *post-hoc* fashion or through default. Cohen describes this process as "shoehorning" [38]. A "band-wagon" effect was created, which fostered further rigid "dichotomizing," with an accompanying loss in quality of fit between the assigned attribute and the data which putatively had engendered it.
4. Given the foregoing, an *absolute model* of hemispheric specialization emerged. It was further bolstered because *inter*hemispheric differences were accentuated, and substantial *intra*hemispheric differences were minimized. Furthermore, the enormous individual differences in cortical organization were largely ignored. Levy argues that the standard laterality pattern is but one among many and that "no more than 15 percent of the population" likely demonstrate the classical and absolute hemispheric pattern of left/right, verbal linguistic/visuospatial [39].
5. It was believed that a strong tendency existed for individuals to preponderantly use one hemisphere to cognize their world and process the information in it [26, 27, 40]:

This was called "hemisphericity." The notion of individual hemisphericity eventually was extended to groups of individuals, implying that different cultures were more prone to display one or the other hemispheric mode of processing information [41].

In short, by the mid-1970s, the stage was set for the wholesale application of the laterality model to education. It was believed that the unique and independent cognitive function of the left and right hemisphere could underpin alterations to course content, curricula, and instructional methodology.

THE LATERALITY MODEL IN THE CLASSROOM

One of the early and significant applications of brain research to the classroom was the work of Orton, who attempted to show a relationship between reading disabilities, especially right/left discrimination, and a lack of lateral dominance [42]. Orton's views had considerable impact on educational theory and practice. They also led to the institution of dominance-enhancing exercises as remedial for reading and writing difficulties. Recent research has failed to establish a causal relationship between lateralization and reading disability [43], and thus, Orton's propositions have been generally discredited. However, Orton's emphasis on left hemispheric "inadequacies" presaged (by about 40 years) an even more fervent concern about the development, education, and exercise of the other hemisphere (e.g., the right) of the contemporary public-school student.

The "Problem:" Left-Brain Education

In the 1970s, a humanistic backlash against a behaviorist orientation in public school education and an accompanying interest in things holistic, imageable/visual, intuitive, creative, and artistic, coalesced with the new research on brain lateralization. At the confluence of these streams of interest was the right hemisphere. For many educators, it then followed that if students were deficient in visual thinking, creative problem solving, artistic endeavors, or other nonlinguistic abilities, these deficits were due to "minimal or haphazard practice in using their right brains" [2, p. 47]. In a superb historical perspective on right-brain education, Harris recounts the wondrous educational benefits claimed from stimulating the right hemisphere [44]. He states that the signs of a "new educational fad" were unmistakable.

If right-brain or whole-brain school programs represent education's latest fad, considerable impetus for the vogue paradoxically came from some of the neuroscientists, who had made sizable empirical contributions to the literature on lateral specialization. Some of these researchers also first articulated the extension of knowledge about cerebral asymmetries to educational policy. For example, Ornstein, in a provocative book, *The Psychology of Consciousness*, popularized the notion of cultural hemisphericity, stating that Western society relies on the left hemisphere's analytic, logical, verbal, and mathematical functions at the cost of limited utilization of the right hemisphere's holistic, artistic, imagery-based faculties [40]. About public school education, Ornstein wrote:

> We deemphasize and even devalue the irrational, nonverbal modes of consciousness. Education consists predominantly of 'reading, ritin', and rithmetic,' and we are taught precious little about our emotions, our bodies, our intuitive capabilities. A strict emphasis on verbal intellectual knowledge has screened out much of what is or could be legitimate for study in contemporary psychology [40, p. 26].

Somewhat similarly Nebes posited:

> If there is any truth in the assertion that our culture stresses left-hemisphere skills, this is especially true of the school system. Selection for higher education is based predominantly on the ability to comprehend and manipulate language . . . we are short-changing ourselves when we educate only left-sided talents in basic schooling [45, p. 16].

Bogen remarks:

> Since education is effective insofar as it affects the working of the brain, we can see that an elementary school program . . . will educate mainly one hemisphere, leaving half of an individual's high level potential unschooled [1, p. 27].

As Kaushansky has discovered, there was an upwelling of articles around 1975, some by neuroscientists, others by educators, interpreting the cerebral laterality data and all inveighing against public schools for neglecting the right hemisphere's educational needs [7]. Bogen put it most bluntly: "The entire student body is being educated lopsidedly" [1, p. 29]. Further, it was suggested that the cultural bias against right hemispheric modes of cognition was perpetuated by public schools.

The consequences of this purported discrimination against the right hemisphere were most dire for the student. It was believed that right hemisphericity students especially would be thwarted by a left hemispheric instructional style. As a result, the student would be prone to frustration, inattentiveness, and acting out [46]. The old "saw" that "unhappy children don't learn" was passionately resurrected, and a left hemispheric educational system was perceived as a potential cause of students' dysphoria. All manner of emotional unrest and lessened academic motivation and achievement presumably were attendant upon a continuance of left hemispheric educational policies. Gazzaniga expressed the concern about such a process:

> [If] (s)he [the student] is being forced into a curriculum that emphasizes the verbal articularity modes of solving a conceptual problem, this child will encounter enormous frustration and difficulty which may well result in hostility toward the teacher and worse toward the learning process itself [47, p. 11].

In short, the educational community responded with alarm to the conclusion, seemingly initially provided by the neuroscientists themselves, that educators were teaching to only half a brain (the left). The upwelling of articles in teacher magazines and education journals, which interpreted and applied the laterality findings, became a flood. Approximately 330 articles on brain laterality and education were published between 1966 and 1981, with over 20 percent of them published in 1981 [7]. From the sample of these articles which we have examined, it seems that the vast majority of the authors argued that educational instruction was pitched towards the left hemisphere's specializations and concomitantly undervalued right hemispheric capacities. Because of this biased teaching methodology, students suffered, and their innate capabilities and potential were not tapped. Instructional methods and curricula which emphasized the right hemisphere, or at least a more balanced approach, were perceived as the remedial answer.

THE SOLUTION: RIGHT-BRAIN AND/OR WHOLE-BRAIN EDUCATION

A host of teaching strategies and curriculum modifications were identified and advocated to redress a perceived educational (and hemispheric) imbalance. Methods for achieving this end included a "language experience" teaching approach and "affective teaching" [13], the ability to move from one process to another at will [48], employing divergent strategies and avoiding reductionist answers [49], diagramming and modeling [14], and direct experience in visual and manual arts [16].

Specific articles in subject area journals stressed right-brain approaches or cooperation between hemispheres in teaching particular subjects. It seemed that presenting material in both verbal/analytic and spatial/wholistic modes assured that no student would be hemispherically handicapped in initial classroom instruction.

Learning to read is perhaps the most important skill acquired in school. The fully functioning, reading teacher in a "symmetric" classroom could utilize "whole-brain" strategies, such as: imagery, the correct mode of questioning, daily exposure of students to literature (with emphasis on themes—a supposed right-hemisphere activity), and diagnostic (that is, of hemisphericity) teaching. Hudgens suggested that students at the junior-college level who were not efficient readers (in her appraisal, due to left-hemisphere difficulties) might become more proficient by involving themselves in concrete or imageable experiences to increase their understanding of abstract learning [50]. Hudgens proposes that the visual arts would be at the core of such a program. The teaching staff would consist of artists, art educators, and art therapists, as well as guided-imagery experts and instructors sensitive to multisensory reading.

Nelson pointed out to the English teacher that the left hemisphere was the scientist, while the right hemisphere was the poet [51]. Wolfe and Reising offered

English teachers strategies to enhance both hemispheres via affective teaching [52]. An educational emphasis on right hemispheric modes of thought seemingly legitimized English as a proper area of study, although previously it often had experienced subtle disparagement because of its metaphoric, nonanalytic or "fuzzy" nature.

The teaching of mathematics, a supposedly prototypic left hemispheric function, was examined under the light of the laterality model and found wanting. Given the new brain approach, mathematics curricula "provide little encouragement of right hemisphere thought" [53]. The raising of mathematics to a "brain-compatible status" would involve; the application of mathematics to everyday, concrete problems, geometry, computer literacy [54], and puzzles [53]. It was argued that these activities would tap right hemispheric capacities.

Right- or whole-brain instructional methods were suggested for chemistry [55], biology [56], art [57], music [58], and even outdoor education [59]. The tenor of these articles is much as described above, and the essence of the genre is captured in the extreme by Staley's conclusion that "outdoor education . . . achieves its ultimate impact on an individual in experiences which are probably sensed and interpreted in the right hemisphere" [59, p. 46].

A perusal of the roster of school subjects for which specific educational techniques, learning aids, and curricula were prescribed, makes it evident that the laterality model cast a wide net. Those who interpreted the cerebral asymmetry research and suggested educational applications of it, also agreed upon the importance of imagery as a means of facilitating new, whole-brain learning. For example, Williams, in the recent book, *Teaching for the Two-sided Mind*, has proposed the use of metaphor, visual thinking, fantasy, multisensory learning, and direct experience as a means of balancing the curriculum [10].

IMAGERY AND VISUALIZATION

Abundant research attests to the use of imagery as a mnemonic and learning aid [60, 61], and its efficacy is largely indisputable. Generally it is accepted that learning can be greatly improved if verbal material is supported or, in some cases, replaced by imagery. In his review of children's learning and imagery, Pressley concluded, "Imposed pictures [imagery] are almost always learned better than words. No more experiments are required to substantiate the positive effect of pictures on children's learning" [62, p. 613]. Although research in both cognitive and educational psychology on imagery, learning, and thinking has proliferated since Paivio [63] enunciated a dual coding model (words vs. pictures) for information processing, an intensification of interest in imagery accompanied the application of the laterality model to the classroom.

The burgeoning excitement about imagery was somewhat predictable given educators' interest in the right hemisphere and the neuropsychological finding that imagery is subserved by the right hemisphere [5]. Virtually every article in education journals which reviews right-brain instructional strategies identifies imagery techniques as being instrumental to them. Descriptions of techniques, such as guided fantasy [64, 65], various visualization methods [10], and imagery-based problem-solving strategies, pervade these articles. For example, Rico introduced readers to "clustering," which supposedly draws heavily upon the nonlinear functions of the right hemisphere [15]. Clustering is described as being similar to "brainstorming" or other "stream of consciousness" techniques. During clustering, the student visually creates a web or labyrinth of related ideas on a central theme; subsequently the web is used in creative writing or problem solving. Specific training programs also were developed to enhance students' spatial-visualization abilities for a variety of subjects, including mathematics [66].

The range of imagery techniques perhaps is limited only by an educator's ability to devise such techniques. Fairly spectacular claims for accelerated learning often accompany those imagery methods which are applied outside of the classroom, especially if they "make it" in the market place. For example, the Lozanow method of foreign-language learning combines deep muscle relaxation training and positive suggestion with imagery-based instruction, which often requires the student to encode words and phrases in bizarre images. The Lozanow method has generated great enthusiasm amongst linguists: Its combination of relaxation, imagery, and a positive emotional context makes it especially tailored to the right hemisphere. Of interest is that the Lozanow method may not differ radically from techniques suggested by Galyeen who recommends imaging, chanting, breathing, and movement, to redress the hemispheric imbalance in the classroom [67].

CREATIVITY

Many educators have linked imagery with the creative act itself [68]. Empirical evidence substantiates this general association [69], although the specific relationship between imagery and creativity is complex, largely, we suspect, because the constructs are multiplex. Our review indicates that educators favor the notion that creativity is housed in the right hemisphere. For example, Wheatley states, "There is evidence that the right hemisphere is the site of creative thought" [53, p. 38].

The belief that creativity is a property of the right hemisphere is perhaps the most appealing dichotomization (to educators) in the cortical spectrum [7]. The popularity of this notion may have been fueled by the humanistic [70] and "confluent education" movements initiated by educators in the late 1960s and early 1970s, who felt that public school education was not meeting the needs of the whole person. Many of these educators further stated that the school system overemphasized the so-called left-hemisphere functions (i.e., "the three Rs"), at the expense of undereducating right hemispheric properties (i.e., arts and creativity). This movement achieved the status of a zeitgeist and many teachers were highly motivated to have "creative," "holistic," and "student-centered" classrooms. The findings of the studies with split-brain patients, specifically, and of the cerebral-laterality research, generally, presumably provided sound evidence for such reconceptualizations.

However, Kaushansky has concluded that the association between creativity and the right hemisphere was not founded on any substantive empirical basis [7]. More than likely, the association evolved inferentially, due to the application of descriptors, such as intuitive, irrational, visual, inarticulate, etc., to both the right hemisphere's cognitive style and to creative thought itself [68].

Given the supposition that the right-brain housed creativity, it naturally followed that right-brain stimulation prompted creative processes.

The belief in an isomorphic correspondence between special exercise for the right hemisphere and enhanced creative output is a naive one. It is reminiscent of the advocacy of the Ambidextral Cultural Society at the turn of the century [44]. These zealots encouraged the development of ambidexterity, particularly among school children, and claimed that it would result in greater proficiency in "manly" arts (especially armed combat), art, education, increased intellectual functioning, and even relief from writer's cramp and spinal curvature (due to angling the body for right-handed writing postures). They proposed motor exercises to increase the activity of the largely inert and unused right hemisphere, with the expectation that such enhancement offered the potential for "doubling mental powers." Also they envisioned that each hemisphere would subserve different languages, and thus, an absolute communication deficit would not result if the speech centers of the left hemisphere were damaged (i.e., the patient could speak the foreign language presumably encoded in the preserved right hemisphere). In an excellent piece of scholarship, Harris has drawn a fascinating parallel between the Ambidextral Cultural Society of the 1890s and the right-brain educators of the 1970s: Harris' description is strongly recommended to the interested reader of matters hemispheric.

Initially, the association between creative thinking and the right hemisphere was a firm one. Consistent with the right hemisphere = creativity equation, many methods were promulgated for improving school children's artistic abilities. The most popular technique was described by Edwards in the best-selling book, *Drawing on the Right Side of the Brain* [12]. Edwards devised exercises which were intended to bypass "L-mode" or left hemispheric faculties, to actualize "R-mode" or right hemispheric drawing abilities, and thereby improving the artistic rendering.

Creativity, for the purposes of right hemispheric assignation, has been construed rather monolithically. This simplistic viewpoint eventually was broadened to encompass those theories which considered creativity to involve two complementary modes of thought, be they described as "lateral" and "vertical" [71], "critical" and "creative" [72], or "active" and "receptive" [73]. Thus, subsequent models of creative-thinking processes assigned important cognitive roles to each hemisphere. Some educators melded Wallas' classic four-stage model of creative thinking (*preparation, incubation, illumination, verification*) with left/right-brain functions [74]. Thus, Wallas' first and fourth stages, preparation and verification, were construed as left hemispheric processes. Conversely, Wallas' second and third stages, incubation and illumination, were construed as right hemispheric functions [75]. Implicit in such formulations was the notion that hemispheric activation would shift from left to right and back to left during the creative process. Consequently, creativity came to be viewed as depending upon the cooperation and interactive efforts of the two hemispheres: Therefore, "whole-brainedness" became the *sine qua non* for creative thought [76].

ASSESSING HEMISPHERICITY

Once educators became committed to right-brain or even whole-brain education, it followed logically that assessment methods or devices were necessary to determine which students had what kind of hemisphericity. The differentiation of left- from right-brained children could serve various purposes, such as, the individual tailoring of instructional methods, classroom organization, and perhaps even identification of the "gifted." Although such differentiation seems contrary to the humanistic spirit of the holistic classroom, many authors and educators extolled the merits of diagnosing students' hemisphericity. For example, by means of the Differential Hemispheric Activation Test, Dunn, Cavanaugh, Eberle, and Zenhausern found that with respect to classroom environment, "right preferred students, because of their need for an informed environment and their ability to either block out extraneous sounds or to work with background sounds, might perform more comfortably in either an open or an alternative program than in a conventional environment" [77, p. 293]. Likewise, Sonnier is unequivocal on the matter of student-teacher matching; she says, "Holistic education has its most natural and coherent status under the guidance of a teacher who ... [has] a dominant right hemisphere—a visualizer" [78, p. 66].

To facilitate these positive experiences, many instruments were developed to determine hemisphericity. Typically, these inventories were self-administered questionnaires which assessed the test-taker's preferences for activities or cognitive modes that reflected a presumed, preponderant reliance on one or the other hemisphere. Three of the more popular hemisphericity tests are Torrance, Reynolds, Riegel, and Ball's [79] Your Style of Learning and Thinking Test (SOLAT), Herrman's [76] Brain Dominance Instrument, and Zenhausern's Differential Hemispheric Activation Test. Although these devices had moderate success in linking particular cognitive-style features to tests of creative ability or visual spatial skills, the majority of these brain inventories are extremely weak psychometrically. Basic psychometric properties, such as various reliability and validity measures, are not systematically reported by the test designers. The construct validity or the extent to which these tests actually measure hemisphericity has not been shown. As an aside, we note that Hermann's Brain Dominance Instrument is now in its fifteenth edition since 1976.

SUMMARY

In summarizing the instructional methods, curriculum changes, and pedagogic philosophy that constituted right-brain or whole-brain educational programs, a number of points can be made. First, educators inferred from the cerebral-asymmetry research that each hemisphere functioned uniquely and independently and that complex cognitive processes could be consigned exclusively to either the left or right hemisphere. Second, it was argued that traditional public-school education ("the three Rs") put a premium on students' left hemispheric capacities. This imbalance was characterized as a disservice to children's learning abilities and intellectual potential. Third, it was inferred that creativity was a property of the right hemisphere and that right-brain stimulation enhanced creative thinking. The school system also was perceived as "lopsided" because, historically, creative thinking and problem solving had not been fostered in the classroom. Fourth, efforts to assess hemisphericity met with mixed success, and the instruments designed for this purpose are weak psychometrically. Sixth, although the few evaluation studies of the efficacy of holistic education are equivocal, the significance of imagery for mediating and augmenting learning is well-established.

CRITIQUE: THE PROS AND CONS OF THE APPLICATION OF THE LATERALITY MODEL TO EDUCATION

Cons

From a strict scientific standpoint, educators have misinterpreted the data on cerebral asymmetries. A statement such as, "the autonomy and independence of the two hemispheres are well established and understood" [78, p. 64] is factually wrong. However, the responsibility for such misunderstanding does not necessarily lie with the educators themselves, because they received much of their information about brain laterality from nonscientific sources, such as popular books [12, 40], their own professional books, journals, and workshops. A review of this literature [7] suggests that much of the "slippage" between the neuropsychological evidence and educators' representation of it, perhaps occurred because of inattention to the complexity of the findings and a failure to consider fully subject factors such as sex, handedness, and attentional strategy, which can significantly modify the observed (and "traditional") asymmetries (e.g., left/verbal, linguistic: right/nonverbal, visuospatial). However, popularizers of scientific data are rarely encharged with the responsibility of presenting the full complexity and extensity of the database: To do so would likely result in a rapid erosion of their popularity. Harris notes about popular writing on cerebral laterality, that "all the subtleties, complexities, sheer inconsistencies, and non-replicable findings are passed over" [44, p. 22].

As indicated elsewhere in the present review, many of the attributes and functions assigned to each hemisphere, such as "creativity," intuition, and metaphor [9], are highly amplified speculations and represent veritable caricatures of the original cognitive-style formulations. Such rigid and radical dichotomizing is perhaps the apotheosis of the tendency to smooth over complex or equivocal experimental findings. Additionally, "dichotomania" represents a complete disavowal of the preexisting (and empirically established) *relative* hemispheric asymmetries, in favor of an *absolute* model of hemispheric asymmetries, which is perhaps "neuromythological" [22]. Such absolutism implies that one hemisphere makes a 100 percent contribution to a particular cognitive task, whereas the other hemisphere is noncontributory. This is simply not the case. For example, even the most robustly lateralized tasks, such as consonant-vowel (cv) identification, yield right-ear (left-hemisphere) recognition accuracies which exceed left-ear (right-hemisphere) recognition rates by perhaps only 15 to 25 percent [4]. Thus, in the main, hemispheric differences are small even for well-lateralized cognitive functions. Perhaps not surprisingly, educators' extension of the laterality model to the classroom neglects to incorporate such subtlety.

A belief in an absolute model of hemispheric functioning necessarily entails the conception that one hemisphere is active for a particular cognitive task, while the other hemisphere lies dormant or awaits its turn. Unfortunately, the hemispheres do not work in such a hydraulic fashion, nor do they "seek out" and isolate hemispherically compatible stimuli for processing. It is only in the rarefied and artificial research labs of cognitive neuropsychologists that stimuli can be selectively controlled and discretely presented to one or the other hemisphere of a subject. Although the physical separation of the left and right hemispheres was clinically necessitated for the split-brain patients, normal human hemispheres are joined and highly interactive, *not* independent and autonomous. Therefore, each hemisphere has a role in any complex cognitive/motor task, be it calculus, calligraphy, or calypso dance. In other words, the three Rs are not the sole property of the left hemisphere, any more than copying or drawing a picture is an exclusive function of the right hemisphere. Levy, one of the seminal laterality researchers, makes this same point in a recent educational journal:

> The realization that the whole brain is actively participating in perception, encoding of information, organization of representations, memory, arousal, planning, thinking, understanding, and all other mental operations whether it be a social interaction, painting a picture, playing the piano, doing mathematics, writing a story, attending a lecture, or seeing a movie, seems to have escaped many, if not most, popular writers [80, p. 68].

In short, many educators over- or misinterpreted the research evidence on cerebral asymmetries and rendered it simpler, "neater," perhaps more romanticized, and thus, more readily applied to educational policy, programs, and procedures.

Despite the above-described misinterpretation of the laterality evidence, it could be that the programs nonetheless work. Unfortunately, it is difficult to tell.

By and large, there is a dearth of methodologically sound, evaluative studies on the efficacy of laterality-based education innovations. Our literature review revealed only seven evaluation studies (four of which were doctoral dissertations) conducted since 1979: a frequency which stands in dramatic contrast to the spate of articles advocating right- and whole-brain educational reform.

Whereas a solid corpus of studies attests to the utility of imagery as a learning aid, whole-brain teaching methods have not been proven superior to other instructional techniques [7]. For example, the best study in this small group compared left hemispheric instructional techniques (i.e., textbook oriented, verbal teaching methods with no demonstrations or visual aids) and right hemispheric techniques (i.e., largely nonverbal, wholistic, activity-centered methods) with an integrative approach which combined both methodologies [81]. Grade 5 science classes (and control classes) were taught in one of these three "experimental" manners for one month, and at the end of this period testing indicated that no significant differences existed between groups. A similar study was carried out with Grade 1 children [82]: A left- or right-brain teaching methodology was applied to different classrooms, but the two approaches yielded no subsequent performance differences on the WISC-R. In contrast, however, when a "whole-brain learning/teaching model" was used with experimental, Grade 10, creative-writing classes, a significant treatment effect was noted [83].

Given the paucity of studies conducted, it is perhaps premature to conclude that whole-brain educational strategies are not superior to traditional instructional methods. Although methodological problems, such as, adequate controls, reliable standardized teaching techniques, "blind" teachers and raters, to name but a few, await the ambitious evaluator, it is clear that the definitive study is sorely needed. In a social and political climate of shrinking educational dollars, we presume that a significant superiority of whole-brain education would have to be convincingly demonstrated in order to justify the sizable resource allocation necessary to "retool" teachers, curricula, and learning aids to right-brain compatibility.

Some authors have taken umbrage at an implied antiliteracy bias which pervades much of the right- or whole-brain educational literature [44]. This concern is perhaps founded on the, at times, overly zealous advocacy by certain educators of "nontraditional" course content or educational experiences (e.g., chanting, basket weaving), and a coexistent disparagement of rationality and the three Rs. Fueling the wrath of critics are comments such as those of Blakeslee:

There is a decadence in the field of higher education . . . a sort of academic dream world has been created in which purely "left-brain" thinkers admire each other's "scholarliness." Many students who earn their Ph.D.'s become so habitually "left-brained" that they are unable to do anything but become "scholars" themselves [84, p. 56].

Such hyperbole is perhaps grossly inaccurate at best and inflammatory at worse: for, the effects of laterality-based educational programs probably are relatively benign.

Has there been any real harm? Not likely. We have mild concerns about the potentially negative impact of identifying (or diagnosing) left- and right-brained students; in essence this represents the latest wrinkle in the "multiple tracking" or "streaming" of students: a practice with a heritage dating from the American Civil War.

Furthermore, it is difficult to imagine that any truly dire consequences (other than boredom and inefficient time management) would result from a teacher's misinterpretation and misapplication of the laterality model to his/her classroom. For example, a student's academic progress is unlikely to be impeded by a right-brain or whole-brain teaching method. If anything, such diversity might enrich the subject matter and create a broader educational experience for the learner.

Pros

Although the efficacy of the new laterality-based educational strategies is unproven in a formal, empirical sense, such programs likely have some positive features. For example, the spirit embodied in right-brain or whole-brain education is perhaps laudatory. We believe that sincere and thoughtful effort to apply scientific findings to the enhancement of learning, academic motivation, creativity, problem-solving, performance in particular school subjects, or to the remediation of learning difficulties should be supported in most cases. A heightened appreciation for the unique learning needs, the individual style and aptitude of each student is implicit in the "symmetric" approach: Such individualized attention and instruction should have salutary effects.

Along the same lines, Kaushansky has hypothesized that the application of brain research to the classroom would serve to break the grip which behaviorism held on public-school instruction [7]. In support of his hypothesis, he cites Fultz-Telzrow who writes,

The influence of the behaviorist school of psychology on education during the last twenty years has been substantial . . . little attention is given to variations in capacities between individuals or groups . . . it does appear that some moderation of the strict behaviorist tradition may provide us with more tenable answers about the ways in which children learn [85, p. 477].

Fultz-Telzrow believes that information about brain development, especially about cerebral laterality, can facilitate understanding of children's learning. Although scientists or educators will have to render the ultimate verdict on Kaushansky's assertion, it does seem that laterality-based educational models inculcated a more humanistic (and less mechanistic) orientation in the classroom. An assessment of the advantages and disadvantages of such a pedagogical shift is, in the absence of objective program evaluation data, a highly subjective judgment and one which we leave to the reader.

Educators not only acquired a heightened appreciation of individual differences in learning, but they also seemingly became more cognizant of and experimented with nonverbal, imagery-based instructional methods or mnemonic aids. In his Nobel Laureate's address, Sperry emphasized the importance of this broadened conceptualization of cognitive processes [86]. Sperry states, "Regardless of remaining uncertainties concerning laterality, one beneficial outcome that appears to hold up is an enhanced awareness in education and elsewhere of the important role of nonverbal components and forms of intellect" [86, p. 1225]. It is presumed, although not proven, that increasing and diversifying teaching techniques leads to greater cognitive flexibility and better problem-solving skills in students.

In short, it may well be that laterality-based educational policies and practices work—but for the wrong reasons. For instance, it would be surprising if the zeal which accompanied right- or whole-brain education, did not lead directly to greater teacher enthusiasm. This positive excitement might have fostered greater student motivation to learn and a concomitant responsiveness to novel, instructional methods and programs.

Similar "nonspecific" educational advantages also might accrue for those students identified as right-brained. Such students might do better academically by virtue of a Pygmalian effect. A Pygmalian effect or self-fulfilling prophecy is one of the well established principles in psychology: According to it, people (and animals) perform better when someone (usually a supervising authority, such as a parent, teacher, or boss) expects them to do well. The whole-brain approach unwittingly capitalizes on the Pygmalian effect to a great extent. Thus, those right-brained students who once were disadvantaged in the left-brained classroom, might be perceived by teachers as achieving more in the right-brained classroom, when in fact no objective performance differences exist.

Somewhat akin to the Pygmalian effect is the Hawthorne effect, which was derived from research demonstrating that workers' productivity increased in response to virtually any change in the work environment or simply whenever people (again usually authority figures) paid attention to them. Like events probably occur in the right-brain classroom. Certainly, many structural innovations occurred in the symmetric classroom, and according to the Hawthorne effect, such changes should lead to greater student productivity. Also it can be expected that the right-brained teacher unintentionally might devote greater attention to right-brained students, with whom he/she is presumably more compatible. According to the Hawthorne effect, these students then should work harder.

SUMMARY

It is not quite clear where the right-brain or whole-brain educational movement is going. Lay, professional, and scientific interest, as reflected by educational-journal publications likely peaked a few years ago. Quite frankly, these days one hears much less about laterality in the classroom. At present, a conservative backlash against radical, experimental, or innovative instructional methods and curricula exists (at least in Canada). The three Rs are being reaffirmed, and this advocacy probably will eclipse laterality-based educational programs. Perhaps, some of the less desirable excesses of the whole-brain movement will drop off, and a nucleus of sound educational practices will remain. It does seem desirable that all teachers attempt to understand each individual learner and instruct each student in a manner that best increases the student's motivation and ability to learn. There is no doubt that imagery-based instructional methods should be a significant part of the teacher's armamentarium.

In summary, in this chapter we have reviewed the neuropsychological evidence and chronicled the events leading to the explosion of educators' interest in hemispheric specialization, as well as the consequent application of this knowledge to the classroom. It seems that educators believed that the hemispheres were autonomous and uniquely specialized for specific cognitive processes, such as creative thought. The public school system was perceived to favor left hemispheric cognition, and this bias was viewed as disadvantageous to many children, especially to those with right hemisphericity. In the extreme, these notions coalesced in the view that the educational system was "lopsided." Efforts to redress this imbalance included changes in curricula and teaching methods which were aimed at educating the right or whole brain. It is our impression that many educators over- or misinterpreted the neuropsychological evidence on which these novel policy and program changes were founded. However, it appears that the effects of such misinterpretation and misapplication are relatively benign. Although the limited experiments in the holistic classroom yielded decidedly equivocal results, laterality-based education may have had subtle, yet positive effects, especially with respect to enhancing student/teacher enthusiasm, as well as capitalizing on Pygmalian or Hawthorne effects. Although formal program evaluations of the symmetric classroom have yielded mixed results, the use of imagery as a mediator in learning is well established.

In conclusion, it should be remembered that the brain is unbelievably complex. Nobel Laureate Sperry has stated that the brain's surface structure "would probably make those differences seen in facial features or fingerprint patterns look relatively simple and crude by comparison" [23, p. 33]. Although the brain is structurally separable into left and right halves and although it is of greater metaphoric appeal and heuristic utility when so dichotomized, functionally the brain is highly interactive. Each hemisphere is relatively rather than absolutely specialized for various cognitive processes. The educational implication to be drawn from this caveat is that "effectiveness in education comes from a fully acknowledged commitment to the function of both hemispheres" [8, p. 123]. We concur whole-heartedly and -brainedly.

REFERENCES

1. J. E. Bogen, Some Educational Aspects of Hemispheric Specialization, *UCLA Educator*, *17*, pp. 24-32, 1975.
2. M. Hunter, Right-Brained Kids in Left-Brained Schools, *Today's Education*, *51*, pp. 45-48, 1976.
3. R. E. Samples, *The Metaphoric Mind*, Addison Wesley, Reading, Massachusetts, 1976.
4. M. P. Bryden, *Laterality: Functional Asymmetry in the Intact Human Brain*, Academic Press, New York, 1982.
5. R. G. Ley, Cerebral Laterality and Imagery, in *Imagery: Current Theory, Research and Application*, A. A. Sheikh (ed.), Wiley and Sons, New York, 1983.
6. S. J. Segalowitz, *Two Sides of the Brain*, Prentice-Hall, Englewood Cliffs, New Jersey, 1983.
7. M. Kaushansky, The Implications of the Lateralized Brain Model for Educational Practice: A Critical Analysis of the Research Base, unpublished doctoral dissertation, Simon Fraser University, Burnaby, B.C., 1983.
8. R. E. Samples, Educating for Both Sides of the Human Mind, *Science Teacher*, *42*, pp. 21-23, 1975.
9. M. R. Rennels, Cerebral Symmetry: An Urgent Concern for Education, *Phi Delta Kappan*, *57*, pp. 471-472, 1976.
10. L. V. Williams, *Teaching for the Two-Sided Mind*, Prentice-Hall, Englewood Cliffs, New Jersey, 1983.
11. T. Buzan, *Use Both Sides of Your Brain*, Dutton, New York, 1976.
12. B. Edwards, *Drawing on the Right Side of the Brain*, Tarcher Press, Los Angeles, 1979.
13. L. Guckes and R. Elkins, *Implications of Brain Research for Educational Practices*, (ERIC Document Reproduction Service NO. ED 211-520) Boise State College, Boise, Idaho, 1981.
14. M. Hunter, The Two Brains of Man, *The Clearing House*, *55*, p. 51, 1978.
15. G. Rico, *Writing the Natural Way*, Tarcher Press, Los Angeles, 1983.
16. E. J. Ogletree, Curriculum for Two Modes of Consciousness, *Contemporary Education*, *4*, pp. 203-206, 1978.
17. M. Critchley, *The Parietal Lobes*, Arnold, London, 1953.
18. S. Springer and G. Deutsch, *Left Brain, Right Brain*, Freeman, San Francisco, 1981.

19. R. W. Sperry, Lateral Specialization in the Surgically Separated Hemispheres, in *The Neurosciences: Third Study Program*, F. O. Schmitt and F. G. Worden (eds.), MIT Press, Cambridge, 1974.

20. R. Sperry, M. Gazzaniga, and J. E. Bogen, Role of the Neocortical Commissures, in *Handbook of Clinical Neurology*, Vol. 4, P. J. Vinken and G. W. Bruyn (eds.), North Holland Publishing, Amsterdam, 1969.

21. J. Levy-Agresti and R. W. Sperry, Differential Perceptual Capacities in Major and Minor Hemispheres, *Proceedings of the National Academy of Science*, *61*, p. 1151, 1968.

22. C. Hardyck and R. Haapanen, Educating Both Halves of the Brain: Educational Breakthrough or Neuromythology?, *Journal of School Psychology*, *17*:3, pp. 219-230, 1979.

23. R. W. Sperry, Left Brain, Right Brain, *Saturday Review*, pp. 30-33, August 9, 1975.

24. M. S. Gazzaniga, *The Bisected Brain*, Appleton-Century-Crofts, New York, 1970.

25. R. W. Sperry, Hemisphere Deconnection and Unity in Conscious Awareness, *American Psychologist*, *22*, pp. 723-733, 1968.

26. J. E. Bogen, The Other Side of the Brain I: Dysgraphia and Dyscopia Following Cerebral Commissurotomy, *Bulletin of the Los Angeles Neurological Societies*, *34*, pp. 73-105, 1969.

27. _____, The Other Side of the Brain II: An Appositional Mind, *Bulletin of the Los Angeles Neurological Societies*, *34*, pp. 135-162, 1969.

28. E. Zaidel, Auditory Language Comprehension in the Right Hemisphere Following Cerebral Commissurotomy and Hemispherectomy: A Comparison with Child Language and Aphasia, in *Language Acquisition and Language Breakdown*, A. Caramazza and E. Zurif (eds.), John Hopkins Press, Baltimore, 1977.

29. M. S. Gazzaniga, Right Hemisphere Language Following Brain Bisection: A 20 Year Perspective, *American Psychologist*, *38*:5, pp. 525-537, 1983.

30. A. Gates and J. L. Bradshaw, The Role of the Cerebral Hemispheres in Music, *Brain and Language*, 4, pp. 403-431, 1977.

31. R. Efron, The Effect of Handedness on the Perception of Simultaneity and Temporal Order, *Brain*, *86*, pp. 261-284, 1963.

32. J. Semmes, Hemispheric Specialization: A Possible Clue to Mechanism, *Neuropsychologia*, *6*, pp. 11-26, 1968.

33. G. Cohen, Hemispheric Differences in Serial Versus Parallel Processing, *Journal of Experimental Psychology*, *97*, pp. 349-356, 1973.

34. R. C. Gur, H. S. Sackheim, and R. E. Gur, Classroom Seating and Psychopathology: Some Initial Data, *Journal of Abnormal Psychology*, *84*, pp. 122-124, 1976.

35. W. T. Gallwey, *The Inner Game*, Random House, New York, 1974.

36. H. Mintzberg, Planning on the Left Side and Managing on the Right, *Harvard Business Review*, *54*, pp. 49-58, 1976.

37. J. L. Bradshaw and N. C. Nettleton, The Nature of Hemispheric Specialization in Man, *The Behavioral and Brain Sciences*, 4, pp. 51-92, 1981.

38. G. Cohen, Explaining Hemispheric Asymmetry: New Dichotomies for Old?, *Behavioral and Brain Science, 4*, p. 67, 1981.
39. J. Levy, Cerebral Asymmetry and the Psychology of Man, in *The Brain and Psychology*, M. Wittrock (ed.), Academic Press, New York, 1980.
40. R. Ornstein, *The Psychology of Consciousness*, Freeman, San Francisco, 1972.
41. J. E. Bogen, R. DeZare, W. D. TenHouten, and J. F. Marsh, The Other Side of the Brain IV: The A/P Ratio, *Bulletin of the Los Angeles Neurological Societies, 37*, pp. 49-61, 1972.
42. S. Orton, *Reading, Writing and Speech Problems in Children*, W. W. Norton, New York, 1937.
43. M. Kinsbourne and M. Hiscock, Cerebral Lateralization and Cognitive Development, in "Education and the Brain," J. S. Chall and A. F. Mirsky (eds.), *The Seventy-seventh Yearbook of the National Society for the Study of Education*, University of Chicago Press, Chicago, 1978.
44. L. J. Harris, Teaching the Right Brain: Historical Perspective on a Contemporary Fad, in *Developmental Neuropsychology and Education*, C. T. Best (ed.), Academic Press, New York, 1982.
45. R. B. Nebes, Man's So-Called 'Minor' Hemisphere, *The UCLA Educator, 2*, pp. 13-16, 1975.
46. J. Stellern, M. Marlowe, and A. Cossairt, Cognitive Mode and Classroom Behavior, *Psychology in the Schools*, in press, 1984.
47. M. S. Gazzaniga, Review of the Split Brain, *The UCLA Educator, 2*, pp. 9-12, 1975.
48. R. D. Konicek, Seeking Synergism for Man's Two Hemisphere Brain, *Phi Delta Kappan*, pp. 37-39, 1975.
49. P. Brandwein and R. Ornstein, The Duality of the Mind, *Instructor, 86*, pp. 54-58, 1977.
50. A. G. Hudgens, Implications of Hemisphericity for Remedial Programs, *Community College Review, 3*, pp. 15-23, 1980.
51. G. L. Nelson, Toward a New English Teacher, *English Education, 8*, pp. 131-138, 1977.
52. D. T. Wolfe and R. W. Reising, Politics and English Teaching, or (Can, Should, Will) We Teach the Whole Brain?, *The English Journal, 67*, pp. 29-32, 1978.
53. G. H. Wheatley, The Right Hemisphere's Role in Problem Solving, *Arithmetic Teacher, 25*, pp. 36-39, 1977.
54. P. Elliot, Going Back to Basics in Mathematics Won't Prove Who's 'Right,' but Who's 'Left' (Brain Duality and Mathematics Learning), *International Journal of Mathematical Education in Science and Technology, 11*, pp. 213-219, 1980.
55. C. Hildebrand, Right-Brained Activities for the Chemistry Classroom, *Journal of Chemical Education, 8*, pp. 597-598, 1980.
56. M. Iannazzi, Brain Asymmetry, *The Science Teacher, 1*, pp. 47-48, 1975.
57. E. Virshup, Art and the Right Hemisphere, *Art Education, 7*, pp. 14-15, 1976.
58. T. A. Regelski, Music Education and the Human Brain, *Education Digest, 44*, pp. 44-47, 1977.

59. F. A. Staley, Hemispheric Brain Research and Outdoor Education, *Education Digest*, *46*, pp. 46-49, 1980.
60. A. A. Sheikh, *Imagery: Current Theory, Research and Application*, Wiley and Sons, New York, 1983.
61. J. Yuille and M. J. Catchpole, Imagery and Children's Associative Learning, in *Cognitive Psychology and Instruction*, A. M. Lesgold, J. W. Pellegrino, S. D. Fokkema and R. Glasser (eds.), Plenum Press, New York, 1977.
62. M. Pressley, Imagery and Children's Learning: Putting the Picture in Developmental Perspective, *Review of Educational Research*, *47*, pp. 585-622, 1977.
63. A. Paivio, *Imagery and the Verbal Processes*, Holt, Rinehart and Winston, New York, 1971.
64. C. MacKinnon, *Implications of the Right Brain Research on Curriculum Development*, (ERIC Document Reproduction Service, No. ED 211519), Western Oregon State College, Monmouth, Oregon, 1981.
65. R. Rose, Guided Fantasies in Elementary Classrooms, in *Imagery: Concepts, Results and Applications*, E. Klinger (ed.), Plenum Press, New York, 1979.
66. N. J. Young, The Effects of Spatial Abilities in Hemispheric Enhancement Through Right-Brain Instructional Techniques (doctoral dissertation, United States International University), *Dissertation Abstracts International*, *42*, 625A, (University Microfilms No. 8116379), 1981.
67. B. Galyeen, Brain Hemispheric Functioning, *Roeper Review*, *4*, pp. 6-9, 1981.
68. E. P. Torrance, Hemisphericity and Creative Functioning, *Journal of Research and Development in Education*, *3*, pp. 29-37, 1982.
69. B. L. Forisha, Relationship Between Creativity and Mental Imagery: A Question of Cognitive Styles, in *Imagery: Current Theory, Research and Application*, A. A. Sheikh (ed.), Wiley and Sons, New York, 1983.
70. J. Kozol, *Death at an Early Age*, Houghton Mifflin, Boston, 1967.
71. E. deBono, *Lateral Thinking*, Harper and Row, New York, 1970.
72. A. F. Osborn, *Applied Imagination*, Scribners, New York, 1963.
73. A. Deikman, Bimodal Consciousness, *Archives of General Psychiatry*, *25*, pp. 481-489, 1970.
74. G. Wallas, *The Art of Thought*, Harcourt, New York, 1926.
75. R. Rubenzer, The Role of the Right Hemisphere in Learning and Creativity: Implications for Enhancing Problem Solving Ability, *Gifted Child Quarterly*, *1*, pp. 78-100, 1979.
76. N. Hermann, The Creative Brain, *Training and Development Journal*, pp. 11-16, 1981.
77. R. Dunn, D. P. Cavanaugh, B. M. Eberle, and R. Zenhausern, Hemispheric Preference: The Newest Element of Learning Style, *American Biology Teacher*, *44*:5, pp. 291-294, 1982.
78. I. L. Sonnier, Holistic Education: How I Do It, *College Student Journal*, *16*:1, pp. 65-69, 1982.
79. E. P. Torrance, R. C. Reynolds, T. Riegel, and O. E. Ball, Your Style of Learning and Thinking, Forms A and B: Preliminary Norms, Abbreviated Technical Notes, Scoring Keys and Selected References, *Gifted Child Quarterly*, *21*, pp. 563-573, 1977.

80. J. Levy, Research Synthesis on Right and Left Hemisphere: We Think with Both Sides of the Brain, *Educational Leadership, 40*, pp. 66-71, 1983.
81. J. B. Kemp, An Investigation of the Effects of Varying Left and Right Hemisphere Activities on Achievement of 5th Grade Science Students (doctoral dissertation, University of Southern Mississippi), *Dissertation Abstracts International, 39A*, 5430A, (University Microfilms No. 7905130), 1978.
82. D. W. Vigil, A Study of Hemispheric Synergism as an Applied Theoretical Construct to Determine the Effects of Contrasting Educational Interventions on Children's Learning Styles, (doctoral dissertation, University of Northern Colorado), *Dissertation Abstracts International, 42*, 994A, University Microfilms No. 8119811), 1981.
83. J. B. Reedy, An Investigation of the Effects of a Whole-Brain Learning/Teaching Model, Bi-Modal Development and Synthesis, on Tenth Grade Student Writers, (doctoral dissertation, Pepperdine University), *Dissertation Abstracts International, 42*, 2544A-2545A, 1981.
84. T. R. Blakeslee, *The Right Brain*, Anchor Press/Doubleday, Garden City, 1980.
85. C. Fultz-Telzrow, The Impact of Brain Development on Curriculum, *Educational Forum, 45*, pp. 477-483, 1981.
86. R. W. Sperry, Some Effects of Disconnecting the Cerebral Hemispheres, *Science, 217*, pp. 1223-1226, 1982.

CHAPTER 5

Mental Imagery and Problem Solving: Implications for the Educational Process

GEIR KAUFMANN
AND TORE HELSTRUP

It is often claimed that imagery has not been carefully studied in relation to problem solving, and that the evidence we have is largely anecdotal [1]. It is correct, as Richardson points out, that problem solving is a less explored territory in imagery research than are the areas of learning and memory [2]. As will be evident in the sequel, however, a quite substantial body of research evidence pertaining to the role of imagery in human problem solving does, in fact, exist. The early research has been extensively reviewed and critically discussed in several works [3-9]. The present chapter is devoted specifically to the role of imagery in problem solving and based mainly on previous works by Kaufmann [5, 6, 10, 11], where a more detailed examination and discussion of relevant theory and research is given (see also [2]).

As Raaheim has pointed out [12], there is a great similarity between different attempts in the literature to define the terms "problem" and "problem solving." Summarizing the different proposals for definitions, it may be said that an individual has a problem when he/she has a goal but is uncertain of how to reach it [9, 13-16]. The uncertainty experienced by the subject may be regarded as resulting from a conflict between the situation at hand and the desired result [17]. Major determinants of the conflict are complexity and/or novelty in the task confronting the individual [12, 18-21].

The term "imagery" is ambiguous. It may be used to denote cognitive content in a general way, both of a sensory and nonsensory kind [5]. More frequently, "imagery" refers to symbolic processes of a specific sensory kind. Whereas some investigations of imagery and problem solving have dealt with imagery in several sense modalities [22-25], usually the reference is to the visual modality. Consequently, in the present context, we shall use the term "imagery" as equivalent to visuo-imaginal symbolic processes.

The present chapter is organized in the following way. Informal studies on the relationship between imagery and problem solving and some early studies of conditions arousing imagery in thought will be reviewed first. A brief presentation of major theories of the functional significance of imagery in problem solving is followed by a fairly comprehensive review of contemporary experimental research on this issue. In the final section, the potential implications for the educational process will be examined.

INFORMAL STUDIES OF THE RELATIONSHIP BETWEEN MENTAL IMAGERY AND PROBLEM SOLVING

A series of reports concerning the development of inventions and scientific discoveries suggest that the inventors were visualizing highly complex situations when their revealing "flash of insight" occurred [5, 6, 26-32]. As an example, one might refer to Einstein's development of the theory of relativity as reported by Shepard [31]. The basic idea first came to him when at the age of sixteen he imagined himself traveling along beside a beam of light. He realized then that the imaginary stationary spatial oscillation did not correspond to anything that could be perceptually experienced. Neither did it fit in with Maxwell's equations for propagation of light. (Cf. Einstein, [33], however, where he emphasizes the importance of language for thought.) A dramatic and often cited example of the use of visual imagery in creative problem solving is the important discovery of the "benzene ring" by the chemist, Kekule [34]. This insight, according to Kekule, was mediated by seeing, in a hypnagogic state of mind, a snake seizing hold of its own tail. Gordon, who worked with "synectics groups", assembled to work out practically useful inventions, also stresses the functional significance of imagery; he holds that it enables the inventor "to get away from the familiar, over-rationalized, word-intoxicated view of a problem" [35, p. 48]. Gordon cites numerous instances of constructive uses of visual imagery, often bizarre, in the process of invention.

The mathematician Hadamard reports that in his creative efforts he often resorted to visual imagery "when matters became too complex" [35, p. 114]. Walkup, an active inventor in the field of engineering, concludes from a study of problem solving among his co-workers in a large industrial research institute, that the ability to visualize is a vital ingredient in the process of making technical inventions [36, 37]. Guilford asked creative scientists to rate the relative importance to their problem-solving endeavors of the different Structure of Intelligence (SI) factors [38]. The highest rank was given to the Figural Adaptive Flexibility factor, which presumably involves imagery processing [39].

Testimonial evidence must, of course, be treated with care. The reported imagery may be the exception rather than the rule, as the results of the pioneering studies of Galton imply [40], or it may be relevant only in particular fields of problem solving, as is suggested by Roe [24]. Also one might claim that the mental imagery constitutes only epiphenomenal traces of underlying mental processes of a different kind. Such a theoretical position appears both in the early literature [22] as well as in contemporary writings (e.g., [41]).

EARLY RESEARCH ON THE CONDITIONS AROUSING MENTAL IMAGERY IN PROBLEM SOLVING

Although Galton concluded his study by arguing that vivid imagery may prove detrimental to abstract thought, he nevertheless claimed that imagery may be an important element in "inventive" thinking [40, p. 68]. In an experiment by Fox, the subjects were to comprehend the meanings of given mathematical, historical, and grammatical statements, and they were asked to give evidence of their mental content during the act of thought [42]. Fox observed that a conflict in consciousness is a favorable condition for the development of imagery, while the contrary condition of "smooth" thinking is unfavorable for the production of imagery. Comstock replicated Fox's experiment and obtained similar results [43].

Findings like those of Fox and Comstock seem closely akin to Titchener's contention that tasks that are familiar, mechanized, and solvable by routine thinking, do not require imagery [44]. The Titchenerian view was adopted also by Pear [45], who argued that the important "working up" of the raw material in thinking was achieved by way of imagery. Pear suggests that imagery has the function of performing "the groundwork in problem solving" [45, p. 7].

In line with the findings and considerations reported above, Woods observed that imagery is richer when the task presented has only a slight degree of familiarity [46]. Furthermore, Finkenbinder observed that problems which presented features novel to the subject were recalled predominantly in imagery [47]. Fisher found that in concept formation tasks, imagery often will fade as a function of repeated solutions, and that a purely verbal representation will take over in the later stages of concept formation [48]. Bartlett arrived at a similar conclusion, linking the function of imagery to the function of *change* in cognition [49]. Bartlett noted that all the subjects who showed a marked orientation towards inventive thinking relied upon imagery as a representational mode. In later works, Bartlett claimed that imagery is particularly useful under the condition of conceptual conflict but also warned that the detailedness of imagery may be counteractive to thinking, in the sense that it may block abstraction and generalization [50, 51]. Altogether, the early research on imagery and problem solving suggests that imagery is particularly important under conditions of "conflict" and "novelty" in problem solving, thus indicating a special role for imagery in the process of creative thinking. However, counterproductive functions of imagery in problem solving also have been suggested.

CURRENT THEORETICAL VIEWS ON THE ROLE OF IMAGERY IN PROBLEM SOLVING

In a comprehensive study of the biographic and autobiographic literature on the requisites for the creative act, Rugg describes the process of problem solving as occurring in two stages [52]. The first stage—discovery—involves an autonomous self-forming and transforming imagery activity. The second stage—verification—is presumed to involve the more logical and directed verbal symbolic system.

A related view has been advanced by McKellar in his distinction between A-(autistic) and R-(realistic) thinking [53-55]. A-thinking is compared to authorship, while R-thinking is seen as a form of editorship. Of particular importance in the present context is McKellar's assertion that the major content of A-thinking consists of imagery, and that receptivity to such activities in many cases may be a requisite for achieving originality in problem solving.

Shepard, focusing specifically on the creativity aspect of problem solving, holds the following characteristics of imagery to be important in this respect [31]: 1) Imagery is less constrained by tradition than is language; 2) the richness of imagery makes it possible to note significant details and relationships not present in verbal representations; 3) the spatial character of images makes them directly accessible to potent competencies for spatial intuition and manipulation; and 4) vivid images may constitute more adequate substitutes for corresponding external objects and events than is purely verbal representation. Thus, images have a stronger tendency to mobilize the affective and motivational system. This latter point also is emphasized by Arieti who assigns a crucial role to imagery as a representational vehicle for creative thinking. In this respect, Arieti points to the expediency of imagery in creating the unreal.

Berlyne makes a distinction between situational and transformational thoughts [56], the former include representational processes with static and stabilizing functions which represent stages in the ongoing problem-solving process. The latter refer to the dynamic function of transitions from one specific thought to another. Berlyne argues that imagery, conceptualized as internalized action, is of special importance in transformational thought. In contrast, language is supposed to operate in situational thought. The rationale for this contention is that visual imagery enables individuals to represent self-generated actions and their consequences, as well as environmental processes of an impersonal kind. In contrast, Berlyne considers words and sentences to be poorly suited for the representation of transformations, since words and sentences can only effect changes in the environment through social mediation, that is, communication. Thus Berlyne regards language as having primarily a *labeling* function in problem solving. From a Gestalt theoretical perspective, Arnheim advocates a similar view [57-59].

In his discussion of the relationship between imagery and problem solving, Richardson advances the hypothesis that uncontrolled vivid imagery might be a hindrance to problem solving by disrupting fruitful lines of thought [60]. However, he also points out that controlled imagery often aids problem solving by helping to break an ineffective set and thus to bring about a "restructuring" and "reorganization" of the elements of the problem.

From an information-processing point of view, Chase and Clark assign a major role to imagery in the restructuring activities during problem solving [61]. They believe that imagery has special utility in the generation of new information during search in the problem space [41, 62].

Paivio's theory although primarily addressed to the areas of learning and memory, also is relevant for the field of problem solving [63-67]. The more *concrete* the task situation is, the more easily imaginal mediators are supposed to be elicited. Verbal processes, on the other hand, are regarded as being more functional as mediators in abstract tasks. Paivio also emphasizes the linkage of imagery to visual perception [30, 68-74]. Paivio thus considers imagery to be a visual-spatial representational system specialized for a *parallel processing* of information. Verbal processes are held to be of an auditory-motor nature, and therefore specialized for sequential processing. Thus Paivio argues that imagery involves synchronously organized informational structures, contributing to the richness of content, flexibility, and speed of thinking [66]. Verbal processes are, on the other hand, characterized by a higher degree of sequential constraint which is held to limit memory capacity, as well as flexibility and speed in thinking. The positive function of language lies in providing logical direction to thinking.

Kaufmann has proposed that language may be considered a superordinate symbolic system, and imagery may play mainly the role of a subsidiary, ancillary symbolic tool, which operates *within* and under *conceptual control* of language [6, 75]. Thus conceived, one may argue that imagery makes possible an increased level of processing in cognition, since imagery adds to linguistic processing. Due to its adaptability to the specifics of a problem situation, imagery is held to be particularly suited for the processing needed in solving tasks which entail a high degree of novelty, and which resist being handled solely through the application of general principles and rules. In general, linguistic representation is believed to be more appropriate and economic the higher the degree of task familiarity. With increasing situational novelty, the functional significance of imagery is assumed to increase. Kaufmann also assumes imagery to have a parallel representational capacity, which may have the function of reducing cognitive strain under conditions of high information load [75]. Using imagery therefore becomes increasingly important with incrementing task complexity.

As seen from the above presentation, most theories agree on relating the usefulness of imagery to the creativity dimension of problem solving. Potential detrimental effects of using imagery in problem solving also are noted and generally are thought to be due to the detailed and particular nature of the image (for a thorough and critical discussion of the theories, the reader is referred to Kaufmann [6]).

CONTEMPORARY EXPERIMENTAL RESEARCH ON THE FUNCTIONAL ROLE OF IMAGERY IN PROBLEM SOLVING

A theory-neutral way of classifying problem-solving tasks is achieved through the distinction drawn by Reitman [76;18] between well-defined and ill-defined tasks. The focus is on the degree of constraint imposed on the problem solver. In a well-defined task, the problem solver is faced with an explicit, initial situation and clearly instructed as to the goal state. The solution proposal can be unambiguously judged as right or wrong. On the other hand, ill-defined problems are ambiguously stated, require the production of new solutions, or have uncertain solutions. Most research has dealt with rather well-defined problems. In the sequel, research on the role of imagery in problem solving will be grouped in categories varying systematically from well-defined to ill-defined tasks.

Linear Syllogisms

By far the most carefully studied type of task in the field is in the category of linear syllogisms. In this category, the role of imagery has been extensively studied in the so-called "three-term-series problem." An example of the task would be the following:

> Anne is taller than Jean
> Mary is shorter than Jean
> Who is tallest?

The pioneering studies of this form of deductive reasoning were performed by Hunter [77].

Of particular interest is the question of whether imagery may be a particularly expedient way of achieving a unified representation of the elements of the problem which in turn may facilitate task performance. This possibility was first suggested by DeSoto, London, and Handel [78]. They hypothesized that the premises are combined into a unitary representation in the form of a mental image. The correct answer then may be straightforwardly read off. The image theory has been further developed by Huttenlocher [79]. According to the image theory, it is easier to place a premise in the representational array, if its first item is an "end-anchor," that is, if it occurs at one end of the final array, rather than in the middle position.

However, the imagery interpretation has been challenged by Clark [80, 81]. Clark claims that the transitive inference required is based upon abstract linguistic representations of the two premises. According to Clark, task performance is better explained by basic psycholinguistic principles. (An example is the principle of congruity, which states that the subject will search for information which is congruent with the form of the question.)

The image theorists cite three kinds of evidence in favor of their interpretation [78, 82-86]. These are: 1) Introspective reports reveal the presence of mental imagery when solving this kind of task. 2) Comparisons of variations in task difficulty found in adult subjects solving the actual three-term series tasks and in children arranging concrete objects in an actual spatial array (placement tasks) tend to converge on the same pattern. The implication is that adult subjects base their inference on an internal analogue (image) of the physical relations described in the task. 3) When subjects write down the elements of the task in a spatial array, the arrangements of the three terms conform to the pattern predicted by the image theory.

The proponents of Clark's linguistic theory have argued that reaction times and error rates reflecting variations in task difficulty fit more precisely with the pattern expected from the operation of the hypothesized linguistic processes, and that the postulation of imagery processes is superfluous [80, 81, 87-90].

However, French has been able to show that the affective value of adjectives can be an even better predictor of problem-solving performance than Clark's psycholinguistic principles [91]. The results suggest that adjectives of high affective value are more easily imaged than their low affective counterparts. Williams made an interesting step towards a possible resolution of the competing theories [92]. He found that syllogisms rated high in imagery-evoking capacity were easier to solve than those rated low. In conflicting cases, both theories gained support, depending on whether one used latency as a measure of difficulty (which supported the linguistic theory) or error rate (which supported the image model). Williams concluded that the image model is more relevant to the problem-solving dimension, and that the linguistic model is more related to the sentence-processing aspect of the task. Potts and Scholz separated time required to encode the two premises of a three-term series problem from the time required to generate an answer to the test question [93]. The results indicated that the subjects tended to integrate the two premises into a single, unified representation in the way hypothesized by the image theory.

In the course of the research that has been done, ad hoc assumptions gradually have made it hard to distinguish the two theories in terms of empirical implications [94]. A most interesting proposal for a resolution between the two theories has been suggested by Wood [95] and Wood, Shotter and Godden [96]. They employed tasks involving up to six premises, which could result in many different types of arrays. All the premises involved the comparative term "taller," and the test question was always in the form "who is taller, X or Y?"

The following example is a typical problem:

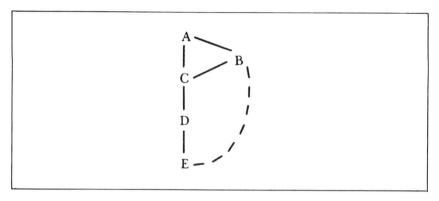

Figure 1. A Haas-diagram of a five-term series problem.

1. D is taller than E
2. C is taller than D
3. A is taller than C
4. A is taller than B
5. B is taller than C

"Who is taller, B or E?"

The structure of such problems can be visually represented by a so-called Haas-diagram (see Figure 1).

The items in the array here are seen to be represented according to their relative heights. The question posed at the end is represented by the dotted line.

Wood examined whether there would be a developmental sequence of problem-solving strategies. A certain number of conventional problems first were given. Then a special test was administered, in which the subject was asked an *unexpected question*, such as, "Who is taller, A or D?" These questions all were formulated so as to be easily answered only by those who had constructed a unified representation (image) of the premises. (The "A or D" question, for instance, is readily answered by reading off from a visual representation, such as the Haas-diagram.) By use of this simple and elegant experimental technique, Wood obtained evidence in support of the hypothesis that subjects attack the problem through imagery in the initial phase of problem solving. As a consequence of increasing familiarity with the problems, they subsequently switch over to linguistic representation.

Sternberg [97] was not able to confirm the strategy shift observed by Wood [98] and argued that a combined spatial-linguistic strategy was used throughout. However, Sternberg used only two premises in contrast to the six employed by Wood, and the imagery construct was operationalized solely through scores on a spatial test, which probably is at best an incomplete and insensitive measure of imagery [63].

A developmental pattern similar to that observed by Wood has been demonstrated by Quinton and Fellows, who recorded reports of strategies used, and, subsequently, gave instructions and training in use of the most effective strategies reported [99]. Kosslyn, Murphy, Bemesderfer, and Feinstein examined performance in a mental comparison task, focusing on the role of different modes of symbolic representations [100]. The subjects were to judge the relative sizes of named objects. The evidence indicated that the subjects initially used both analogue (image) and discrete (linguistic) representation simultaneously. With overlearning, there was a transition to a purely discrete representational strategy, where the category labels served as cues for the size comparisons.

Kinship Problems

Kinship problems are structurally close to syllogisms. The task consists of inferring correct kinship relations from specifically stated questions, such as, "What relationship to her is her mother's mother?" Wood and Shotter inferred the use of imagery strategies from the subjects' reports and examination of patterns of task difficulty [101]. The results indicated that the subjects used an imagery strategy in the initial phase of the task. Later, they switched over to faster, linguistic short-cut strategies (e.g., "up-across" in the image means "cousin"). Wood and Shotter emphasize specifically the functional usefulness of imagery for the *understanding process*.

Imagery in Anagram Performance and in Other Complex Verbal Tasks

The most popular word problem in the experimental study of problem solving undoubtedly has been the anagram: A set of letters (e.g., "albet") is presented with instructions to transform it into a meaningful word (e.g., "table"). Gavurin observed a significant positive correlation between time to solve ten six-letter anagrams and scores on a test of spatial aptitude, when the subjects were instructed to perform the anagram task "in their head" [102]. But the correlation disappeared when overt rearrangement of the letters was permitted. Gavurin assumed that a spatial representational layout was used to perform the required transformations in the "covert" condition. Furby examined the role of spatial visualization under nonsense and word conditions [103]: In the first condition, the subject was presented with the usual nonsense arrangement of letters, and the task was to rearrange the letters into a meaningful word. In the latter condition, the subject was given a word and asked to make another one using all letters. Furby found that scores on the spatial visualization test predicted performance in the nonsense condition but not in the word condition.

Wallace performed a factorial experiment with two levels of spatial aptitude, two levels of anagram difficulty, and a covert rearrangement condition [104]. Wallace obtained significant main effects for spatial aptitude and anagram difficulty but no interaction effects. These results counter Gavurin's finding of the special utility of spatial aptitude in the covert condition. These experiments are suggestive, but they lack control for general level of intellectual ability. Thus the findings are difficult to interpret.

A more comprehensive and carefully controlled experiment was carried out by Frandsen and Holder who investigated the role of spatial visualization in solving anagrams [105], as well as other complex verbal tasks (syllogisms, logical-deduction problems, and time-rate-distance travel problems). Unlike the above studies, this one did include a control test of verbal-reasoning ability. Both verbal-reasoning and spatial-visualization scores were found to correlate with success in solving the complex verbal problems. A partial correlation analysis revealed that both factors made independent contributions. Also the results showed that presenting the tasks with diagrams significantly influenced problem-solving performance. This last effect was restricted to the subjects low in spatial aptitude.

Jablonski and Mueller found a significant difference in solution time in favor of high-imagery items [106]; whereas, Dewing and Hetherington [107] found high-imagery words to be solved significantly faster when other variables known to influence anagram solution time were controlled (word length, number of possible solutions, frequency of successive letter pairs, and letter order). The subjects were provided with structural cues (initial and final letter of the solution word) and semantic cues (the word's superordinate), and the result was that structural cues affected performance on the low-imagery words, and that semantic clues facilitated the solution time of high-imagery words. Stratton and Jacobus also found a significant effect on anagram solution performance for high-imagery words, when word frequency was controlled [108].

The interpretation of the effect of imageability is straightforward in the case of verbal learning and memory, but it is harder to conceive of a similar mediational function for imagery in anagram performance. It is possible that imageability has been confounded with other variables not controlled for, such as concreteness (see Richardson [109-111], who emphasizes the importance of controlling for concreteness when examining effects of imageability).

Cox [112, 113] employed a spy game word problem worked out by Hayes [114] and found that the concrete word problems were more easily solved and better memorized than abstract ones. These findings are interpreted in terms of imaginal coding, assumed to aid both problem solving and memory.

Imagery in Abstract Tasks

Paivio's contention [63] that imagery is linked to task concreteness and that verbal processes are tied to abstract stimulus materials, has been challenged by several independent lines of evidence which suggest that imagery does play an important role also in highly abstract tasks. Skemp has provided testimonial evidence that visual imagery has an important function in mathematical thinking, not only in geometry problems but also in the area of algebra [115]. Hadamard, as quoted above, emphasized the need for imagery in order to solve mathematical problems of high complexity.

More controlled tests have demonstrated that mathematical ability might be closely related to Spearman's g-factor [116]. The question then is whether spatial imagery makes an independent contribution, in addition to the g-factor. The answer seems to be in the positive. Barabat (reported in Smith [116]), controlled for the g-factor and found that the geometry test had a substantial loading on the spatial factor for both sexes; whereas, tests of algebra had significant loadings on the spatial factor for girls but not for boys. For both sexes, negative effects were demonstrated for the verbal factor. Wrigley similarly obtained negative loadings on the mathematical group factor for the verbal tests but positive ones for spatial visualization tasks [117]. This pattern showed up in algebra as well as in geometry tasks. Werdelin also has observed positive effects for the spatial factor in relation to mathematical aptitude [118]. The verbal factor had the lowest correlation of all factors included. In a large-scale investigation using Guilford-tests, Hill (1957, reported in Smith [116]) found a positive relationship between scores on visualization tests and general mathematical aptitude, and a lack of significant correlations with verbal ability (measured by a vocabulary test). Of considerable interest is Vernon's study of mathematical abilities in college students and army cadets [119]. He claimed that the effect of spatial ability was particularly pronounced at the *high-grade* levels. More recent research points in the same direction. Spatial ability seems, in many cases, to constitute an essential component in mathematical aptitude [120-123]. However, the negative relationship to verbal ability has not been replicated [122].

Burnett, McLane, and Dratt also emphasized the importance of spatial visualization in mathematical-quantitative ability, particularly for complex problems [123]. They suggested that the frequently noted sex difference in spatial visualization ability [120] might be a possible cause of the high attrition rate for females in mathematics courses beyond the tenth grade level. (But see [125 and [126] for an alternative interpretation which emphasizes sociocultural and corresponding attitudinal factors.) Burnett et al. found in their study of mathematics performance at advanced levels that there was a clearly significant correlation between scores on a spatial visualization test and mathematical-quantitative ability. General level of intelligence was held constant. With the spatial visualization factor statistically controlled, no significant sex differences were observed in high-level mathematical-quantitative ability. Taken together, these findings indicate that imagery may play a crucial role in abstract problem solving, particularly at the advanced level.

The research in this area is largely correlational, and the results should therefore be interpreted with care. Alternative research on the role of imagery is based mainly on protocol studies, whose data consists of reports from the subjects on procedures used during problem solving.

Hayes has obtained protocol data indicating that use of imagery is more important for solving relatively complex mathematical problems [127]. Paige and Simon discovered systematic individual differences in strategies used to solve algebra problems [128]. An interesting difference is that between *verbal* and *physical* strategies. With a verbal strategy, the problem essentially was represented as a set of equations. With physical strategies, various forms of spatial representational aids were reportedly used (e.g., in the form of diagrams, graphs, or models) in solving the problems. Contradictions and impossible combinations of information were most easily detected with such spatial representations.

The Role of Imagery in Insight Problems and Complex Search Tasks

With an insight task, one usually has to "invent" a workable construction that is to serve some specified purpose. It has been argued by Kaufmann that this type of task is likely to involve imagery processes, since it requires both the generation of novel information and a simultaneous organizing of the problem elements [56]. He has tested the imagery hypothesis by studying the relationship between the solution of practical construction problems as a function of the ability to construct pictorial analogies. A very close relationship was found between task difficulty and pictorial analogy production, and the solvers produced significantly more pictorial analogies than did the nonsolvers. A verbal analogy test was incorporated as a control factor, and a slightly negative correlation was found between performance on this test and the ability to construct helpful pictorial analogies. A significant effect of mode of presentation, favoring the visual mode, was also obtained. Overall, these findings are in line with results obtained by Katona [129] and Fitzpatrick [130].

In other experiments, Kaufmann has examined the role of spatial manipulation ability in solving practical construction problems [56]. In order to hold the simultaneous organization dimension constant, all subjects were given a visual presentation of the problem. Scores on the spatial tests were shown to predict success in problem solving; whereas, scores on verbal tests were unrelated to problem-solving performance.

It may, of course, be argued that practical construction problems represent highly concrete stimulus situations, and that concreteness (rather than novelty) is responsible for the imagery effect. These contrasting interpretations were tested in an experiment performed by Kaufmann and Bengtsson [131]. The task could be solved by way of a rather well-known physical principle. As no difference was observed between visual and verbal presentation, the results were taken to support a novelty interpretation. The concreteness hypothesis also has been examined by Fitzpatrick [130], who assumed that scores on a verbal ability test would predict performance in verbally presented tasks; whereas, spatial ability correspondingly should predict performance under a visual presentation condition. The hypothesis was not supported [132]. (Cf. 132, for a similar prediction and a similar finding.)

Several investigators working with insight problems [133, 134] have reported that visual representational processes are particularly important in the exploratory phase of problem solving. Emphasis on verbalization in the initial phase in fact has been found to inhibit subsequent problem solving performance. Corman has further shown that the importance of verbal rule information increases with practice, particularly in the phase of generalizing to transfer tasks [135].

Some negative findings concerning the role of imagery in insight problems also must be noted. Wicker, Weinstein and Brooks asked their subjects to form clear and detailed visual images of the problem components, but they obtained no effect of these instructions [136]. Hollenberg [137] and Runquist and Hutt [138] obtained similar negative results for imagery in the area of concept formation. These results are in line with Bartlett's and Richardson's views previously cited, and they indicate that detailed visualization of a problem situation may have detrimental effects on problem solving. In another study by Durndell and Wetherick [139], no relationship was found between reported imagery and ability to solve the task. Time to reach solution in fact correlated positively with rated use of imagery during attempted solution.

A group of Russian researchers, Zinchenco, Munipov, and Gordon, have made an interesting examination of the functional usefulness of imagery in problem solving [140]. Complex search tasks were employed in the experimental setup. Imagery was operationalized through 1) the duration and amplitude of eye movements and 2) the degree of depression of the EEG of the occipital region of the cortex. Verbal processes were measured through EMG recordings from the lower lip. Their results indicate that the more complex the task, the greater the incidence of visualizing. Verbal processes seemed to be most important in the terminating phase of problem solving. It was suggested that "inner speech" is functional in planning activity and in summarizing the results obtained, and that imagery occupies a major role in the search space of the problem solver.

Imagery in Ideational Fluency and Other Creativity Tasks

Major theories in the field seem to emphasize the role of imagery in the creativity aspect of problem solving. A convenient task for testing this general hypothesis is the ideational-fluency situation [39], since it is generally regarded a valid measure of cognitive flexibility [141]. Thus one should expect imagery to play a significant part in ideational fluency performance.

Forisha and Nagy and Ernest (both reported in [142]) found low significant correlations between scores on an imagery questionnaire (Betts QMI) and performance on the Unusual Uses and Alternate Uses tests, respectively [143]. A weak but significant effect for vividness of imagery in relation to ideational fluency production also was found by Rhodes [25]. However, Durdell and Wetherick, who categorized subjects both in terms of imagery vividness (Betts QMI) and imagery control (Gordon TVIC) observed no relation between the vividness scores and performance on ideational fluency tasks [139], but imagery control was significantly related to three of the four scores derived from the ideational fluency tasks—a finding corroborated by Ernest (reported in [142]). Forisha found a significant relationship between vividness of imagery and ideational fluency performance for females but not for males [144]. No relationship was found between vividness of imagery scores and performance on the Remote Associates Test [145].

The inconsistency in these results may be due to serious methodological flaws inherent in the imagery questionnaire technique, for example, differences in subjective conceptions of the rating scale employed (see [146-149] for detailed discussions on this point).

In line with this argument, Hargreaves and Bolton obtained quite strong correlations with measures of ideational fluency performance when they used a paired-associate technique as measure of imagery ability [150]. A similar finding has been reported by Schmidt who used a spatial visualization test in his study [151].

Using an experimental method, Davis and Manske induced higher ideational fluency production under instructions to visualize an object (a screwdriver) in a particular setting (a picnic) than without such instructions [152]. Kaufmann [153] has experimentally studied the function of imagery in ideational-fluency performance by using a selective-interference technique (cf. [68, 70]) aimed at disrupting visual or verbal representational processes by presenting the subjects with irrelevant visual and auditory stimuli during task performance. The results showed an interaction between type of interference and sex. The performance of the males was more disrupted by visual interference; whereas the females responded in the opposite direction.

Results from several experiments with ideational fluency tasks have quite consistently shown that ideas given early in the production sequence tend to be conventional and stereotyped; whereas high-quality and original ideas appear at a later stage [143, 154, 155]. On the basis of these findings, Kaufmann predicted that the utility of imagery should increase with production time [6, 11]. In an experiment designed to test this hypothesis [148], the imagery construct was operationalized through scores on a spatial manipulation test. When the predictor effect for the spatial manipulation test was calculated in relation to ideational fluency performance at different time intervals (1, 2, 3 and 4 min.) in the production sequence, the results showed a systematic increase in predictor efficiency from nonsignificance at 1 minute to strong significance at 4 minutes. No systematic effect was found for scores on a verbal reasoning test. In a recently performed experiment, where a more appropriate index of verbal representational capacity was included (WAIS Vocabulary), Kaufmann [156] found that linguistic representation seems to be most appropriate in the initial, reproductive phase in ideational fluency production.

Schmeidler used a different measure of creativity (Barron Independence of Judgment Scale), and he found a small but significant relationship with scores on an imagery questionnaire of the Galton type [157]. When Schmeidler examined the scatterplots of the scores, however, she found that the quadrant which contained low creativity scores and high imagery scores was sparsely populated, in contrast to all the other quadrants. These results may be taken to mean that imagery is a useful symbolic instrument in creative thinking but is not necessary. This agrees with the observation made in some investigations that blind subjects are equal to their sighted peers on ideational fluency performance [158, 159]. In one study, Johnson even found that blind subjects surpassed sighted subjects in creative analogy production [160]. As Johnson notes, however, the superior performance of the blind may have been due to the onomatopoeic stimulus words employed. In an earlier study, however, Singer and Streiner found blind subjects to be inferior to their sighted peers in the area of imagination and cognitive flexibility [161].

Role of Imagery in Problem Solving

Let us now present some general issues about the potential role of imagery in problem solving and try to answer them on the basis of the available research evidence.

(1) **Does imagery play a functional role in problem solving?** The most basic question is whether available data indicate that imagery has a *causal* and truly *functional* place in the operations involved in problem solving, or if imagery is merely an *irrelevant by-product* or even a *distractor*, disrupting efficient cognitive processes.

The evidence as a whole clearly suggests that imagery is truly functional and may aid problem solving in significant ways. This conclusion seems warranted on different grounds:

- Experimental research, where imagery is manipulated systematically, indicates quite consistently that use of imagery strategies does lead to enhanced task performance.
- There is a systematic trend in this research evidence which suggests that the functional utility of imagery strategies increases with increasing *task difficulty*. It may be argued that this is exactly the condition in which the problem solver *cannot* afford any irrelevant cognitive luxury.

Whether it is possible to compensate by using other types of cognitive strategies is a question not readily answered by the data available. We will return to this in the sequel. Also our conclusion does not rule out the possibility that use of imagery in thinking under certain conditions might prove detrimental to thinking as compared to alternative strategies.

(2) Is imagery related to type of process used in problem solving, level of programming or abstractness-concreteness of the task? Greeno has grouped the tasks examined above with reference to particular information-processing functions assumed to be differentially involved in the various tasks [162] (e.g., understanding, planning, and constructive search processes).

The evidence shows that imagery does not seem to be exclusively tied to specific cognitive process functions or to certain general modes of operation. Indeed, the research seems to show that imagery is functional over the whole process spectrum. However, the evidence is scanty and must be regarded as tentative. It may, indeed, turn out that imagery is *particularly* valuable in certain process functions (e.g., understanding). But the results suggest quite definitely that the functional utility of imagery is not limited to a particular type of cognitive process function or mode of processing, as has been proposed by Berlyne [56] and Paivio [63]. As yet, it has not been possible to pinpoint the functional usefulness of imagery to certain specific cognitive process functions and/or modes of processing. There are, however, clear indications that *level of programming* in the task is a major determinant of the functional usefulness of imagery. We may conceive problems as falling on a continuum from *programmed* to *nonprogrammed*. A task is programmed if the subject possesses a definite procedure to handle it and nonprogrammed when it appears novel, unstructured, or unusually complicated and consequential to the subject [163]. In particular, the evidence concerning the imagery-task *novelty* link is quite suggestive, and it seems to be replicable over a broad spectrum of different tasks. Task *complexity* also seems to be an important determinant of the appropriateness of using imagery. This seems implied in the research suggesting a particular role for imagery in high-level quantitative thinking. In a computer simulation study of problem solving, Baylor found a pictorial representation to be particularly useful when the problem structure was complex [164]. The research by Paige and Simon reviewed above also indicates that imagery strategies may be particularly appropriate as a means of resolving *ambiguity* and *inconsistency*. Related to these findings are reports indicating that imagery is a useful strategy under conditions of *low meaning* (see experiments by Furby reviewed above, and also Kaufmann [11]).

Again, we emphasize that the research evidence is scarce and that the above conclusions should be regarded primarily as an interesting working hypothesis. A convincing demonstration of a systematic relationship between imagery and level of programming however would have considerable importance both for basic theory and for educational-technological application.

The results pertaining to the abstractness-concreteness dimension are quite intriguing. The research evidence suggests quite definitely that imagery does not impede abstract thinking. Neither does the functional usefulness of imagery seem to be tied to task concreteness, as claimed by Paivio. Quite to the contrary, several independent lines of research indicate that imagery is highly functional under *abstract* task conditions. This may seem paradoxical and contrary to much research evidence [63], but it is really not so. When addressing the question of the possible functional properties of imagery, it is important to make a distinction between the conditions that *naturally* or most *easily* give rise to imagery, and the conditions under which imagery is most urgently *needed* for most *efficient* task performance [11]. Paivio tends to run these two senses of the functional significance of imagery together; whereas we believe that it is important to keep them apart. This is illustrated by the following point: Imagery may be most easily *evoked* in relation to concrete stimulus material; whereas, imagery may be most highly *needed* in dealing with abstract tasks. Since Paivio leans toward the behavioristic S-R-scheme with its implications that the individual is a passive "response-system," it comes as no surprise that he concentrates on the conditions that most naturally elicit imagery, rather than focusing on the conditions in which an active information processor has the strongest *need* for the use of imagery as a representational strategy. In the present context, we concentrate on the latter aspect, which we think is the most appropriate for demonstrating the true nature and functional significance of imagery in cognition. This is not to say that significant, positive interactions between imagery and performance in concrete, perceptual tasks do not exist. Indeed, it would be strange if there were no such relationships. However, it should be noted that even in clear-cut perceptual tasks, visualization seems to be most appropriate under conditions of high task difficulty [164, 165].

In conclusion, then, imagery definitely does not appear to be the primitive form of thinking used primarily by children and housewives, as Galton [40] suggested and as many scholars still believe [166]. On the contrary, imagery seems to make possible an *increased amount of processing in cognition* [11] and is a symbolic tool that seems most appropriate in *high-grade thinking*.

Implications for Education

We deal with the implications of the above reviewed research for the educational process, a word of caution is necessary. Neither the quantity nor the quality of the research that has been done permits the formulation of definite precepts for educational practice. Thus, the points made in the sequel should be regarded mainly as tentative suggestions and as proposals for *further research*.

A primary question is whether imagery should be regarded primarily as a *structurally dependent capacity* or if it is more appropriately regarded as belonging to the category of *functional control operations*, which are more *optional* in use than are the structurally dependent capacities. A third and very reasonable possibility is that imagery represents an intricate interplay in which structural factors regulate the function of optional strategies.

Research has indicated that the brain processes underlying imagery representations primarily are located in the nondominant hemisphere [167, 168]. However, recent research reviewed by Marks points to a topographical organization across both hemispheres [169]. Also, experimental findings indicate quite strongly that, to a large extent, imagery can fruitfully be regarded as a functional strategy. A striking observation is how easy it is to manipulate imagery by way of simple instructions or through a brief training program. As we have seen, such experimental manipulations have significant effects on task performance. The research findings thus tend to confirm the subtle distinction made by Richardson [60], McKellar [55], and Marks [170] that the *potential* for imagery may be universal, but that the *ability* to generate and employ imagery may vary across people, as a result of experience and training. Recently, Marks and McKellar have restated and elaborated this point in an interesting way [171]. Such a view of imagery is in line with the one advocated by Kolers and Smythe [172], who regard imagery primarily as a skill. If this is essentially correct, the utilization of imagery naturally will be responsive to training and environmental influences, and great possibilities for educational stimulation will open up.

In an early study which deserves renewed attention, Boisbaudran presented systematic evidence in favor of the thesis that imagery skills may be influenced to a considerable degree through training [173]. Boisbaudran used a procedure consisting of tasks carefully graded from simple to complex ones. Several contemporary studies have corroborated this finding [174-178]. A series of recently performed experiments by Khatena deserve special attention [179]. Khatena demonstrated that it was possible to increase the level of imagination imagery by way of a relatively short training program. The implications of these findings are highly interesting, since imagery seems to be particularly useful for the processing needed in creative thinking tasks.

However, negative findings also appear in the literature [168]. One crucial variable seems to be the relatedness of the training program to the criterion task [180]. Another may be the training procedure itself. It seems well advised to follow the systematic procedure used by Boisbaudran [173] and carefully build up visualization skills along the simple-complex dimension.

Research on instructions to use imagery has indicated that most people possess potent cognitive competencies that are not used to the degree they deserve. Many writers in the educational field [181, 182] argue that in our educational system, too heavy emphasis is placed on the use and development of a discrete, linguistic-propositional mode of representation. We can speculate that this may be one of the reasons why people are reluctant to use imagery strategies even when these would be highly efficient for dealing with the task at hand. For educational purposes, future research should specify the conditions under which imagery is most useful as a symbolic tool, and it should instigate the development of efficient procedures for instructing students in the use of their imagery powers under those conditions. This suggestion is premised on the view that most people do possess the required capacity, but they neither know the conditions under which imagery is workable nor the best way to monitor this representational system.

In the following, we will discuss potential educational implications of imagery research in relation to

1. *content* (curriculum, topics, and task conditions);
2. *method* (instructional strategies, general approaches, and individual differences);
3. *evaluation* (procedures for assessing attainment).

At the outset, we must emphasize the general lack of educational research specifically relating imagery to *problem solving* functions. To a great extent, then, we have to extrapolate from laboratory research and from educational research in the fields of learning and memory. However, we will stay as close as possible to the problem solving domain and refer to research on cognitive processes with clear relevance to problem solving functions.

(1) Content. In an important essay on cognition and curriculum, Eisner warns against the return-to-the-basics trend in American educational practice [181]. According to Eisner, the emphasis on the three R's may lead to excessive restriction of the individual's possibilities for developing a full-fledged cognitive competence. Different modes of representation are differently suited for different sorts of information pick-ups and cannot fully compensate for each other. In Eisner's opinion, the return-to-the-basics trend implies overfocusing on a discrete, linguistic-propositional mode of representation at the expense of other valuable and functionally important modes of representation. Of primary concern is the neglect of the opportunities for fostering imagery representations. Although the return-to-the-basics movement has never gained the same momentum in the European school debate, it is still true that curriculum, teaching, and evaluation here too are largely geared to a linguistic-propositional mode of representation. The results of research on imagery and problem solving tend to support Eisner's view. We have seen that imagery may be particularly important as a symbolic working space for high-grade, productive thinking. If we wish to foster creativity in our educational practice, we must provide the opportunities for developing the imagery mode of representation, rather than restricting it. We therefore agree with Eisner that a *broadening of the curriculum* to include subjects, themes, and activities that naturally develop the individual's capacity for using imagery is an important educational challenge (see [181] for specific suggestions for the implementation of this goal in educational practice).

Eisner is concerned with the importance of upgrading the esthetic subjects for this purpose. The relevance of this point is validated by the close relationship between imagery and creativity that is often observed in the literature. However, problem solving activity in other subjects also seems to benefit from the use of imagery strategies. Contrary to common expectations, the research evidence suggests quite strongly that imagery is particularly important in highly *abstract* tasks and quantitative thinking, particularly at advanced levels. In general, research seems to show that imagery is particularly functional as a representational technique under the task conditions of *high novelty, high complexity* and *high ambiguity*. If this hypothesis is substantiated by future research, the educational implications seem to be quite important. In the following, we will suggest some potential applications from this hypothesis for educational method.

(2) **Method.** Alesandrini has distinguished between three main strategies for eliciting imagery and has discussed the role of these imagery-eliciting strategies in the context of meaningful learning [183]. These are: 1) *pictorial stimuli*, such as pictures, graphs, etc., 2) *imagery instructions* or direct inducements, and 3) *concretization* (concrete verbal stimuli). It is reasonable to argue that there is a continuous dimension of strength in inducement from 1), which is generally strongest, to 3) which is generally weakest. However, it seems appropriate to point out some possible *disadvantages* of using the different strategies. Specifically, the three strategies may differ systematically in degree of tying the individual up in *specific details* of the information provided, which may *disrupt* efficient problem solving. Pictorial stimuli may foster this potential dysfunctional consequence to the greatest extent, imagery-instruction would be less likely to do so, and concretization represents the least danger in this respect. As seen above, the research literature contains clear examples of this potential dysfunctional effect of using pictorial material and imagery-based strategies.

The implication seems to be that the imagery inducement strength must be carefully monitored according to the real *need* for using visualization as a problem solving strategy. On the basis of the general conclusions we have tentatively drawn from the research on imagery and problem solving, we suggest that strength of inducement should be monitored systematically according to *level of programming* in the problem-solving task: The strongest inducement is required in nonprogrammed tasks and lowest (or no) inducement is needed in highly programmed tasks. Research findings also clearly point to the need for strong inducement in highly *abstract* tasks. There is further some evidence to the effect that strong inducement may be particularly favorable in tasks drawing heavily upon *understanding processes*.

Educational research evidence relevant to the hypotheses framed above is, unfortunately, rather scarce. However, there are some interesting results reported which indicate that our assumptions have some validity.

Several studies indicate that under the condition of learning *novel concepts* (nonprogrammed tasks) a pictorial strategy (strong inducement) facilitates problem solving to a significant degree both for children and adults [184-186]. In tasks with a higher degree of programming (partly known material), instructing subjects to use mental imagery seems to be more effective than the picture strategy [187]. We may speculate that in highly programmed tasks, purely verbal strategies may be the most economic and efficient procedures (see [6] for a detailed discussion of this proposition).

Level of programming is, of course, not exclusively a task variable, but rather is a result of interaction between an individual, having certain skills, competencies, and capacities, and a particular task which relates to these resources (i.e., what is a difficult task for one individual, may be a very easy one for another). Therefore, our working hypothesis implies, among other things, that an individual who is low in general problem solving capacity or suffers from a general experiential deprivation may profit particularly from using imagery strategies, since imagery strategies *ex hypothesis* promote a higher level of processing in cognition.

Support for this hypothesis comes from studies by Rohwer and Harris who found that socially disadvantaged children may benefit more from seeing pictures in concept formation tasks than children from a richer social background [188]. Of particular interest in this context is a study by Bender and Levin which demonstrates that retardates can benefit greatly from a picture strategy [189]. Gustavsson also suggests that pictorial information is most effective with individuals of *low verbal and low general intellectual ability* [190, 191].

Such findings may be explained by assuming that due to experiential deprivation and low ability, these individuals are often faced with a high level of task difficulty in their problem solving transactions with the environment.

This view implies that we should find a similar pattern when examining the effect of strong inducement in relation to *age*; that is, the effect of pictorial strategies should decrease with increasing age. The research literature offers firm support for this hypothesis [183, 192]. In general, picture strategies are more effective with children than with adults; the latter profit more from imagery instructions and concretization strategies. It is particularly interesting to note that children below the age of five or six years experience great difficulty in generating imagery from instructions. This finding supports the view that *constructive use* of imagery may presuppose the mastery of a more basic linguistic-conceptual mode of representation [75].

Another individual difference variable of particular interest is *sex*. Research findings strongly suggest that males are superior to females in visualization ability [120, 169]. The sex difference may be due to biological factors (such as differences in lateralization), or to differences in socialization practices and play activities for the two sexes, or to an interaction between both factors (see [169] for a general discussion of this issue). Of considerable importance for the educational process is the quite consistent finding reported above that sex differences in quantitative ability are systematically related to sex differences in visualization ability. Research evidence points to the important finding that visual adjuncts (graphs) significantly aid mathematical problem solving ability (e.g., [193]), and they are of greater help to females than to males [194-196]. It is important to explore the implications of such findings with the aim of discovering to what degree a more imagery-based training program in mathematics may accelerate general performance, and in particular how it may affect sex differences in quantitative ability.

Individual differences in ability profiles already have been mentioned above. The research findings tend to show that low verbal ability, low general intellectual ability, and high spatial ability are important determinants of the efficiency of pictorial strategies (see e.g., [183, 197]). Of course, the effect for high spatial ability may merely reflect that tuning in to the preferred mode of representation yields a significant effect in tasks that are congruent with the preferred strategies. More important is the effect of *training* in visualization on problem solving performance. The results suggest that those who are initially *low* in spatial ability may profit the most [196] but see also [168] for conflicting evidence.

(3) **Evaluation.** Evaluation methods are assumed to make possible precise and fair assessment of attainments in relation to goals independently established. However, as Eisner has cogently argued [181], there can be little doubt that the form and content of evaluation methods also have a *prescriptive* effect on the choice of curriculum and methods of teaching. If it is desirable to strengthen the basis for teaching children to develop imagery-based representational skills, this factor must be taken into account.

This may be achieved *within* the current evaluation paradigm by requiring students to manifest their knowledge and competencies in imagery-based forms, either in multiple-choice type of tasks (e.g., select the best visual, graphic illustration of a particular principle or concept) or in free-response format where the task is to express knowledge in visualized and imagery-based form (such as drawings, playacting, etc.). It may be achieved also by going outside the current evaluation paradigm to nontraditional evaluation techniques, such as films and audio-visual programs (see [181] for a more detailed discussion of such nontraditional methods of evaluation).

CONCLUDING REMARKS

What we have said about implications of imagery research in problem solving for the educational process admittedly has been spectulative and should be regarded more as suggestions for further research than as specific advices for immediate and direct educational application. Imagery research, particularly in the domain of problem solving, is still in an early state. Some psychologists even will argue that it has not been established that imagery plays a functional role in cognition [198, 199]. In our opinion, this view is difficult to uphold given the evidence in stock [11, 200].

However, a general inadequacy of existing imagery research is that we do not know to what extent the benefits of using imagery strategies may be achieved by way of other cognitive strategies. Research on congenitally blind subjects (see e.g., [72, 201]) suggests that the human problem solver is very flexible and that inadequate development in certain areas may be offset to a considerable degree by accelerated development in other functions. On logical grounds, we can distinguish between three categories of functional utility, as far as imagery strategies are concerned:

- The category of the *optional* signifies that other strategies (e.g., linguistic) may be used as effectively as imagery strategies.
- The category of the *expedient* indicates that imagery strategies are preferable but may be compensated by accelerated development in other strategy functions.
- The category of the *necessary* implies that imagery strategies are definitely superior to other strategies and necessary in order to reach a certain level of performance.

In general, we agree with Eisner who claims that different forms of representation are specialized to deal with different aspects of information pick-up and information processing, and that there are limits to mutual translatability between different types of representational strategies [181]. However, this is basically an empirical question and cannot be decided by *a priori* armchair speculations. Mapping the location of the imagery variable in the conceptual domains outlined above is a major task for imagery research, and it is of great importance both for the advancement of basic theory and for the establishment of a firmer basis for more detailed and precise educational applications.

REFERENCES

1. S. M. Kosslyn, Research on Mental Imagery: Some Goals and Directions, *Cognition, 10*:3, pp. 173-179, 1981.
2. J. T. E. Richardson, Mental Imagery in Thinking and Problem Solving, in *Thinking and Reasoning: Psychological Approaches*, J. St. B. T. Evans (ed.), Routledge and Kegan Paul, London, 1983.
3. M. J. Horowitz, *Image Formation and Cognition*, Butterworths, London, 1970.
4. G. Humphrey, *Thinking*, Methuen and Co., Ltd., London, 1959.
5. G. Kaufmann, *Visual Imagery and Its Relation to Problem Solving: A Theoretical and Experimental Inquiry*, Universitetsforlaget, Oslo/Bergen/Tromsø, 1979.
6. _____, *Imagery, Language and Cognition*, Universitetsforlaget, Oslo/Bergen/Tromsø, 1980.
7. S. M. Kosslyn, *Image and Mind*, Harvard University Press, Cambridge, 1980.
8. J. M. Mandler and G. Mandler, (eds.), *Thinking: From Association to Gestalt*, Wiley, New York, 1964.
9. R. S. Woodworth and H. Schlosberg, *Experimental Psychology*, Holt, Rinehart and Winston, New York, 1955.
10. G. Kaufmann, Mental Imagery and Problem Solving, *International Review of Mental Imagery*, in press.
11. _____, On the Conceptual Basis of Imagery Models: A Critique and a Theory, in *Theories of Imagery Formation*, D. Marks (ed.), Brandon House, New York, in press.
12. K. Raaheim, *Problem Solving: A New Approach*, Universitetsforlaget, Oslo/Bergen/Tromsø, 1961.
13. J. Dewey, *How We Think*, D. C. Heath Company, Boston, 1910.

14. D. M. Johnson, *The Psychology of Thought and Judgment*, Harper and Row, New York, 1955.
15. W. Køhler, *The Mentality of Apes*, Harcourt, Brace and World, New York, 1927.
16. A. Newell and H. A. Simon, *Human Problem Solving*, Prentice-Hall, New Jersey, 1972.
17. K. Duncker, On Problem Solving, *Psychological Monographs*, No. 5. (Whole No. 270), 1945.
18. L. E. Bourne, B. R. Ekstrand, and R. L. Dominowski, *The Psychology of Thinking*, Prentice-Hall, London, 1971.
19. K. Raaheim, *Problem Solving and Intelligence*, Universitetsforlaget, Oslo/ Bergen/Tromsø, 1974.
20. W. S. Ray, Complex Tasks for Use in Human Problem Solving Research, *Psychological Bulletin*, *52*, pp. 134-149, 1955.
21. W. S. Ray, *The Experimental Psychology of Original Thinking*, Macmillan, New York, 1967.
22. G. H. Betts, *The Distributions and Functions of Mental Imagery*, Columbia University Teachers' College Press, New York, 1909.
23. C. H. Griffith, Individual Differences in Imagery, *Psychological Monographs*, *37*, pp. 1-91, 1927.
24. A. Roe, *The Making of a Scientist*, Dodd, Mead, New York, 1952.
25. J. W. Rhodes, Relationship between Vividness of Mental Imagery and Creative Thinking, *Journal of Creative Behavior*, *15*:2, pp. 235-249, 1981.
26. S. Arieti, *Creativity: The Magic Synthesis*, Basic Books, New York, 1976.
27. R. Dreistadt, An Analysis of the Use of Analogies and Metaphors in Science, *The Journal of Psychology*, *68*, pp. 97-116, 1968.
28. E. S. Ferguson, The Mind's Eye: Nonverbal Thought in Technology, *Science*, *197*, pp. 827-836, 1977.
29. M. I. Posner, *Cognition: An Introduction*, Scott, Foresman, Glenview, Illinois, 1973.
30. R. N. Shepard, The Mental Image, *American Psychologist*, pp. 125-137, February, 1978.
31. _____, Externalization of the Image and the Act of Creation, in *Visual Learning, Thinking and Communication*, B. S. Randhawa (ed.), Academic Press, New York, pp. 133-189, 1978.
32. H. Nash, The Role of Metaphor in Psychological Theory, *Behavioral Science*, *8*, pp. 336-345, 1963.
33. A. Einstein, *Out of My Later Years*, Philosophical Library, New York, 1950.
34. A. Koestler, *The Act of Creation*, Macmillan, New York, 1964.
35. W. J. Gordon, *Synetics: The Development of Creative Capacity*, Harper and Row, New York, 1961.
36. L. E. Walkup, Creativity in Science through Visualization, *Perceptual and Motor Skills*, *21*, pp. 35-41, 1965.
37. D. Taylor, Creative Design through Functional Visualization, *The Journal of Creative Behavior*, *3*:2, pp. 122-127, 1969.

38. J. P. Guilford, Intellectual Resources and their Values as Seen by Scientists, in *Scientific Creativity: Its Recognition and Development*, C. W. Taylor and F. Barron (eds.), Wiley, New York, pp. 101-117, 1963.

39. _____, *The Nature of Human Intelligence*, McGraw-Hill, New York, 1967.

40. F. Galton, *Inquiries into Human Faculty and Its Development*, Macmillan, London, 1883.

41. Z. W. Pylyshyn, What the Mind's Eye Tells the Mind's Brain: A Critique of Mental Imagery, *Psychological Bulletin, 80*:1, pp. 1-23, 1973.

42. C. Fox, The Conditions which Arouse Mental Images in Thought, *British Journal of Psychology, 6*, pp. 420-431, 1914.

43. C. Comstock, On the Relevancy of Imagery to the Process of Thought, *American Journal of Psychology, 32*, pp. 196-230, 1921.

44. E. B. Tichener, *A Textbook of Psychology*, Macmillan, New York, 1910.

45. T. H. Pear, The Relevance of Visual Imagery to the Process of Thought, *British Journal of Psychology, 28*, pp. 1-14, 1927.

46. E. L. Woods, An Experimental Study of the Process of Recognizing, *American Journal of Psychology, 26*, pp. 313-387, 1915.

47. E. O. Finkenbinder, The Remembrance of Problems and of Their Solutions: A Study in Logical Memory, *American Journal of Psychology, 6*, pp. 440-413, 1914.

48. C. S. Fisher, The Process of Generalizing Abstraction, and Its Product, the General Concept, *Psychological Monographs, 21*:90, pp. 150-180, 1916.

49. F. C. Bartlett, The Function of Images, *British Journal of Psychology, 11*, pp. 320-337, 1921.

50. _____, Feeling, Imagery and Thinking, *British Journal of Psychology, 16*, pp. 16-28, 1925.

51. _____, The Relevance of Visual Imagery to Thinking, *British Journal of Psychology, 18*, pp. 23-29, 1927.

52. H. Rugg, *Imagination*, Harper and Row, New York, 1963.

53. P. McKellar, *Imagination and Thinking*, Basic Books, New York, 1957.

54. _____, Three Aspects of the Psychology of Originality in Human Thinking, *British Journal of Aesthetics, 3*, pp. 129-147, 1963.

55. _____, Imagery from the Standpoint of Introspection, in *The Function and Nature of Imagery*, P. W. Sheehan (ed.), Academic Press, New York, 1972.

56. D. Berlyne, *Structure and Direction in Thinking*, Wiley, New York, 1965.

57. R. Arnheim, *Art and Visual Perception: A Psychology of the Creative Eye*, University of California Press, Berkeley, 1954.

58. _____, *Visual Thinking*, University of California Press, Berkeley, 1969.

59. _____, *Toward a Psychology of Art*, University of California Press, Berkeley, 1972.

60. A. Richardson, *Mental Imagery*, Springer, New York, 1969.

61. W. G. Chase and H. H. Clark, Mental Operations in the Comparison of Sentences and Pictures, in *Cognition in Learning and Memory*, L. W. Gregg (ed.), Wiley, New York, 1972.

62. W. G. Chase and H. A. Simon, The Mind's Eye in Chess, in *Visual Information Processing*, W. G. Chase (ed.), Academic Press, New York, pp. 215-281, 1973.

63. A. Paivio, *Imagery and Verbal Processes*, Holt, New York, 1971.
64. _____, A Theoretical Analysis of the Role of Imagery in Learning and Memory, in *The Function and Nature of Imagery*, P. W. Sheehan (ed.), Academic Press, London, 1972.
65. _____, Psychophysiological Correlates of Imagery, in *The Psychophysiology of Covert Processes*, F. J. Mcguigan and R. A. Schoonover (eds.), Academic Press, London, 1973.
66. _____, Imagery and Synchronic Thinking, *Canadian Psychological Review*, pp. 147-163, 1975.
67. _____, Neomentalism, *Canadian Journal of Psychology*, *29*, pp. 263-291, 1975.
68. G. Atwood, An Experimental Study of Visual Imagination and Memory, *Cognitive Psychology*, *2*, pp. 290-299, 1971.
69. G. H. Bower, Mental Imagery and Associative Learning, in *Cognition in Learning and Memory*, L. W. Gregg (ed.), Wiley, New York, 1972.
70. L. R. Brooks, The Suppression of Visualization by Reading, *Quarterly Journal of Experimental Psychology*, *19*, pp. 289-299, 1967.
71. J. S. Bruner, R. R. Olver, and P. M. Greenfield, *Studies in Cognitive Growth*, Wiley, New York, 1966.
72. B. R. Bugelski, The Definition of the Image, in *Imagery: Current Cognitive Approaches*, S. J. Segal (ed.), Academic Press, New York, 1971.
73. D. D. Hebb, Concerning Imagery, *Psychological Review*, *75*, pp. 466-477, 1968.
74. O. R. Mowrer, *Learning Theory and the Symbolic Processes*, Wiley, New York, 1960.
75. G. Kaufmann, The Conceptual Status of Imagery as a Symbolic System, paper presented at the Fourth American Imagery Conference, San Francisco, November 13-16, 1980b.
76. W. R. Reitman, *Cognition and Thought: An Information Processing Approach*, Wiley, New York, 1965.
77. I. M. L. Hunter, The Solving of Three-Term Series Problems, *British Journal of Psychology*, *48*, pp. 286-298, 1957.
78. C. B. De Soto, M. London, and S. Handel, Social Reasoning and Spatial Paralogic, *Journal of Personality and Social Psychology*, *2*, pp. 513-521, 1965.
79. J. Huttenlocher, Constructing Spatial Images: A Strategy in Reasoning, *Psychological Review*, *75*, pp. 556-560, 1968.
80. H. H. Clark, Linguistic Processes in Deductive Reasoning, *Psychological Review*, *76*, pp. 387-404, 1969.
81. _____, The Influence of Language in Solving Three-Term Series Problems, *Journal of Experimental Psychology*, *82*, pp. 205-215, 1969.
82. J. Huttenlocher, K. Eisenberg, and S. Strauss, Comprehension: Relation between Perceived Action and Logical Subject, *Journal of Verbal Learning and Verbal Behavior*, *7*, pp. 527-530, 1968.
83. J. Huttenlocher and E. T. Higgins, Adjectives, Comparitives and Syllogisms, *Psychological Review*, *78*, pp. 487–504, 1971.
84. _____, On Reasoning, Congruence, and Other Matters, *Psychological Review*, *79*, pp. 402-407, 1972.

85. J. Huttenlocher, E. T. Higgins, C. Milligan, and B. Kauffman, The Mystery of the 'Negative Equative' Construction, *Journal of Verbal Learning and Verbal Behavior, 9*, pp. 334-341, 1970.

86. P. Shaver, L. Pierson, and S. Lang, Converging Evidence of the Functional Significance of Imagery in Problem Solving, *Cognition, 1*, pp. 359-374, 1976.

87. H. H. Clark, More about "Adjectives, Comparatives and Syllogisms:" A Reply to Huttenlocher and Higgins, *Psychological Review, 78*, pp. 505-514, 1971.

88. _____, On the Evidence Concerning J. Huttenlocher and E. T. Higgins' Theory of Reasoning: A Second Reply, *Psychological Review, 79*, pp. 428-432, 1972.

89. M. G. Eley, The Suitability of Placement Tasks as Analogues for Syllogistic Reasoning, *British Journal of Psychology, 70*:4, pp. 541-546, 1979.

90. S. Jones, Visual and Verbal Processes in Problem-Solving, *Cognitive Psychology, 1*, pp. 201-214, 1970.

91. P. L. French, Linguistic Marking, Strategy, and Affect in Syllogistic Reasoning, *Journal of Psycholinguistic Research, 8*, pp. 425-449, 1979.

92. R. L. Williams, Imagery and Linguistic Factors Affecting the Solution of Linear Syllogisms, *Journal of Psycholinguistic Research, 8*:2, pp. 123-140, 1977.

93. G. R. Potts and K. W. Scholz, The Internal Representation of a Three-Term Series Problem, *Journal of Verbal Learning and Verbal Behavior, 14*, pp. 439-452, 1975.

94. P. N. Johnson-Laird, The Three-Term Series Problem, *Cognition, 1*, pp. 57-82, 1972.

95. D. Wood, Approach to the Study of Human Reasoning, *Nature, 223*, pp. 101-102. 1969.

96. D. Wood, J. Shotter, and D. Godden, An Investigation of the Relationship between Problem Solving Strategies, Representation and Memory, *Quarterly Journal of Experimental Psychology, 26*, pp. 252-257, 1974.

97. R. J. Sternberg, Representation and Process in Linear Syllogistic Reasoning, *Journal of Experimental Psychology: General, 109*, pp. 119-159, 1980.

98. R. J. Sternberg and G. M. Weil, An Aptitude-Strategy Interaction in Linear Syllogistic Reasoning, *Journal of Educational Psychology, 72*, pp. 226-234, 1980.

99. G. Quinton and B. J. Fellows, 'Perceptual' Strategies in the Solving of Three-Term Series Problems, *British Journal of Psychology, 66*, pp. 69-78, 1975.

100. S. M. Kosslyn, G. L. Murphy, M. E. Bemesderfer, and K. J. Feinstein, Category and Continuum in Mental Comparisons, *Journal of Experimental Psychology, 104*:4, pp. 341-375, 1977.

101. D. Wood and J. Shotter, A Preliminary Study of Distinctive Features in Problem Solving, *Quarterly Journal of Experimental Psychology, 25*, pp. 504-510, 1973.

102. E. I. Gavurin, Anagram Solving and Spatial Aptitude, *Journal of Psychology, 65*, pp. 65-68, 1967.

103. L. Furby, The Role of Spatial Visualization in Verbal Problem Solving, *Journal of General Psychology*, *85*, pp. 149-152, 1971.
104. I. G. Wallace, The Role of Overt Rearrangement in Anagram Solving in Subjects of High and Low Spatial Ability and Anagrams of Two Levels of Difficulty, *The Journal of General Psychology*, *96*, pp. 117-124, 1977.
105. A. N. Frandsen and J. R. Holder, Spatial Visualization in Solving Complex Verbal Problems, *The Journal of Psychology*, *73*, pp. 229-233, 1969.
106. E. M. Jablonski and J. H. Mueller, Anagram Solution as a Function of Instructions, Priming and Imagery, *Journal of Experimental Psychology*, *94*:1, pp. 84-89, 1972.
107. K. Dewing and P. Hetherington, Anagram Solving as a Function of Word Imagery, *Journal of Experimental Psychology*, *102*:5, pp. 764-767, 1974.
108. R. P. Stratton and K. A. Jacobus, Solving Anagrams as Function of Word Frequency, Imagery and Distribution of Practice, *Canadian Journal of Psychology*, *29*, pp. 22-31, 1975.
109. J. T. E. Richardson, Imagery, Concreteness and Lexical Complexity, *Quarterly Journal of Experimental Psychology*, *27*:2, pp. 211-223, 1975.
110. _____, Concreteness and Imageability, *Quarterly Journal of Experimental Psychology*, *27*:2, pp. 235-249, 1975b.
111. _____, Imageability and Concreteness, *Bulletin of the Psychonomic Society*, *7*:5, pp. 429-431, 1976.
112. W. F. Cox, Problem Solving as Influenced by Stimulus Abstractness-Concreteness, *Psychology*, pp. 37-44, 1976.
113. _____, Problem Solving as a Function of Abstract or Concrete Words, *Contemporary Educational Psychology*, *3*, pp. 95-101, 1978.
114. J. R. Hayes, Problem Typology and the Solution Process, *Journal of Verbal Learning and Verbal Behavior*, *4*, pp. 371-379, 1965.
115. R. R. Skemp, *The Psychology of Learning Mathematics*, Penguin, New York, 1971.
116. I. M. Smith, *Spatial Ability*, University of London Press Ltd., London, 1964.
117. J. Wrigley, The Factorial Nature of Ability in Elementary Mathematics, *British Journal of Educational Psychology*, *2*, pp. 61-78, 1958.
118. I. Werdelin, *The Mathematical Ability: Experimental and Factorial Studies*, Ohlsson, Lund, 1958.
119. P. E. Vernon, *The Structure of Human Abilities*, Methuen, London, 1950.
120. E. Maccoby and D. Jacklin, *The Psychology of Sex Differences*, Stanford University Press, Stanford, 1974.
121. C. Poole and G. Stanley, A Factorial and Predictive Study of Spatial Abilities, *Australian Journal of Psychology*, *24*:3, pp. 317-320, 1972.
122. J. A. Sherman, Predicting Mathematics Performance in High School Girls and Boys, *Journal of Educational Psychology*, *71*, pp. 242-249, 1979.
123. _____, Predicting Mathematics Grades of High School Girls: A Further Study, *Contemporary Educational Psychology*, *5*, pp. 249-255, 1980.
124. S. A. Burnett, D. M. McLane, and L. M. Dratt, Spatial Visualization and Sex Differences in Quantitative Ability, *Intelligence*, *3*:4, pp. 345-354, 1979.

125. E. Fennema and J. Sherman, Sex-Related Differences in Mathematics Achievement, Spatial Visualization and Affective Factors, *American Educational Research Journal, 14*:1, pp. 51-71, 1977.

126. J. A. Sherman, Mathematics, Spatial Visualization and Related Factors: Changes in Girls and Boys, Grades 8-11, *Journal of Educational Psychology, 72*:4, pp. 476-482, 1980b.

127. J. R. Hayes, On the Function of Visual Imagery in Elementary Mathematics, in *Visual Information Processing*, W. G. Chase (ed.), Academic Press, New York, pp. 117-124, 1973.

128. J. M. Paige and H. A. Simon, Cognitive Processes in Solving Algebra Problems, in *Problem Solving: Research Method and Theory*, B. Kleinmuntz (ed.), Wiley, New York, 1966.

129. G. Katona, *Organizing and Memorizing*, Columbia University Press, New York, 1940.

130. T. J. Fitzpatrick, The Relation of Imagery and Word Association Abilities to Various Problem Solving Tasks, unpublished Ph.D. dissertation, New York University, 1978.

131. G. Kaufmann and G. Bengtsson, Effect of Mode of Presentation on Performance in a Familiar Task, *Scandinavian Journal of Psychology, 21*, pp. 61-63, 1980.

132. C. H. Ernest, Imagery Ability and the Identification of Fragmented Pictures and Words, *Acta Psychologica, 44*, pp. 51-57, 1980.

133. G. M. Haslerud and S. Meyers, The Transfer Value of Given and Individually Derived Principles, *Journal of Educational Psychology, 49*, pp. 293-298, 1958.

134. G. Hendrix, Prerequisite for Meaning, *Mathematics Teacher, 43*, pp. 334-339, 1950.

135. B. R. Corman, The Effect of Varying Amounts of Information as Guidance in Problem Solving, *Psychological Monographs, 71*:2 (Whole No. 431), 1957.

136. F. W. Wicker, C. A. Weinstein, and J. D. Brooks, Problem Reformulation Training and Visualization Training with Insight Problems, *Journal of Educational Psychology, 70*:3, pp. 372-377, 1978.

137. C. K. Hollenberg, Function of Visual Imagery in the Learning and Concept Formation of Children, *Child Development, 41*, pp. 1003-1015, 1970.

138. W. N. Runquist and U. H. Hutt, Verbal Concept Learning in High School Students with Pictorial and Verbal Representation of Stimuli, *Journal of Educational Psychology, 52*, pp. 108-111, 1961.

139. A. J. Durndell and N. E. Wetherick, The Relation of Reported Imagery to Cognitive Performance, *British Journal of Psychology, 67*, pp. 501-506, 1979.

140. U. P. Zinchenko, U. M. Munipov, and V. M. Gordon, The Study of Visual Thinking, *Voprosy Psikhologii, 2*, pp. 3-14, 1973.

141. M. A. Wallach, Creativity, in *Carmichael's Manual of Child Psychology*, Vol. 1, P. Mussen (ed.), Wiley, New York, 1970.

142. C. H. Ernest, Imagery Ability and Cognition: A Critical Review, *Journal of Mental Imagery, 2*, pp. 181-216, 1977.

143. P. R. Christensen, J. P. Guilford, and R. C. Wilson, Relation of Creative Responses to Working Time and Instructions, *Journal of Experimental Psychology*, *53*, pp. 82-88, 1957.

144. B. L. Forisha, Creativity and Imagery in Men and Women, *Perceptual and Motor Skills*, *47*:3, pp. 1255-1264, 1978.

145. S. Mednick and M. Mednick, *Remote Associates Test*, Houghton and Mifflin, New York, 1967.

146. G. Kaufmann, Metaphors and Creative Thinking: II, The Relationship to Visual Imagery, *Reports from the Institute of Psychology, University of Bergen*, No. 2, 1973.

147. _____, Is Imagery a Cognitive Appendix?, *Reports from the Institute of Psychology, University of Bergen*, No. 1, 1976.

148. _____, What Is Wrong with Imagery Questionnaires?, *Scandinavian Journal of Psychology*, *22*, pp. 59-64, 1981.

149. J. T. E. Richardson, Correlations between Imagery and Memory Across Stimuli and across Subjects, *Bulletin of the Psychonomic Society*, *14*:5, pp. 368-370, 1979.

150. D. J. Hargreaves and N. Bolton, Selecting Creativity Tests for Use in Research, *British Journal of Psychology*, *63*, pp. 451-462, 1972.

151. H. E. Schmidt, The Identification of High and Low Creativity in Architecture Students, *Psychologica Africana*, *15*, pp. 15-40, 1973.

152. G. A. Davis and M. E. Manske, An Instructional Method of Increasing Originality, *Psychonomic Science*, *6*, pp. 73-74, 1966.

153. G. Kaufmann, Visual Imagery and Problem Solving: II, Effect of Visual and Auditory Inference on Ideational Fluency Performance, *Reports from the Institute of Psychology, University of Bergen*, No. 1, 1974.

154. A. Meadow and S. J. Parnes, Evaluation of Training in Creative Problem Solving, *Journal of Applied Psychology*, *43*, pp. 189-194, 1959.

155. S. J. Parnes, Effects of Extended Effort in Creative Problem Solving, *Journal of Educational Psychology*, *3*, pp. 117-122, 1961.

156. G. Kaufmann, The Functional Significance of Visual Imagery in Ideational Fluency Performance, *Journal of Mental Imagery*, *5*, pp. 115-120, 1981.

157. G. R. Schmeidler, Visual Imagery Correlated to a Measure of Creativity, *Journal of Consulting Psychology*, *29*, pp. 78-80, 1965.

158. W. J. Tisdall, E. A. Blackhurst, and C. H. Marks, Divergent Thinking in Blind Children, *Journal of Educational Psychology*, *62*:6, pp. 468-473, 1971.

159. G. Halpin, G. Halpin, and E. P. Torrance, Effects of Blindness on Creative Thinking Abilities of Children, *Developmental Psychology*, *9*:2, pp. 268-274, 1973.

160. R. Johnson, Creative Imagery in Blind and Sighted Adolescents, *Journal of Mental Imagery*, *3*, pp. 23-30, 1979.

161. J. L. Singer and B. F. Streiner, Imaginative Content in the Dreams and Fantasy Play of Blind and Sighted Children, *Perceptual and Motor Skills*, *22*, pp. 475-482, 1966.

162. J. G. Greeno, Natures of Problem-Solving Abilities, in *Handbook of Learning and Cognitive Processes. Vol. 5. Human Information Processing*, W. K. Estes (ed.), Lawrence Erlbaum, Hillsdale, New Jersey, 1978.

163. H. A. Simon, Information-Processing Theory of Human Problem Solving, in *Handbook of Learning and Cognitive Processes. Vol. 5. Human Information Processing*, W. K. Estes (ed.), Lawrence Erlbaum, Hillsdale, New Jersey, 1978.

164. G. W. Baylor, A Trestise on the Mind's Eye: An Empirical Investigation of Visual Mental Imagery, unpublished Ph.D. dissertation, Carnegie-Mellon University, 1971.

165. W. S. Zimmerman, The Influence of Item Complexity upon the Factor Composition of a Spatial Visualization Test, *Educational and Psychological Measurement, 14*, pp. 106-109, 1954.

166. N. Postman, *The Disappearance of Childhood*, Delacorte, New York, 1982.

167. R. G. Ley, Cerebral Laterality and Imagery, in *Imagery: Current Theory, Research and Application*, A. A. Sheikh (ed.), Wiley, New York, 1983.

168. M. G. McGee, *Human Spatial Abilities*, Praeger, New York, 1979.

169. D. Marks, The Neuropsychological Basis of Memory: Theory and Experiment, in *Theories of Imagery Formation*, D. Marks (ed.), Brandon House, New York, 1984.

170. _____, Individual Differences in the Vividness of Visual Imagery and Their Effects on Function, in *The Function and Nature of Imagery*, P. W. Sheehan (ed.), Academic Press, New York, 1972.

171. D. Marks and P. McKellar, The Nature and Function of Imagery, *Journal of Mental Imagery, 6*:1, pp. 1-124, 1982.

172. P. A. Kolers and W. E. Smythe, Images, Symbols and Skills, *Canadian Journal of Psychology, 33*, pp. 158-184, 1979.

173. H. L. de Boisbaudran, *The Training of the Memory in Art*, L. D. Luard (ed. and trans.), MacMillian, London, 1911.

174. M. F. Blade and W. S. Watson, Increase in Spatial Visualization Test-Scores during Engineering Study, *Psychological Monographs*, No. 397, 1955.

175. E. H. Brinkmann, Programmed Instruction as a Technique for Spatial Visualization, *Journal of Applied Psychology, 50*, pp. 179-184, 1966.

176. R. A. Ciganko, The Effect of Spatial Information Training and Drawing Practice upon Spatial Visualization Ability and Representational Drawings of Ninth Grade Students, unpublished doctoral dissertation, Illinois State University, 1973.

177. J. F. Mundy, Spatial Ability, Mathematics Achievement, and Spatial Training in Male and Female Calculus Students, unpublished doctoral dissertation, University of New Hampshire, 1980.

178. J. E. Platt and S. Cohen, Mental Rotation Task Performance as a Function of Age and Training, *The Journal of Psychology, 108*, pp. 173-178, 1981.

179. J. Khatena, *Educational Psychology of the Gifted*, Wiley, New York, 1982.

180. G. L. Duncan, Visual Imagery Training and Skill in Chess, unpublished doctoral dissertation, Virginia Commonwealth University, 1979.

181. E. W. Eisner, *Cognition and Curriculum*, Longman, New York, 1982.

182. R. R. Holt, Imagery: The Return of the Ostracized, *American Psychologist, 19*, pp. 254-264, 1964.

183. K. L. Alesandrini, Imagery-Eliciting Strategies and Meaningful Learning, *Journal of Mental Imagery, 6*, pp. 125-140, 1982.

184. T. C. Arnold and F. M. Dwyer, Realism in Visualized Instruction, *Perceptual and Motor Skills, 40*, pp. 369-370, 1975.

185. F. M. Dwyer, The Effect of Overt Responses in Improving Visually Programmed Science Instruction, *Journal of Research in Science Teaching, 9*, pp. 47-55, 1972.

186. W. H. Holliday, The Effects of Verbal and Adjunct Pictorial-Verbal Information in Science Instruction, *Journal of Research in Science Teaching, 12*, pp. 77-83, 1975.

187. R. V. Rasco, R. D. Tennyson, and R. C. Boutwell, Imagery Instructions and Drawings in Learning Prose, *Journal of Educational Psychology, 67*, pp. 188-192, 1975.

188. W. D. Rohwer and W. J. Harris, Media Effects on Prose Learning in Two Populations of Children, *Journal of Educational Psychology, 67*, pp. 651-657, 1975.

189. B. G. Bender and J. R. Levin, Pictures, Imagery and Retarded Children's Prose Learning, *Journal of Educational Psychology, 70*, pp. 583-588, 1978.

190. J. E. Gustavsson, Verbal versus Figural in Aptitude-Treatment Interactions, Review of the Literature and an Empirical Study, *Report from the Institute of Education, University of Goetenburg*, No. 26, 1974.

191. _____, Verbal and Figural Aptitudes in Relation to Instructional Methods, *Goteborg Studies in Educational Sciences, 17*, Goteborg, 1976.

192. J. B. Levin and M. A. Pressley, A Test of the Developmental Imagery Hypothesis in Children's Associative Learning, *Journal of Educational Psychology, 70*:5, pp. 691-694, 1978.

193. J. Threadgill-Sowder and L. Sowder, Drawn versus Verbal Formats for Mathematical Story Problems, *Journal of Research in Mathematics Education, 13*:5, pp. 324-331, 1982.

194. S. W. Garrard, Sex Differences, Spatial Visualization Ability, and the Effects of Induced and Imposed Imagery on Problem Solving Performance, unpublished Ph.D. dissertation, University of Southern California, 1982.

195. M. A. Konsin, Spatial Visualization and Mathematical Problem Solving, unpublished Ph.D. dissertation, The University of Wisconsin, 1980.

196. J. F. Mundy, Spatial Ability, Mathematics Achievement and Spatial Training in Male and Female Calculus Students, unpublished Ph.D. dissertation, University of New Hampshire, 1980.

197. C. H. Ernest, Spatial Imagery Ability, Sex Differences, and Hemispheric Function, in *Imagery, Memory and Cognition*, J. C. Yuille (ed.), Lawrence Erlbaum, Hillsdale, New Jersey, 1983.

198. K. J. Gilhooley, *Thinking: Directed, Undirected and Creative*, Academic Press, New York, 1982.

199. Z. W. Pylyshyn, The Imagery Debate: Analogue Media versus Tacit Knowledge, *Psychological Review, 88*, pp. 16-45, 1981.

200. A. A. Sheikh, *Imagery: Current Theory, Research, and Application*, Wiley, New York, 1983.

201. N. H. Kerr, The Role of Vision in "Visual Imagery" Experiments, Evidence from the Congenitally Blind, *Journal of Experimental Psychology: General, 112*, pp. 265–277, 1983.

CHAPTER 6
Imagery and the Readability of Textbooks
WILLIAM P. WHARTON

In his "War Memoirs" Winston Churchill described an historical moment in a meeting with Joseph Stalin [1]. The Russians were restless for the Allies to open a second front. Long delays had made Stalin glum and critical. There were tense oppressive silences in their conversations. Then Churchill explained the plans for "Operation Torch" (the invasion of North Africa):

> I then described the military advantages of freeing the Mediter-ranean, whence still another front could be opened. To illustrate my point I had meanwhile drawn a picture of a crocodile, and explained to Stalin with the help of this picture how it was our intention to attack the soft belly of the crocodile as we attacked his hard snout. And, Stalin, whose interest was now at high pitch, said: "May God prosper this undertaking."
> This marked the turning-point of our conversation.

This incident indicates how the power of imagery to get attention, arouse interest, and carry conviction has helped to turn the tide of history. Without this clear metaphoric concept of the contribution to be made by Allied support, who knows how the suspicious and disgruntled teamwork might have affected the outcome of the war. To help the reader visualize people, ideas, and actions is a vital task of the historian.

Are images, then, merely "mental luxuries" [2, p. 60] or are they "our readi-est instruments for abstracting concepts from the tumbling stream of actual impressions" [3, pp. 32, 113, 117, 217].

This chapter will illustrate how imagery helps educational communication. It will focus on a careful experiment to explore how imagery affects readability. Then it will discuss how those findings may be used to improve texts.

IMAGERY IN EDUCATIONAL COMMUNICATION

The value of imagery as a tool of communication has long been assumed by writers and debated by psychologists. The ancients, such as Homer, Aristotle, Cicero, and Longinus, believed that imagery appealed to both the heart and the mind. It seemed to place the things of which they spoke "under the eyes of their hearers" [4, pp. 17-19, 36].

Yet, there was little relevant scientific data until the work of Sir Francis Galton, the father of correlation. He decided that "the highest minds are probably those in which the faculty [of imagery] is not lost but subordinated, and is ready for use on suitable occasions" [5, p. 61]. His own writing style, considered very readable by eminent scientists, illustrates that images are more than ornaments. For, although he wrote, "Statistics are the only tools by which an opening can be cut through the formidable thicket of difficulties that bar the path of those who pursue the science of man" [6, p. 28], he used images to drive home his point.

Every teacher knows that new ideas are explained by linking them with older experiences. When astronomers observed that the starlight from distant galaxies, under spectrum analysis, shifted towards red, they deemed that the universe was expanding.

The "red shift" in light was explained by analogy to the "Doppler effect" in sound. As a locomotive whistle recedes into the distance, it seems lower-pitched. So, light shifting toward a lower wavelength must mean that distant worlds are moving still farther apart.

Thus, the bridge for new ideas is analogy. Analogy, in turn, often rests on metaphor. Metaphor rests on images, and imagery rests on sensory impressions, guided by psychic needs.

Images based on sensory impressions sparkled from Stanley Williams' lectures on Washington Irving. He might have said abstractly, "Irving's ability consisted largely in his proclivity for describing natural settings and legendary material." But, what he said was much more memorable: "The power of Irving lay in the blue ribbon of the Hudson under a blue sky, the caw of the crow, Rip Van Winkle—mood of reverie" [7].

Does he achieve his purpose? To anyone who has tramped high in the Catskills, the Hudson does look just like that—a blue ribbon in the distance. By such description, the teacher stimulated speculation in reviving sensory impressions. He also made his general point about style, and in such a way that it stuck.

Who would doubt that this specific description gives more pleasure and more understanding? For the mind moves readily from such linked concrete images to induce the general idea. This tendency of the mind is what Binet once called: "L'essor vers le général"—the flight toward generality [8, p. 95].

Indeed, the order in which concepts are formed, as Heidbreder showed, proceeds from the concrete to the abstract [9, pp. 121, 173-223]. That finding ties into our problem of bridging new concepts. For, studding general ideas with concrete images should stimulate learning.

Here, the *Encyclopedia of Educational Research* [10, p. 1231], clues us to a main fault of textbook language: Language has sometimes failed as a medium of instruction. . . . Specifically it has too often dealt with abstraction, with too little attention to descriptions of concrete details. . . . Sensory and lower mental processes are the windows, instruments and foundations for the higher mental processes. (As William James once observed: "All our inward images tend invincibly to attach themselves to something sensible so as to gain in corporeity and life" [11, pp. 29-30].)

Readability

Too many textbooks, especially in the social sciences, are needlessly dull. But as the scope of education widens, as information explodes, the demand grows for readable texts. Just in the last few decades some history books have doubled in size. Or, if size is held down, a dense compression results. Texts compete with each other, with television, and even with our society's speeded-up pace of living. No longer is there room for a dull textbook.

What are the keys, then, for unlocking readability? The Readability Laboratory of the American Association for Adult Education set up under Lyman Bryson found that readable prose has three main traits: lucidity, comprehensibility, and appeal [12, pp. 397-389].

Lucidity means a logical clarity of message wherein one says what he means [13, p. 159]. John Dewey's writing, for instance, is lucid, but not comprehensible to most readers.

Comprehensibility goes beyond lucidity. Comprehensible writing touches experiences that readers have had, so that they understand its meaning. One cannot fully grasp the meaning of ice skates until one has skated on them. Kinaesthesia is bound up in the meaning. Thus, comprehensible writing usually has some sensory referents.

Appeal touches emotive functions. Does the text hold attention? Does it tune into readers' motives and interests? Does it help readers to develop new perspectives and to see relationships?

The need for further study of interest-making factors was pointed out by Lorge as he reviewed readability formulas: "These formulas give little, if any, attention to the vividness of imagery or to the emphasis of dramatic expression" [14, p. 93].

We cannot measure lucidity by only readers' responses. But we have measured the other two elements in the experiment to be described.

Images in Readability

Now, although our main thrust in this chapter is aimed at college texts, it may be interesting to note that elementary-school teachers have long worked with the importance of images. For example, an early pamphlet, *Successful Teaching with "My Weekly Reader"* cited an exercise like visualizing Paul Bunyan's pancakes, cooked on a griddle as big as a pond [15, p. 22]. It asked pupils: "Can you *see* the pancakes, and *smell* the bacon sizzling?" This teaching-tool for teachers contained these remarks: How does one comprehend? Unfortunately, far too little attention has been given to training pupils on all grade levels to visualize details as they read. Students must be trained to build mental pictures as they read, to be aware of the richness of imagery or sensory impression [15, p. 22].

On the adult level, Wiese studied the popularity of best sellers, as determined by announcements in *The Publisher's Weekly* and by discussion with librarians. She wrote:

> Stimulating the imagination by many devices which create mental images helps to maintain interest. Active verbs and active nouns create vivid pictures. . . .
> Such words as "popped," "fluttered," "lurched," and "rumbling," "whistling" are more likely to bring a mental image than such broad and indefinite words as "moved," "asked," or "said" [16, p. 42].

Even so, one may say: "But college students are grown-up. They should think in abstractions." But, hear what Robert Browning once answered [17, pp. 52-53]:

> But here's your fault; grown men want thought, you think. . .
> Boys seek for images and melody.
> Men must have reason—so you aim at men.
> Quite otherwise! . . .
> . . . by the time youth slips a stage or two
> While reading prose in that tough book (Boehme) wrote. . .
> We shut the clasps and find life's summer past.
> Then who helps more, pray, to repair our loss—
> Another Boehme with a tougher book
> And subtler meanings of what roses say—
> Or some stout Mage like him of Halberstad,
> John, who made things Boehme wrote thoughts about?
>
> * * * * *
>
> He with a "look you!" vents a brace of rhymes
> And in there breaks the sudden rose herself,
> Over us, under, round us every side,
> Nay, in and out the tables and the chairs
> And musty volumes, Boehme's book and all—
> Buries us with a glory, young once more,
> Pouring heaven into this shut house of life!

RELATED STUDIES

Because space is limited here and because this experiment [18, 19, pp. 3-6] antedates most modern research into imagery, I shall restrict these citations to those specifically germane to imagery and readability. Memory, for instance, is not quite the same as comprehension. There are very few references. For, even during the "rediscovery" of mental imagery in the last two decades, as a variable for semantics, memory and psychotherapy, there seems to have been no other experiment carried out with a large sample of college students, that aims directly at assessing the impact of imagery on the readability of texts.

More generally, Richardson had remarked that: "Certain traditional topics such as the relation of mental imagery to literature or to education have been almost completely ignored" [20, p. xi].

In regard to the psychology of teaching and reading, E. B. Huey believed that "even an irrelevant sense image may help a word to hold attention on the real meaning, which, however, was not the image" [21, pp. 163, 167]. But, finding no images in the little connective words (e.g., "and," "if," "on") may have diverted him from the further research that he had glimpsed was possible by using sentences as units.

But, viewing the psychology of reading within the context of learning and teaching, Bugelski pictured that in reading for meaning we are exciting for ourselves a fleeting "succession of images," within relationships, accompanied by flows of feeling [22, p. 324].

After meticulous studies with paired associates, Paivio and Begg developed data on sentences. Their findings suggest that although "imagery and comprehension cannot be equated, they are closely related generally" and that "imagery is more closely related to comprehension when the material is concrete rather than when it is abstract" [23, p. 443].

Litt reviewed reports of interest to schoolteachers [24, pp. 27-33]. He estimated that, with appropriate instructional methods, alterations in imagery experience may accompany improvements in learning. He suggested more research on the imagery value of words to children, similar to the studies with adults.

Cramer tested 124 eleventh and twelfth grade high school students [25]. He found a combined imagery and comprehension score was significantly related to reading attitude, and he encouraged further research on the use of imagery during reading.

Finally, Holden in the Sunday *New York Times* pointed up the urgent need for more readable writing of texts [26, p. E19].

THE EXPERIMENT

The major question now is whether imagery can be shown experimentally to increase interest and understanding. What is the effect of images, specifically, on the readability of college textbooks? Does it make them more interesting, better understood, or as rapidly read?

These questions are answered in more scientific detail, with statistical tables in the *Journal of Mental Imagery* [27, pp. 129-147]. But a brief description here of the methods and findings may serve.

Materials and Methods

The field studied was American History. That was partly because history texts have sometimes been accused of being too abstract, and partly because I wanted to deal with a subject of common interest to students, regardless of their majors. Moreover, the problem of how wars start is of perennial concern.

Accordingly, from a standard American history text, four different war periods were chosen. Each passage was whittled to exactly 500 words in length. Each passage had two treatments. The original treatment followed the textbook almost exactly. The revised treatment injected just one new variable—namely, words that seemed more clearly image-building to the writer. (Later on, the results proved that they were more clearly image building, also, to readers.)

To hold "difficulty" constant, both treatments of each passage were equated as to "reading ease" by Flesch formula. The "Human interest" factor in all eight passages was similarly held constant. This was a hairspring-delicate task, requiring close control. The passages were then reviewed separately by two Columbia professors, who agreed that the revised treatments did not change the essential meanings of the original text treatments.

It should be made clear that I do not consider my revisions to be "good writing." For, the structure and pace of these pages were already set. To introduce a more journalistic staccato, for example, would have created an extraneous variable for the study. Moreover, at times, I pressed too hard, for good writing, in order to make the image-bearing words stand out as a distinct variable. For, since higher images were injected into only about one word in eight, I wondered if this sprinkling would be enough to have any effect. A few short examples will illustrate the two treatments:

Illustration #2-o "The War of Orders and Decrees"—Original Text. With England in control of the seas and France invincible on land the war became an economic contest. Unable to reach his chief antagonist with armed forces, Napoleon devised the "Continental System." Under military pressure a combination of European states was formed, pledged to exclude British commerce from the markets of the continent. England's trade was the source of her economic strength, and to undermine it would be to destroy England's power in war.

Illustration #2-r "The War of Orders and Decrees"—Revised Text. With England sweeping the seas and France overrunning the land the war lapsed into an economic tussle. Unable to grapple with his chief antagonist by armed forces, Napoleon devised the "Continental System." Under military pressure a bloc of European nations was welded together, pledged to exclude British exchange from the markets of Europe. England's trade was the sinew of her economic strength, and to shrivel it would be to cripple England's power in war.

Illustration #4-o "The Pre-Civil War Period"—Original Text. Only seven states were represented at Montgomery, but the architects of the new republic expected the early adhesion of the eight slave states, which, as yet, continued loyal to the old Union. Indeed in their high enthusiasm, they expected an extension beyond these natural limits. Stephens, with secession an accomplished fact had promptly become an ardent supporter of the Confederacy. He predicted in a notable speech at Savannah, that it was "not beyond the range of possibility, and even probability that all the great states of the north-west will gravitate this way."

Illustration #4-r "The Pre-Civil War Period"–Revised Text.   Only seven states sent delegates to Montgomery, but the architects of the new republic looked for an early joining-up of the eight slave states which, as yet, continued loyal to the old Union. Indeed, in their brimming enthusiasm, they anticipated attracting states beyond these natural boundaries. Stephens, with secession an accomplished fact, had promptly become an ardent supporter of the Confederacy. He predicted in a notable speech in Savannah, that it was "not beyond the range of possibility, and even probability, that all of the great states of the north-west will swing over this way."

Interest was measured by students' expressed comparisons of the two treatments and also by a 5-point scale.

Comprehension was measured by objective tests. I built these objective tests so as to gauge not only grasp of literal meaning but also the other three elements in the N.S.S.E.'s 47th Yearbook analysis [28, p. 93] : interpreting broadly, reacting critically, and applying what was read. (This Yearbook had, further, pointed out that, in the study of social sciences and of history in particular, it is important to visualize historical persons, ideas, and events. It is important, moreover, to relate ideas to present-day affairs and to understand time relationships and cause and effect.)

In the light of these criteria, the foils of the objective tests were built—each on the same rational hypotheses [29, p. 24; 30, p. 128-137]. The foils later gave us clues for the early prevention of certain reading problems for some students tested. In the objective-test stems, neutral synonyms had been used, and experts in test construction judged that the stems and foils did not favor either treatment.

Pilot studies were made with graduate classes at Teachers College and with freshmen classes at Hofstra University. These trial runs established the reliability and homogeneous variability of the tests.

Design.   It was vital to avoid "practice effect." For if any students were tested on two treatments of the *same* passage, their comprehension scores might be raised and interest scores reduced on the second try. To avoid this problem, the design of the experiment was completely balanced. That is, the *two treatments* of *different passages* were presented in every possible combination and order, equally often—making twenty-four arrangements altogether. In this way, certain sources of error were washed out in an analysis of variance.

Subjects.   Booklets containing the material were distributed to the entire Dickinson College freshman class present at orientation week testing. The final sample, sifted by random numbers for even subsets, comprised 192 students.

Since the majority of them were aiming at the sciences or law, this sample, if anything, seems conservative toward the figurative language of many images.

RESULTS

When the data were analyzed, the findings supported our hypothesis that appropriate imagery improves readability.

First, *interest* in the revisions was *very significantly* higher.

Second, *comprehension* of the revised treatment was *significantly* higher.

Finally, speed of reading was not affected. The revisions took only a half-second more, on the average, to read. Although hypothesized, this result seems curious. For, one might think that imagery would be savored like a vintage wine. Perhaps any lingering was balanced by a quicker mediation of meaning.

It may be concluded that appropriate imagery improves the readability of college history texts.

AGREEMENTS ON IMAGE-FORMING WORDS

A rather astonishing subsidiary finding emerged from the data. To a *very significant* extent, students agreed that the words injected into the revised treatments were more image forming to them than were the respective original words in the text.

For example, if mere blind chance were operating, only 1.5 percent of the students could be expected to agree on twenty-three or more choices (out of 32). Yet, a clear majority of 61.5 percent reached that many agreements. Furthermore, there was only *one* chance *in ten million*, statistically, that *any* student would reach thirty out of thirty-two agreements with the writer. Nevertheless, *16 percent* of the students attained that score [31, pp. 279-283].

Interestingly, too, there was no significant difference between the numbers of college men and women who reached agreements at the 99 percent level of confidence.

IMPLICATIONS

Our findings, then, support the intuitively high valuation that writers for years have placed on images as springboards for ideas.

For one thing, it is evident that readability formulas need another dimension beyond the syllable count and word length elements of the Flesch formula, or the word rarity and prepositional-phrase factors of the Lorge formula. That dimension is imagibility. But, if further imagery word-scales are developed, they will be needed for verbs as well as for nouns [32]. Meanwhile, the degree of higher imagery probably can be estimated very roughly by the *specificity* and *concreteness* as well as the *number of different kinds of sensory referents* apparently entailed in a word or phrase. (These kinds of sensory experiences, of course, include, sight, hearing, touch, taste, smell, motion, heat, and pain.)

If a word or phrase calls up several kinds of sensory experiences at the same time, it probably is one of the highest imagery-producing words. For example, "splash" may call up not only a visual image of a spray of water, but also an auditory image of a hand or object whacking the water, the motion of the flung spray, the touch of drops against one's face, and even the coolness of the drops. Even without scientific scaling, it seems obvious that a word with so many clear sensory roots should be very high in yielding imagery.

Another type of word that is probably high in stimulating imagery is any specific verb of motion that carries with it the force of an adverb. To "lurch" means to move; but it also means to do so suddenly, jerkily, or heavily, to one side. Such words help to transmit finely tuned images. "Cherchez le mot juste," as Flaubert did, is one prescription for writers encoding images.

Sir James Barrie tells the story of a young "genius" in an essay contest, who spent an hour delving for one right word. "Why?" demanded his preceptors, "it's so easy . . . to find the right word." "It's not," said the lad, "it's as difficult as to hit a squirrel" [33, p. 488].

But the main application of this chapter simply lies in the clear possibility of improving texts by harnessing images.

IMPROVING TEXTS WITH IMAGES

People read in conscious, or subconscious, expectation of a reward, either immediate or delayed [34, pp. 149-159]. Perhaps imagery brings readers greater psychological closure. A spark needs voltage to pull it across a spark gap. As ideas move from the concrete to the abstract, image-bearing words may be like sensory stimuli which supply the "voltage" to pull ideas across synaptic connections [35, p. 214]. Fanciful as this analogy sounds, it is not out of line with certain previous theories about the anticipation of needs. For instance, Mowrer had stressed that a person may be motivated not only by needs, but by the anticipation of needs [36, pp. 553-565]. Images, then, may not only *produce* anxiety and motivate behavior, but they may also *reduce* anxiety. Therapists often ask tense clients to imagine themselves in a peaceful meadow or at a calm beach on a beautiful day. Images, with their basis of sensory impressions, may be the kinds of signs which permit readers to reduce their inner tensions and achieve closure.

The problem of a reward is an essential consideration for text writers. The grimly assiduous doctoral candidate will suffer through almost any welter of abstract complexities because the reward is greater. He or she is held to the task by the energy of the will and by the "pull of the problem." The undergraduate and the adult general public are much less motivated. The professor must select. Why burden the student of literature with the furniture in the bard's home at

Stratford-on-Avon? What students really want to know is: How does this relate to them, and how will this subject help them to lead happier or more successful lives?

Denotative Images

We have mentioned the bridge of analogy for imparting new ideas. But *imagery does not require metaphor.* Some text images simply bring a literal word-picture which reinforces meaning. For example, in the history passages mentioned, the oirginal text of the "War of Orders and Decrees" read: "Our direct trade with England, France lacked the means of stopping." But the "means" that France lacked was the "navy." Why not say so?

In the "French and Indian War," the original passage, describing the ambushing of General Braddock's army, read: "From a shelter of the forest the unseen foe fired upon the regulars, who were unable to make effective reply." But the revision substitutes for the last phrase "whose return fire volleyed aimlessly through the underbrush." It is the same idea but easier to picture and factual.

Again, in the "Mexican War," the original treatment read: "A succession of revolutionary governments had ruled Mexico, resulting in political instability at home and irresponsibility in foreign relations." *We now ask ourselves: "Of what, then, did the 'instability' and 'irresponsibility' consist?"* Or, *"How, behaviorally, was it shown?"* And so, the revision denotes the key indicators of these abstractions, by reading: "producing political explosiveness at home and treaty-breaking in foreign relations." When a writer can add more precision of meaning through images, why be vague?

Connotative Images

Specific images, as we see, can add factual meaning. But images also can be effective in a metaphoric way. In this passage, the "succession of unstable Mexican governments" became a "firecracker-string of Mexican governments." In another passage's revision, statesmen who had been called "over-optimistic" were, instead, called "rainbow-chasing."

We also can *extend a useful metaphor* and *keep it coherent:* For instance, the original text about the pre-Civil-War period said: "The responsibility for formulating a policy to deal with the crisis devolved upon the outgoing President and the Congress, but the government's course was inevitably influenced by the uncertain state of public opinion."

Now, the Ship-of-State has long been a familiar metaphor in American lore. We can put it to work here in a consistent way:

"The responsibility for mapping-out a course to steer against these crisis-headwinds rested upon the outgoing President and Congress, but the government's course was inevitably influenced by the wavering tides of public opinion."

A Few Text Examples

These are simple ways of using images in writing history—an art familiar to Pulitzer-Prize winner, Bruce Catton [37]. He describes how Lee and Stonewall Jackson, vastly outnumbered at Chancellorsville, sat on a cracker box a few miles away from Hooker, the Union Commander, and planned an attack:

> The plan was the distilled and concentrated essence of pure daring.
>
> Jackson would take twenty-five thousand men, march the length of Hooker's front, circle around until he was due west of him, and attack his exposed right flank. The march would take the better part of the day, and to form a line of battle in the trackless wilderness where Hooker's flank rested might take hours; it would be early evening before Jackson could make his fight. Until then Lee with fewer than twenty thousand men would have to confront Hooker and his eighty thousand. Indeed, merely to confront him would not be enough; he would have to pretend to be fighting an offensive battle, and the pretense would have to be convincing, because if Hooker ever found out what Jackson was up to or learned how small Lee's force really was he could destroy the Army of Northern Virginia before the sun went down.
>
> Hooker would find out nothing, for Lee had him in his hands and was toying with him. Jackson made his march (it was discovered, but in the paralysis that had come upon his spirit Hooker was quite unable to interpret the meaning of his discovery; he concluded finally that part of Lee's Army must be retreating, and he sent out a couple of divisions to prod the fugitives along). Lee gave a masterful imitation of a general who is about to open a crushing attack all along the line, and kept Hooker looking his way without inducing him to look so attentively that he could discover anything. And a little while before sundown Jackson struck Hooker's exposed flank like the crack of doom [37, pp. 241-242].   B. Catton, *This Hallowed Ground*

The excitement created by his writings comes too seldom. A panel of historians, educators, and staff members of the National Foundation for the Humanities in 1979 agreed that "the lifelessness of so many textbooks was inexcusable" [38, p. 60].

The panel's finding was nothing new. For, some years ago, Lewerenz, author of an astute readability formula for the Los Angeles public schools, had remarked that it was "perhaps unfortunate that textbooks are written more often by college professors than by newspapermen, inasmuch as few college professors could write sentences that tingled and snapped" [39].

And, more recently, a New York book publisher's Editorial Director wrote in the Sunday *New York Times*: "Like most of my friends in book publishing, I groan when I get a thick packet from a university. . . . Publishers know that most professors are bad writers . . . the star of the book is not the writer, but the reader" [26, p. 19].

"Good scholarly writing, like good teaching," he adds, "isn't an ego-trip. . . . To write well you must put yourself in that stranger's shoes and imagine that you are the reader" [26, p. 19].

Even "the dismal science" of Economics revives with a few images seeded into its generalities. Here is Robert Heilbroner whom J. K. Galbraith has called "a gifted writer . . . lucid and concise," condensing an economic idea that still, painfully, applies today:

> Hence in the final analysis, the economy hung on the amount of investment which business carried out. When investment was low, the economy shrank in size; when investment was high, it pulled the nation up with it; if investment failed to *remain* high, it permitted the process of contraction to begin again. Riches and poverty, boom and slump, all depended on the willingness of business to invest. . . . Not only is investment limited in size, but typically it proceeds in spurts. You cannot build a railway line mile by mile to keep pace with demand; you build one entire line at a time [40, pp. 237-238].

But, generalities, unrelieved by images, even when they express a complex idea logically, can border on jargon. It may be amusing to contrast an early semanticist's and an advertising copy-writer's description of effective sentence structure: The semanticist says:

> The motivating force behind all these changes . . . is, as far as one can perceive, the desire on the one hand to be comprehensible and the desire on the other to be vivid against the general background of an ever-growing crystallization of configuration and decrease in variegation [41, p. 261].

Now, the advertising man: "Good copy has 'cut' and 'bounce'."

What of the sciences? Reports must be factually accurate and conclusions must be drawn without adjectives of value or coloration. But an award-winning science writer says there is no need for books to be "stereotypically dry." For, he claims, there is something of the poet in every scientist, for all experience the sense of wonder and the thrill of exploring a mystery. "And, if none of us can communicate that vision with the sure touch of a Shakespeare, it is the privilege of every one of us to try if we choose" [42, pp. 9-11]. Significantly, he entitles one of his books *From Earth to Heaven*—a phrase drawn from Shakespeare's *Midsummer Night's Dream*.

The dryness of many psychology texts has not escaped the public's notice. Recall the Peanuts cartoon where Peppermint Patty, sitting behind Franklin in the schoolroom, asks him: "What are you reading, Franklin?" [43]

"It's a book on psychology," he says. "From what I understand, it seems to be pretty good."

"Forget it, Franklin," she says. "No book on psychology can be any good if one can understand it."

But, what writers like Catton, Heilbroner, and Azimov have done for their disciplines, occasionally writers have done for psychology.

Here, briefly, is Gardner Murphy guiding us through his scholarly (999-page) tome on personality [44]. He explains elusive theories about needs, perception, autism, and imagination, pulling them together as he builds to the section on creativity. Now, see how he relieves abstruseness with active images:

> There are at least four factors in the creative process which involve nervous wear and tear on the individual. First, his craving is intense. He may rest perfunctorily because it is good for him; but he takes his incompleted work to bed with him, and while others sleep, he leaps downstairs two at a time to add a stroke or a phrase, or like Leonardo, he crosses Milan to put a touch of blue on Matthew's restless figure in the Last Supper. The intellectual processes are screwed to a pitch which would batter any nervous system. . . .
>
> Second, not only is the drive sustained without release, but it may take the individual out of context with most of his environment. Just one thing, one's creation is of value. When Gauss locks himself up for two days in his attic, or Newton, having dined, demands of his servant that dinner be served, or Archimedes runs naked from the bath, shouting, 'I have found it,' we cannot avoid the impression that the mind not only turns ceaselessly on its narrow pivot at a pace which allows no rest, but also permits itself no contact with the normal world of perspective and sanity [44, p. 467].

In such text writing the principles are brought out clearly and anchored to interesting concrete images. Science and art are at work on genius and one can hardly drop the chapter.

Does It Matter?

"As soon as we have the thing before our eyes," writes the philosopher, Heidegger, "and in our hearts an ear for the word, thinking prospers" [45, p. 5]. Isn't that just about what Aristotle and the ancients had said, long ago?

Our brief account has demonstrated that appropriate images make texts more readable. And, we have cited some ways in which images may be harnessed by educators.

Is it really important to use every means to improve texts?

For the American Council on Education, Astin followed up 36,000 college students in 246 institutions, four years after their matriculation, in order to determine the effects of higher educational institutions on college students [46]. The conclusion was gloomy: "The major influence of the university is to increase the student's chances of dropping out of college, and to lower his educational aspirations" [46, pp. 141-142]. The reasons for this jolting result are unclear. Probably it bespeaks a relative lack of faculty interaction with students in universities, Astin thought, as compared with liberal-arts colleges. Nevertheless, the Council's report poses a serious challenge for higher education.

Moreover, when the alumni of a world-renowned university, in their 15th Yearbook write: "We clearly have had enough of study," it is time to polish *every teaching tool* at our disposal. With a little more work and imagination perhaps we can make study more of an adventure.

REFERENCES

1. W. Churchill, Face to Face with Stalin, (The War Memoirs of Winston Churchill), *Life*, October 30, 1950.
2. C. K. Ogden and I. A. Richards, *The Meaning of Meaning*, Harcourt, Brace, New York, 1927.
3. S. K. Langer, *Philosophy in a New Key*, Penguin Books, New York, 1942.
4. D. L. Clark, *Rhetoric and Poetry in the Renaissance*, Columbia University, New York, 1922.
5. Sir F. Galton, *Inquiries Into Human Faculty and Its Development*, J. M. Dent, London, 1973. (Reprint of 1907).
6. Sir F. Galton, in *Elementary Statistical Methods*, H. M. Walker (ed.), Henry Holt, New York, 1943.
7. S. T. Williams, *Lectures on American Literature*, Yale University, New Haven, 1933.
8. A. Binet, *L' Étude Experimentale de L'Intelligence*, C. Reinwald, Paris, 1903.
9. E. Heidbreder, The Attainment of Concepts, *British Journal of Psychology*, *35*, pp. 121, 173-223, 1946.
10. W. Monroe (ed.), *Encyclopedia of Educational Research*, Macmillan, New York, 1950.
11. W. James, *Principles of Psychology*, Henry Holt, New York, *2*, 1890–1918.
12. L. Bryson, What Are Readable Books? *Educational Forum*, *1*, pp. 397-398, 1927.
13. J. M. Clarke, Science and Writing, in *The Communication of Ideas*, Lyman Bryson (ed.), Harper, New York, 1948.
14. I. Lorge, Readability Formulas: An Evaluation, in *Elementary English*, February, 1949.
15. *Successful Teaching with My Weekly Reader*, American Education Press, Columbus, Ohio, 1950.
16. M. J. Wiese, Why Is Popular Writing More Readable? *Typed Ed.D. Project*, Teacher's College, Columbia University, 1938.
17. R. Browning, in *Robert Browning*, W. L. Phelps (ed.), Bobbs-Merrill, Indianapolis, 1932.
18. W. P. Wharton, *Picture-Forming Words and the Readability of College History Texts*, doctoral dissertation, Columbia University, 1952, University Microfilms, Ann Arbor, Michigan, No. 4601.
19. W. P. Wharton, Ideas and Imagery, "Phi Betta Kappa Presidential Address, Eta Chapter of Pennsylvania" 1959, in *Allegheny College Alumni Bulletin*, April 1960.

20. A. Richardson, *Mental Imagery*, Springer, New York, 1969.
21. E. B. Huey, *The Psychology and Pedagogy of Reading*, The M.I.T. Press, Cambridge, 4th Printing, 1977.
22. B. R. Bugelski, *The Psychology of Learning Applied to Teaching*, 2nd Edition, Bobbs-Merrill, Indianapolis, 1971.
23. A. Paivio and I. Begg, Imagery and Comprehension Latencies as a Function of Sentence Concreteness and Structure, *Research Bulletin 154*, Department of Psychology, University of Western Ontario, 1970, in *Imagery and Verbal Processes*, A. Paivio (ed.), Holt, Rinehart and Winston, New York, 1971.
24. L. Litt, Mental Imagery and Reading, *Reading*, 7:2, 1973.
25. E. H. Cramer, Pictures in Your Head: A Discussion of Relationships Among Mental Imagery, Reading Comprehension, and Reading Attitude, paper presented at the Annual Meeting of the International Reading Association, Anaheim, May 1976.
26. D. Holden, Why Profs Can't Write, *New York Times*, Sunday, February 4, 1979.
27. W. P. Wharton, Higher Imagery and the Readability of College History Texts, *Journal of Mental Imagery*, 4:2, Fall 1980.
28. National Society for the Study of Education, *Forty-Seventh Yearbook, Part II: Reading in the High School and College*, University of Chicago Press, Chicago, 1948.
29. M. M. Conant, *The Construction of a Diagnostic Reading Test: For Senior High School and College Freshmen*, Bureau of Publications, Teacher's College, Columbia University, New York, 1942.
30. R. W. Travers, Rational Hypotheses in the Construction of Tests, *Educational and Psychological Measurement*, 11, 1951.
31. Department of Commerce, National Bureau of Standards, *Applied Mathematics Series No. 6: Tables of the Binomial Probability Distribution*, U.S. Government Printing Office, Washington, D.C., 1950.
32. A. Paivio, J. C. Yuille and S. A. Madigan, Concreteness, Imagery and Meaningfulness Values for 925 Nouns, *Journal of Experimental Psychology Monograph*, 76: Part II, 1968.
33. J. M. Barrie, *Sentimental Tommy*, Scribner, New York, 1923.
34. W. Schramm, The Nature of News, *Journalism Quarterly*, 26, June, 1949.
35. M. F. Washburn, *Movement and Mental Imagery*, Houghton-Mifflin, Boston, 1916.
36. O. H. Mowrer, A Stimulus-Response Analysis of Anxiety and Its Role as a Reinforcing Agent, *Psychological Review*, 46, pp. 533-565, 1939.
37. B. Catton, *This Hallowed Ground*, Doubleday, New York, 1955.
38. R. Eder, Miss Fitzgerald Traces History of History Texts, *The New York Times*, Sunday, October 31, 1979.
39. A. S. Lewerenz, *Talk at the Curriculum Conference of Southern California Cities*, University of California at Los Angeles, November 21, 1931.
40. R. L. Heilbroner, *The Worldly Philosophers*, Simon and Schuster, New York, 1961.
41. G. K. Zipf, *The Psycho-Biology of Language*, Houghton-Mifflin, Boston, 1935.

42. I. Azimov, *From Earth to Heaven*, Avon, New York, 1972.
43. C. Schulz, *Peanuts*, United Features Syndicate, Inc., 1972.
44. G. Murphy, *Personality*, Harper, New York, 1947, as cited in W. P. Wharton [18]: *Picture-Forming Words and the Readability of College History Texts*, doctoral dissertation, Columbia University, 1952. University Microfilms, Ann Arbor, Michigan, No. 4601.
45. M. Heidegger, *Poetry, Language, Thought*, Harper and Row, New York, 1971.
46. A. Astin and R. J. Panos, *The Educational and Vocational Development of College Students*, American Council on Education, Washington, D.C., 1969.

CHAPTER 7

Guided Imagery in Education

BEVERLY-COLLEENE GALYEAN

With the introduction of affective/holistic teaching techniques in the mid-60s came an increased use of visualization and guided-imagery techniques in elementary, secondary, and college/university settings. Influenced by advances in medical, biomedical, neurophysiological, and psychological research pointing to the desirable effects on physical, emotional, and mental performance, some educators were quick to study and utilize adaptations of these techniques in their respective education settings. A review of the literature related to affective/holistic education reveals that educators ordinarily use visualization and guided-imagery activities in one or more of four ways [1-3]:

1. They employ it as a means of relaxing, centering, and sharpening perception (focusing), thereby preparing individuals for the learning task at hand.
2. They use it for teaching basic subject matter. This is referred to as *guided cognitive imagery*.
3. They see imagery as a vehicle for affective development, such as the increased awareness of inner senses and feelings and the expression of these wherever appropriate, expanded inner cognizance of personal images and symbols, introspective means to conflict resolution, culling feelings of self-love and appreciation, strengthening one's personal values schema and belief systems, and bonding with others. This is called *guided affective imagery*.
4. They utilize imagery as a means of recognizing and working with altered states of consciousness, experiencing energies beyond the normal field of awakened consciousness, probing the spiritual, mystical, and transcendental aspects of life, experiencing concepts such as unity of being, oneness, wisdom, beauty, joy, love, and self. This is labeled *guided transpersonal imagery*.

These four types of imagery techniques often encompass health-producing or health-maintaining activities, such as deep breathing, stress-reducing visualizations [4-7], sensory-awareness trips [5-7], positive-thought producing and/or pleasureful memory trips [5-9], psychophysical visualizations [5-6, 10-11], and covert rehearsal strategies [12-13]. These activities are being recommended by a growing number of health professionals in hopes that individuals will become increasingly more responsible for managing their own health care [14-16].

IMAGERY IN THE CURRICULUM

In order to use visualization and guided imagery (VGI) on a regular basis, educators have incorporated it into the standard curriculum. In most schools, the curriculum is divided into two parts: the *orientation factor* and the *lesson factor*. Thus imagery work usually takes place prior to the lessons (readiness) or during the lessons.

The Orientation Factor

What teachers do to prepare the room environment for learning and what they do to help students prepare their bodies, minds, and emotions for learning is as important as the lessons themselves. Nonreadiness to learn can impede digestion of the most exciting lessons; thus, the readiness factor is of major importance in the overall curricular plan.

Soft relaxing music, such as classical baroque, renaissance, flute, harp, and mellow guitar, sets the tone for reflective activity. After students have entered the room and class has begun, the teacher or another student leads the group in a two to three minute deep-breathing centering/focusing activity that not only quiets overactive mental vibrations but also enlarges the scope of inner imaging, thus enabling the students to see and experience more of the material being presented in class. The following is an example:

> Close your eyes . . . take a slow . . . deep breath . . . hold it . . . now exhale any tiredness or distractions you might be feeling. (Repeat as often as necessary) [6].

This shortened form is often expanded to include an exercise in basic sensory awareness to sharpen inner feelings and sensing. To achieve this, the above exercise would continue in the following manner:

> Now picture yourself eating something you like very much . . . see this food . . . feel it . . . listen to any sounds it makes . . . smell it . . . taste it. . . . Decide now if you will eat the whole thing or only take a bite (pause). . . . On the count of three, open your eyes and be fully refreshed, alert, and ready to work [6].

The basic aim is to give students the opportunity to experience something pleasurable, and often flowers, beaches, cars, skies, mountains, and trees are substituted for foods. The more specific the suggestions, the more expansive the inner visioning. Thus the above short form of the exercise can continue with very specific instructions:

> Now picture a delicious apple in your mind. . . . This is the most beautiful apple you've ever seen. . . . Notice what color it is . . . if it has any other colors (variegations) running through it. . . . What shape is it . . . round? . . . oval? . . . squarish? . . . flat? . . . Are there any blemishes or thumb prints on it? . . . Is the skin shiny or dull? . . .

> Now take it in your hand and draw it close to your nose. . . . Can you smell the scent, as the apple gets closer to your nose? . . . What happens in your mouth as you begin to smell the apple? . . . in your stomach? . . . Now decide if you want to take a bite . . . and if you do . . . take a bite right now . . . taste this apple in your mouth. . . . Now finish your apple . . . and on the count of three, open your eyes and be fully refreshed, alert, and ready to work [6].

Teachers in our projects have noticed that students' retention of material improves after these exercises have been provided at the beginning of lessons [5].

There is a second aspect of orientation: The students use VGI to plant and reinforce an image of themselves being successful learners and/or successfully completing the tasks prescribed in the lessons for the day. The teacher designs the imagery to fit the learning task. For example, the following format is being used in mathematics classes, after the breathing exercise:

> Today we are going to work with constructing angles. This involves you learning how to use a protractor to draw angles according to given formulas. Picture yourself drawing these angles with ease. . . . You have comprehended the basic formulas and are now drawing the angles. . . . See your hand moving with great ease across the page. . . . Now you finish your drawing . . . you check it with the answer on the board . . . and you are correct. . . . Feel this success right now (pause). . . . Keep this image of success with you throughout the entire lesson. . . . On the count of three, take a deep breath, and be fully refreshed, alert, and ready to work [6].

Some teachers reinforce VGI work with a physical component, such as suggestions that students move their hands as if they were constructing the angles during a VGI activity. This gives students triple reinforcement, mental, physical, and emotional, and is highly desirable.

The Lesson Factor

Once the room environment and the mental set of the students are ready for learning, the lesson begins. VGI is a learning activity that is used either to introduce or to reinforce concepts within the lesson. The teacher will cite a cognitive objective, which is usually presented in the mandated curriculum guide, and will add both an affective experiential objective that displays how VGI will be used to teach the lesson and an interpersonal objective that demonstrates what group dynamics (group mix) will be used [6]. The following example is taken from a science class.

Lesson: "Machines: What They Can Do" [6]

> Cognitive Objective: The students will master the material related to how machines work, that is found on pages 67–82 of the text *Machines and People.*

Affective Objective: The students will picture themselves building a machine using the parts portrayed in the text. They will take a guided-imagery trip 1,000 years into the future and will look at the most helpful machine ever created by people. They will picture themselves building this machine. The imagery will be followed by a discussion and art activity.

Interpersonal Objective: The students will work alone for the VGI activity, but they will share their experiences in small groups of three to four before participating in a whole-class comparison of experiences. They will then work alone to draw their machine and will follow the same procedure for discussing it with others.

VGI Activity:

(Repeat deep-breathing/relaxation activity as already given and continue in the following manner:)

Travel away 1,000 years into the future. . . . And when you arrive there . . . look around and see everything that is there. . . . Notice the people . . . the buildings . . . the cars or other means of transportation . . . the shops . . . the roads . . . clothes . . . food . . . anything else that is there in your future (pause). . . . Now look around and see a fabulous machine . . . a machine that makes yours and everyone's life much happier. . . . What does this machine look like? . . . What does it do? . . . Where is it located? (pause). . . . On the count of three, take a deep breath . . . exhale . . . and return to us here in the room . . . fully refreshed, alert, and ready to work [6].

The above is an example of guided cognitive imagery or imagery used to present cognitive objectives. Guided affective imagery is also prevalent in the curriculum. These are VGI activities that target an affective feeling awareness level of human capability. The following affective VGI is often used by teachers, counselors, and psychologists as a means of enabling students to identify and take command of subtle self-defeating feelings that can inhibit academic or other achievement.

(Repeat deep-breathing/relaxation activity as already given and continue in the following manner:)

In a moment you will visit a house that contains any concerns you might have about succeeding in this class (in this school, in this lesson, etc.). In your mind, picture a comfortable road leading through a beautiful valley where there are many trees and flowers . . . perhaps even small friendly animals, such as birds, chipmunks, and squirrels (pause). . . . Now begin walking down your road . . . enjoying the day . . . taking in the sights . . . smells . . . wonderful sounds . . . happy feelings (pause). . . . As you walk along you notice a house on one side of the road. . . . Examine the house . . . check out the colors . . . building materials, such as wood . . . brick . . . plaster . . . the landscape around it . . . the frame (pause). . . . Inside the house you might find a concern or fear you have about not learning in this class (in this school, in this lesson, etc.). If you do have such a concern and want to meet it and change it into good positive energy for yourself, go into your house now and ask it to appear. . . . Remember that you are totally in command of your images and have nothing to fear about entering this house (pause). . . . When you meet this concern, ask it to tell you about itself . . . where and when it started . . . how it could be changed into a "can do" helpful attitude for you (pause). . . . Now picture yourself having this concern as a friend who helps you achieve in this class (school, lesson, etc.). . . . How does the concern act? (Pause) . . . Now picture yourself succeeding in this class (lesson, school, etc.). . . . What does this look like? . . . feel like? (pause). . . . On the count of three, open your eyes . . . fully refreshed, alert, and ready to work with the imagery [6].

VGI also is used for the purpose of presenting students with newly emerging mind skills promulgated by many futurists. Although VGI, with its emphasis on inner imaging and sensing, is a mind skill in itself, specific imageries are used to develop other mind skills, such as synergic problem solving, transpersonal feeling, altered states of consciousness, and intuition. The following is an example of an exercise to encourage synergic problem solving:

(Repeat basic deep-breathing/relaxation activity as already given and continue in the following manner:)

In your mind picture our entire group (i.e., the group charged with solving a problem) sitting in a circle. . . . Suddenly the center of our circle becomes filled with a lovely light . . . warm and brilliant. . . . This is the light of our intelligence . . . wisdom . . . and care for each other (pause). . . . Suddenly the light spreads to each of us, and we begin to experience this light in our bodies, making us feel lighter and lighter and brighter and brighter (pause). . . . Now fill yourself with this light of intelligence . . . wisdom . . . and care (pause). . . . You might want to take a deep breath to help you fully absorb this wonderful energy (pause). . . . When you have filled yourself with it . . . send it out your right arm into the left arm of the person next to you . . . and let us circulate this energy through our entire group (pause). . . . Remember that what we are sharing is the corporate power of our intelligence, wisdom, and care, all blending together (pause). . . . Now place our problem in the center of the group and send the light energy, that has been flowing through you, out through your heart to the problem . . . and let this energy "shed some light" on how the problem can best be solved. . . . You have one minute of clocktime, which is all the time you need to watch our problem being resolved. . . . At this time, we will all have many ideas about how this problem can best be resolved for the good of everyone concerned (pause). . . . Now complete this imagery and on the count of three, take a deep breath . . . and return to us here in the room . . . fully refreshed, alert, and ready to work [6].

Because this type of VGI seems to expand awareness beyond ordinary awakening of mental capabilities, and leads to heightened energy, sensing, and feeling, it is often called guided transpersonal imagery [3, 4]. More research is needed to determine what new mind skills are actually opened up when this type of VGI is used on a regular basis; however, teacher self-reports, based on observation of student outcomes, indicate that guided transpersonal imagery: 1) enables students to understand aspects of their minds that are often not talked about in ordinary settings; 2) develops extrasensory perceptual skills; 3) refines intuitive communication, such as direct mind to mind links (communicating telepathically); 4) stimulates awareness of subtle energy shifts, such as the effect of various emotions on physical well-being; and 5) awakens a sense of a universal, cosmic or spiritual dimension of life [7].

SIX BASIC STEPS

As we examine the imagery techniques just presented, it becomes evident that there are six basic steps involved in the successful implementation of imagery work in education:

1. relaxing/centering
2. focusing
3. multisensing
4. imaging
5. communicating
6. reflecting/interpreting

Students first are taught how to assume comfortable positions (i.e., lying on the floor, sitting upright with palms folded in lap, etc.) and then to breathe deeply and relax body-muscular tension. They are then presented with a series of short focusing exercises, such as, "Close your eyes and picture a red circle in front of you. . . . Now change the color to orange . . . now to green . . . now change the shape to a square." Focusing exercises help students to sharpen inner perception, to pay greater attention to detail, and to control their images.

Next they are prompted to experience simple sensory images and to "see, feel, touch, hear, taste, and smell" their images. This exercise enables them to experience their images in much greater depth than if they were only to "look at" them. The multisensory mode targets all learners: visual, auditory, and kinesthetic imagers are given an equal opportunity.

After mastering these techniques, students are ready for the longer imagery journeys which take them to various places, involve them in new situations, and bring them in contact with different people and objects. When the journeys are completed, students communicate their experiences orally, through writing and/or the arts. Finally, they are invited to reflect upon the deeper meaning of their images and to determine what new insights might be gleaned from the imagery work.

Sometimes the insights are profound and show an intellectual/spiritual maturation that often does not surface in the more analytical verbal types of learning activities. Two samples of work, one carried out in an elementary school and the other in a secondary school, illustrate this observation.

In one of our imagery activities, called "Love Circle" [6], the children stand in a circle and hold hands. They close their eyes and journey into the center of their hearts where they find love and give it a color. These "love colors" are then sent down the right arm into the left arm of the next person and eventually travel through each person's body and return to the "owner." While the children are sending these love vibrations, they are asked to feel this love in their bodies and to let the love make them feel good all over. Finally, they think about someone not in the room whom they would like to receive this love, and they imagine this person to be in the circle receiving love.

After the activity has ended, the teacher asks the children to share what happened during the experience. One second grader, labeled "incorrigible" and "learning disabled" by the school, described the experience: There were "bubbles with all of the colors of the rainbow floating through my body and down my arms and through the arms of all the other kids. It seemed as if our circle became one big color wheel and you couldn't see individual people anymore. We sort of became like one big ring. Then we changed to reds and pinks and I got very hot. I liked it better when we were all one circle because everyone seemed to really care for each other. In the real world people don't care sometimes, and they hurt you." The ability to see and sense these bubbles of energy is quite mature: Many adults working in consciousness research report similar experiences. The child's interpretation of the event shows a great deal of sensitivity to his own feelings as well as to those of the other children. The maturity of his response indicates that he is far more intelligent than the school had determined him to be.

In one of our high-school classes where the teacher used imagery two or three times per week, the students became expert at scanning their body/mind responses to the activities and often revealed insights that could serve as seeds for future consciousness research. In one of the imagery activities, the students were asked to travel to a two-dimensional planet and to experience what it would be like to be two dimensional. One seventeen-year-old described his experience in the following manner:

> When people walked by you, they disappeared into thin air. You could see only what was right in front of you; yet you knew other things existed. This is sort of how the mind works. There are lots of things out there to be known, but we can't know them until we're willing to look at them. Just because we can't see them, doesn't mean they aren't there. This is what intuition does—it helps us see what's not obvious. Logic, on the other hand, helps us explain things once we've seen them. But logic can't tell us anything new—just clarify the old. Without intuition, the world always would be the same. I also think that beliefs help us see new things. If we're too rigid in our beliefs, then we can't learn very much. Also, one person's beliefs aren't any better than anyone else's since they all show us pieces of what's possible to know. That's why it's important to listen to what others have to say about their experiences."

In comparison to the compositions of most seventeen-year-olds, this response is unusually rich and profound. The teachers believe that the imagery activities spawn these expansive insights. The students themselves often tell us that the "imageries change their ability to think and to understand what's going on in their heads," and that "they learn more when they work with the imageries."

EXAMINING THE EFFECTS
OF IMAGERY WORK IN EDUCATION

Despite the popularization of imagery activities in education settings as reported in various texts [17-18], professional journals,[1] education-related conferences,[2] and education networks aimed at promulgating holistic practices in the schools,[3] very little empirical data are available to guide further research in the area of implementation and evaluation of visualization and imagery work in elementary, secondary, and postsecondary education. The following studies provide us with some data concerning outcomes of imagery work being done in various education settings.

Elligett, Danielson, and Holland reported increases in fifth-grade students' self-esteem and academic achievement as indicated by improved test-taking skills [19]. Shaw found increases in creative and divergent thinking in high I.Q. students [20]. Lange discovered that elementary-school and secondary-school learning-disabled students learned more of the material presented in their science classes, were more highly motivated to learn the material, and showed more creativity than comparison groups. A secondary effect was that they appeared calmer and more ready to work than comparison groups [21]. Piccolo and Render reported gains in reading achievement of high-school students [22]. Groff and Render found gains in social-studies achievement of fourth graders [23]. Boyle and Render reported higher scores in creative thinking among seventh graders [24]. Galyean found decreases in frequencies of disruptive behaviors among high-school students and increases in vocabulary and complexity scores of high-school remedial-English students [25, 26]. She also reported that visualization and guided imagery combined with a variety of other affective holistic language-learning activities helped primary-school language-deficient children to increase their proficiency in oral and written communication skills [27], and high-school foreign-language students to increase their proficiency in oral and written composition skills [28]. Toomim found that visualization and guided-imagery activities combined with various stress-reducing techniques

---

[1] *Journal of Humanistic Psychology, Journal of Transpersonal Psychology, Journal of Suggestive-Accelerative Learning and Teaching, Journal of Humanistic Education, Teacher, Learning,* and *Social Education.*

[2] Conferences sponsored by: Association for Humanistic Psychology, Association for Transpersonal Psychology, Society for Accelerative Learning and Teaching, American Education Research Association, American Association of Mental Imagery, National Council of Teachers of English, Teachers of English to Speakers of Other Languages, and American Council on the Teaching of Foreign Languages.

[3] Networks sponsored by: Association for Humanistic Psychology, Wholistic Educators Network, Association for Humanistic Education, and the National Coalition for Democracy in Education.

help elementary-school children perform better academically, reduce physical and emotional tension, improve test-taking skills, handwriting skills, I.Q.; and learning-disabled students improved in reading recognition, comprehension, and spelling [29]. Schuster and Martin, combining imagery with biofeedback, found gains among college students in the learning of rare words [30]. Edwards reported gains in creativity among fifth, eighth, and ninth graders [31]. Steingart and Glock claimed that reading skills of college students improve with the addition of imagery exercises to the passages being read [32].

Other reports indicate, that, although significant gains were not seen, higher mean scores on various instruments tend to support hypotheses that visualization and guided-imagery work improve self-esteem and assertive behaviors among college students [33], self-concept among third and fourth graders [34], and vocabulary and complexity scores of eighth-grade English students [35].

Along with these empirical studies, informal observational reports from fifty educators, participating in our affective/holistic education projects in the Los Angeles area schools, mentioned the following results: Students seemed to 1) be more attentive and less distracted, 2) be more involved in the work being done in class, 3) learn more of the material being taught, 4) enjoy their learning experiences more than before imagery was introduced to them, 5) do more original and/or creative work, especially in art and writing, 6) get along better with their classmates, 7) be more kind and helpful to one another, 8) feel more confident, 9) be more relaxed, and 10) do better on tests.

A PILOT STUDY

The purpose of this preliminary study was to gather these diverse claims, both empirical and anecdotal, to study the relationships among them, to report major trends, to design a topographical overview of the emergent variables, and to make recommendations for further implementation, curriculum design, evaluation, and research.

Procedure

Beginning in December 1981 and ending in October 1982, 150 educators, recognized as actively using visualization and guided-imagery techniques in their respective elementary, secondary, and college/university settings, were sent a questionnaire to determine their opinions concerning the effects of using these techniques with their own students. To meet the criterion for answering this questionnaire, the educators must have been using visualization and guided imagery for at least one year. No attempt was made to select equal numbers of respondents among the three major populations. One shortcoming of this study is that individuals were not asked to indicate how long they had been using guided imagery; thus, it is not possible to analyze variances that might be related to length of experience in using these techniques.

The questionnaire was based upon seven years of personal experience with guided imagery in various school and therapeutic settings, as well as upon data gleaned from five studies directed by this researcher (three federally funded affective/holistic education projects in Los Angeles area schools, and two privately funded projects to implement and evaluate imagery work in public-school classes) and from the empirical and anecdotal studies just cited. The behaviors which occurred most frequently in each of these situations served as the basis for the statements appearing on the research questionnaire. An assumption was made that the behaviors cited in these preliminary reports would most likely appear in other education settings where imagery techniques were used on a regular basis, and that they could serve as the foundation for constructing observation instruments designed to identify the effects of using imagery techniques in a variety of elementary, secondary, and college/university settings.

The questionnaire was divided into two parts. The first part consisted of eleven statements reflecting the finding of the empirical and observational research just cited. According to these findings, visualization and imagery activities seem to affect student 1) achievement, 2) attention, 3) cohesiveness, 4) productivity, 5) creativity, 6) initiative, 7) listening skills, 8) nonstandard test skills, 9) standard test skills, 10) self-esteem in school, and 11) self-esteem outside of school. The statements were ranked according to degree of occurrence or truth, with 0 meaning "not at all" to 5 meaning "very much." In analyzing scores, raw numbers were changed into mean scores: 4.0 to 5.0 indicated high rating, 3.0 to 3.9 signified moderate to high moderate rating, 2.0 to 2.9 meant low to low moderate rating, 0 to 1.9 indicated very low rating. The second part of the questionnaire was designed to elaborate information based on the eleven statements (see Appendix). Data were analyzed according to the following groups: kindergarten to Grade 3, Grades 4 to 6, junior high, senior high, and college/university.

Findings

All eleven categories received high ratings from almost all groups. The exceptions follow: Kindergarten to Grade 3 ratings were high moderate for the categories productivity and standard proficiency; Grades 4 to 6 were high moderate for productivity, standard proficiency, and self-esteem; junior high ratings were high moderate for self-esteem; senior-high ratings were high moderate for initiative and standard proficiency; and college/university ratings were high moderate for initiative. A separate analysis of gifted, regular, and low achieving students of kindergarten to Grade 8 showed slightly lower scores overall for the low achieving group.

Teachers made these observations: Kindergarten to Grade 3 teachers reported primarily "less disruptive," "calm and relaxed" behavior and "greater achievement, success, and confidence." The Grade 4 to 6 teachers mainly found students to be "less disruptive," "more attentive, focused," "sensitive to selves and inner processes," and to display "more empathy, cohesiveness, and trust," "greater achievement, success, confidence," and "better attendance." The junior-high teachers mentioned "less disruptive" behavior and "more creative work" most often. The senior-high teachers reported above all behaviors, "less disruptive," "more empathy, cohesiveness, and trust," and "more attentive, focused, better concentration." The college/university instructors saw primarily "more interested and involved in work" and "greater sensitivity toward others."

A few respondents indicated areas of difficulty and/or caution in working with VGI:

1. Caution should be exercised when working with students who have emotional problems and/or who take drugs;
2. activities should be used on a voluntary basis;
3. students should be provided with some theoretical basis for doing VGI work;
4. the entire group might better be broken up into smaller groups when doing VGI work;
5. care should be taken that students complete the VGI experiences "alert and ready to work," and
6. terminology should be used with care.

Several teachers added comments to help those just beginning to use VGI in education. They mentioned that some children will resist at first, but with teacher and peer encouragement, they later will agree to do VGI work. Some children are unwilling to share their inner experiences and should never be pressured to do so. Visual/kinesthetic learners work best with VGI (this has never been documented empirically), and some children need visual, tactile experiences to help them with imaging. Some children never manage to do imagery work and fall asleep; they need to be given alternate work. When asked about their own *preparation for using VGI*, nearly half the teachers said that they had attended workshops and seminars where VGI skills were taught. About one-fifth indicated that they were "self starters" and had learned from reading books and articles. Others mentioned staff development programs conducted in their schools.

We also looked at the *frequency* with which educators were using VGI activities in their classes. Kindergarten to Grade 3 teachers used the activities on a frequent to moderate basis, with more tending toward frequent use. Grades 4 to 6 made frequent to moderate use of the activities, with more tending toward moderate use. Junior-high teachers were somewhat balanced between frequent and moderate use. Senior-high teachers used the activities on a frequent to moderate basis, with more tending toward moderate use. College/university instructors used the activities on a frequent to moderate basis, with more tending toward frequent use. (Frequent = three to five times per week; moderate = one to two times per week; infrequent = less than one time per week.)

Respondents were asked to describe *student responses* to VGI work. Eighty percent of these reported that students commented that "they enjoyed VGI work, wanted more and asked to continue doing VGI." Others mentioned that the students described themselves as "feeling more relaxed," "better able to get along with the others," "more cohesive in the group," and "better able to understand their minds."

Also, we wanted to determine if *daily use of VGI (as opposed to infrequent use) would influence student gains* in the eleven areas. We recognize that these are not true students gains but are teacher observations of outcomes and thus are subject to teacher personal bias. Mean scores in the eleven categories for teachers who reported daily use were compared with scores from teachers reporting infrequent use. The following trends were discovered:

In the kindergarten to Grade 3 group, daily users reported higher scores in all categories except for achievement, creativity, and standard proficiency. The group of daily users reported the greatest advantage in attitudes and self-esteem.

In the Grade 4 to 6 group, daily users reported higher scores in all categories except for creativity, listening, and standard proficiency. The daily users of VGI had the most marked advantage in achievement and initiative.

In the junior-high group, daily users reported higher scores in all categories except achievement, productivity, creativity, listening, nonstandard proficiency, and self-esteem.

In the senior-high group, infrequent users reported higher scores in all categories. The greatest differences in favor of infrequent use were in the categories of initative, listening, and nonstandard proficiency.

In the college/university group, daily users reported higher scores in all categories except attention, nonstandard proficiency, and standard proficiency. Because of the small number of respondents in this group, differences in scores reported by daily users and infrequent users connot be used to indicate trends in favor of either group.

The teachers also were asked to add any other observations, especially those not targeted by the eleven areas, that might be significant for predicting future trends in using VGI. These observations revealed that the teachers were noting subtle changes in the interests and levels of thinking of many of their students. This was noted especially among Grade 4 through senior-high students. Teachers frequently made comments such as "The VGI activities tap spiritual depths in the kids," "My students seem more sensitive to global as well as local issues," "They seem better able to understand one another and empathize with each other," "They are becoming more interested in future capabilities such as out-of-body, ESP, and psychic kinds of phenomena," "They are able to transcend their usual ways of seeing things—like becoming more aware of energy in them and in others," and "They talk more frequently about spiritual kinds of experiences." Conversations with the teachers, especially with those who had been teaching five or more years and who were familiar with many teaching methods, revealed that they believed that the students may experience a major shift in focus of interest and intellectual/spiritual capabilities by regularly doing VGI—especially transpersonal VGI.

CONCLUSIONS AND RECOMMENDATIONS

VGI activities are a potentially powerful aspect of the curriculum and can serve to effect highly desirable gains in: 1) cognitive areas of academic-skills acquisition and proficiency; 2) affective areas of attention, creativity, initiative, listening, and self-esteem; and 3) the interpersonal area of cohesiveness.

Along with these effects, VGI also enables participants to experience enjoyment and a desire to do more VGI work; to feel calm and relaxed; to be more focused—less distracted—and thus to learn more easily; and to experience success, which engenders in them a feeling of confidence that they can use their minds for varying benefits, and can use their imaging ability to accelerate and enlarge the scope of learning both on an intrapersonal (inner sensitivity) and an extrapersonal (outer sensitivity) level.

School personnel, such as teachers, counselors, and school psychologists, wishing to use VGI activities are cautioned that some students may resist at first, but with voluntarism as a rule and acceptance by the teacher, and moved by the successes and the enthusiasm of their peers, most find VGI work enjoyable and do well working with it. Students who are hyperactive, have severe emotional problems, and/or are taking drugs may find VGI work difficult. These students should be identified beforehand and given special assistance, and, at all times, they should be given the option of doing alternative work while other students are working with VGI.

Teachers continually should seek evaluation feedback from students concerning their reaction to VGI work, what they learned from it and what changes they would make. Teachers should encourage students to disclose only those personal experiences from the VGI activities that they feel are appropriate for sharing. Teachers also should inform students why VGI work is valuable and introduce it as an aspect of the standard curriculum, either as a "readiness-orientation to learning" exercise or as an activity within the lesson itself. The use of cognitive, affective, transpersonal, and interpersonal objectives could be helpful here [1-3]. Due to the newness of VGI work, teachers should solicit support from administrators and colleagues. Some controversy surrounds the term "meditation," and it is advisable to use other terms, such as "imagery," "centering," "visualization," in order to distinguish between meditation as a religious event and VGI as an educational tool.

Frequency of use should be decided by each teacher, on the basis of his/her curricular demands, district-mandated continua of skills, course requirements, as well as by student (and teacher) readiness to use and preference for working with VGI. Most teachers like to use VGI at least once a week, and many use it three to five times per week. Preparatory and background experiences and materials should be provided to every teacher wishing to use VGI.

More research is needed with larger numbers and with subjects drawn from a general education setting. Most respondents in this study were from holistically oriented groups. We also need to know the length of time as well as the regularity with which teachers use VGI. It also would be helpful to distinguish subject areas, such as mathematics, science, and English, to determine if VGI is more effective for certain disciplines. We also recommend grouping students according to proficiency levels, such as emotional handicaps, learning disability, language deficiency, and giftedness, and also according to physical handicaps, such as visual impairment and hearing impairment, to determine the effectiveness of VGI with these students. Furthermore, it would be worthwhile to determine if cultural biases influence the effectiveness of VGI work. Such research could be carried out among populations representing various ethnic groups, and an analysis of variance applied to the overall data, could distinguish possible culturally influenced effects. Some teachers indicated that they reinforced and/or expanded VGI work with activities in art, music, drama, movement, etc. A comparison of the effects of using VGI with and without adjunct arts activities could clarify the role of the arts combined with VGI in effecting achievement in each of the eleven areas. A frequency profile of occasions when teachers use the four types of imagery (i.e., relaxation-sensory, guided cognitive, guided affective, and guided transpersonal) and subsequent outcomes in each of the eleven areas and in other areas as they emerge within further research, would enable curriculum planners to decide when and how to weave the four types into already existing and emerging curricular materials. Finally, a content analysis of student compositions and taped recordings of their experiences resulting from the various types of imagery activities would give us clues as to the mental/spiritual openings and levels of development being triggered by the various activities. Several teachers who participated in a follow-up study to this report, mentioned that their students were showing an increased interest in consciousness, spiritual and psychic themes treated in transpersonal activities.

Visualization and guided imagery certainly deserve a place in the standard curriculum of elementary, secondary, and postsecondary schools. In fact, VGI may become a *central aspect* of curricula in the future. Reports from both teachers and students, using VGI on a regular basis, continue to be encouraging. Due to increased understanding of what the imaging mind can do, and how it affects physical and emotional material in accord with a mental picture or blueprint, teachers using VGI are providing their students with a survival skill that well may become a "basic" of the future. This basic skill promises to enhance intellectual functioning, expand previously conceived Cartesian-Newtonian mental limitations, enlist intellectual energies beyond those of ordinary awakened consciousness, transcend ordinary values and biased perceptions of human possibility, and heal physical matter. Once VGI is accepted as a core aspect of the curriculum, this transformation may happen much sooner than we think.

APPENDIX

RESEARCH PROJECT ON GUIDED IMAGERY

Name _____ School _____

Address _____ City _____ Zipcode _____

Grade Level Taught

(If secondary, specify subject(s) where you use guided imagery)

Are there any subjects and/or special times during the day
when you use imagery activities?

Using a code from *0 not at all* to *5 very much* indicate the degree to
which you have noted the following results while using imagery activities with your students.

_____ They learn more of the material being taught. *Achievement*

_____ They are more attentive to the lesson. *Attentive*

_____ They work better together. *Cohesiveness*

_____ They do more work. *Productivity*

_____ Their work is more creative (develop their own ideas as opposed to repeating ideas of the text, teacher or others). *Creativity*

_____ They show more initiative (originate projects, ideas and opinions without
teacher prompt). *Initiative*

_____ They listen well to each other's ideas, feelings and opinions. *Listening*

_____ Their test scores are higher in my class. *Nonstandard Proficiency*

_____ Their test scores are higher on standardized tests. *Standard Proficiency*

_____ They talk more about themselves, their own abilities to achieve in school.
Self-Esteem

_____ They talk more about themselves, their own abilities to achieve outside
school. *Self-Esteem*

_____ Any other observations you have noted (i.e., better attendance, less dis-
ruptiveness). Include any problems or cautions.

How often do you use imagery? Be as specific as possible.

Describe how the children respond to (feel about) the activities.

Have you received any training in how to use imagery or did you just start
on your own?

REFERENCES

1. B. Galyean, Guided Imagery in Education, *Journal of Humanistic Psychology, 21*:4, pp. 57–68, Fall, 1981.
2. B. Galyean, The Use of Guided Imagery in Elementary and Secondary Schools, *Imagination, Cognition, and Personality, 2*:2, pp. 145–151, 1982-83.
3. B. Galyean, Guided Imagery in the Curriculum, in *Educational Leadership*, R. Brandt (ed.), Forthcoming, March, 1983.
4. F. Lenz, *Total Relaxation*, Bobbs-Merrill, New York, 1980.
5. M. Murdock, *Spinning Inward*, Peace Press, Culver City, California, 1982.
6. B. Galyean, *Mind Sight: Learning through Imaging*, Center for Integrative Learning, Long Beach, California, 1983.
7. D. Rozman, *Meditation with Children*, University of Trees Press, Boulder Creek, California, 1975.
8. G. Hendricks and R. Wills, *The Centering Book: Awareness Activities for Children, Parents and Teachers*, Prentice-Hall, New Jersey, 1975.
9. G. Hendricks and T. Roberts, *The Second Centering Book: More Awareness Activities for Children, Parents and Teachers*, Prentice-Hall, New Jersey, 1977.
10. M. Feldenkrais, *Awareness through Movement: Health Exercises for Personal Growth*, Harper-Row, New York, 1972.
11. R. Masters and J. Houston, *Listening to the Body*, Delacorte, New York, 1978.
12. J. Shorr, *Psychotherapy through Imagery*, Intercontinental Medical Book Corporation, New York, 1974.
13. J. Singer, *Imagery and Daydream Methods in Psychotherapy and Behavior Modification*, Academic Press, New York, 1974.
14. I. Oyle, *The Healing Mind*, Celestial Arts, Millbrae, California, 1974.
15. C. Simonton and S. Simonton, *Getting Well Again*, Tarcher, Los Angeles, 1978.
16. B. Joy, *Joy's Way*, Tarcher, Los Angeles, 1979.
17. J. Canfield and H. Wells, *100 Ways to Enhance Self-Concept in the Classroom*, Prentice-Hall, New Jersey, 1977.
18. G. Hendricks and J. Fadiman, *Transpersonal Education*, Prentice-Hall, New Jersey, 1975.
19. J. Elligett, H. Danielson, and M. Holland, A Preliminary Evaluation of the Success Imagery Program in Seven Schools, report presented at the Mental Imagery Conference, University of Southern California, Los Angeles, June 25-27, 1982.
20. G. Shaw, Imagery Use in Creative and High I.Q. School Children, report presented at the Mental Imagery Conference, University of Southern California, Los Angeles, June 25-27, 1982.
21. H. Lange, *Increase of Learning Achievement through the Use of Guided Imagery*, unpublished master's thesis, Mount St. Mary's College, Los Angeles, May, 1982.
22. M. Piccolo and G. Render, The Relationship Between Mental Imagery and SRA Reading Comprehension in High School Students, paper presented at

the annual meeting of the American Educational Research Association, New York, March, 1982.

23. E. Groff and G. Render, The Effectiveness of Three Classroom Teaching Methods: Programmed Instruction, Simulation, and Guided Imagery, paper presented at the annual meeting of the American Educational Research Association, New York, March, 1982.

24. C. Boyle and G. Render, The Relationship Between the Use of Fantasy Journeys and Creativity, paper presented at the annual meeting of the American Educational Research Association, New York, March, 1982.

25. B. Galyean, The Effects of a Guided-Imagery Activity on Various Behaviors of Low Achieving Students, *Journal of Suggestive-Accelerative Learning and Teaching*, 5:2, 87–96, 1980.

26. B. Galyean, The Effects of Guided Imagery on the Writing Skills of Tenth-Grade Remedial-English Students, report presented at the annual meeting of the Association for Humanistic Psychology, Washington, D.C., July 24, 1982. (On file at the Center for Integrative Learning, Long Beach, California.)

27. Year End Report, in *A Confluent Language Program for K-3 NES/LES Students*, Los Angeles, California, 1978-81. (On file at the Center for Integrative Learning, Long Beach, California.)

28. Year End Report, in *Confluent Teaching of Foreign Languages*, Los Angeles, California, 1977-80. (On file at the Center for Integrative Learning, Long Beach, California.)

29. M. Toomim, Biofeedback and Imagery in the Schools: Summary of Several Research Projects in Education, report presented at the Brain/Mind Revolution Conference, Upland, California, June 26, 1982.

30. D. Schuster and D. Martin, Effects of Biofeedback-induced Tension or Relaxation, Chronic Anxiety, Vocabulary Easiness, Suggestion and Sex of Subject on Learning Rare Words, *Journal of Suggestive-Accelerative Learning and Teaching*, 5:4, pp. 275-287, 1980.

31. J. Edwards, The Effects of Suggestive-Accelerative Learning and Teaching on Creativity, *Journal of Suggestive-Accelerative Learning and Teaching*, 5:4, pp. 235–253, 1980.

32. S. Steingart and M. Glock, Imagery and the Recall of Connected Discourse, *Reading Research Quarterly*, 1, pp. 66-83, 1979.

33. H. LaRoche, The Use of Guided Imagery as a Treatment Intervention in Assertion Training, unpublished doctoral dissertation, California Graduate Institute, Los Angeles, January, 1983.

34. R. Kruse, The Relationship between Student Self-Concept and the Use of a Fantasy Journey, paper presented at the annual meeting of the American Educational Research Association, New York, March, 1982.

35. B. Galyean, The Effects of a Guided-Imagery Activity on the Writing Skills of Eighth-Grade Students, report presented at the Holistic Educators Workshop Series, Los Angeles, November 14, 1982. (On file at the Center for Integrative Learning, Long Beach, California.)

CHAPTER 8
Imagery Research with Children: Implications for Education
NANCY S. SUZUKI

INTRODUCTION

A considerable amount of research, conducted over the last two decades, has revealed that the maturing learner becomes increasingly proficient at learning and remembering. This increase in proficiency is generally attributed to an increase with age of the spontaneous generation and utilization of appropriate strategies, such as imagery, elaboration, rehearsal, and category clustering in various learning and memory tasks [1-7].

Imaginal and verbal elaboration strategies, however, generally are not systematically taught in schools [8,9], as illustrated by some self-report data obtained by Greer from learners in Grades 6, 8, 10, and 12, after they had completed a paired associate learning task [10]. The majority of students indicated that they preferred an imagery strategy over verbal elaboration, rehearsal, or doing nothing, when they were asked to sort concrete items they had just learned, into strategy categories. Yet, when asked if they had in their past received information regarding ways in which materials could be remembered easily, only 55 percent of the learners reported that they had received some sort of instruction in remembering. Of these students, 69 percent (38% of the total) mentioned receiving mnemonic information from teachers, and 31 percent (17% of the total) mentioned receiving instructions from parents or older siblings. Of the students who reported receiving information from teachers, 61 percent spoke of learning rote strategies, and 39 percent reported learning elaborative strategies. However, of those students who had received information from family members, 24 percent reported rote strategies and 75 percent reported elaborative strategies. In the entire sample, then, 45 percent reported receiving no information, 27 percent

The preparation of this manuscript was facilitated by the author's tenure as a visiting scholar at the State University of New York at Buffalo in the Department of Counseling and Educational Psychology.

reported receiving instruction in rote strategies, and only 28 percent reported receiving instruction in imaginal and elaborative strategies.

Since educators are concerned with producing self-activated and independent learners, it is of interest to examine research investigating the effect of strategic instruction on children's learning, as well as research dealing with learner characteristics and instructional conditions related to performance reflecting self-activated learning. The purpose of the present chapter is to review some of this research. The chapter is organized into four parts: It begins with an introductory statement on the theoretical processes underlying strategies, such as imagery and verbal elaboration. The second section includes primarily research in which strategic instructions to learners have been manipulated in list learning and school-related tasks. The third section covers studies examining characteristics of learners engaging in self-activated activities and work on metamemorial development. Finally, the summary highlights educational implications of the reviewed research.

IMAGERY AND ELABORATION

Paivio has advanced a dual-coding hypothesis of memory which suggests that there is an imaginal and a verbal system available for the organization of information in memory [11]. The two are viewed as separate but complimentary cognitive processing systems. The imagery system is characterized as specialized for parallel and simultaneous processing, while the verbal system is used for sequential and successive processing. Thus, concrete words can be stored in both systems, and abstract words which do not readily evoke an image are stored in the verbal system.

Rohwer has proposed that associative learning involves the creating of shared meanings or a common referential event for two or more initially unrelated items [7]. The process of elaboration consists of the generating of a common referent for the items, by combining memories, by direct involvement, by observation of an interaction, by pure mental interaction, or through some "event" or "episode" in which the separate items interact. One member of the pair or set of items would then act as a retrieval cue for the common referential event. The other members can then be easily retrieved as an integral part of the shared meaning. Rohwer's position is that elaboration is the underlying process, and that modality questions about imagery processes versus verbal processes are secondary to questions about prompting the underlying process. The position is thus amodal. Much of the research on associative learning in children is consistent with such a single-process model, as minimal differences have been found between visual and verbal elaborations of items to be learned but substantial differences have been found due to explicitness of elaborative prompting instructions [5, 7, 12]. Furthermore, although Paivio has provided considerable evidence for the validity of the dual-coding model, his position has been criticized for not dealing adequately with what learners already know and for not easily accommodating linguistic notions of deep or conceptual structures of sentences [13, 14]. The present chapter will therefore view imagery as a form of prompting the underlying elaboration process rather than deal extensively with the distinction between imagery and verbal codes.

Before reviewing the research studies, a description of some basic tasks is in order. The effects of imagery on children's learning have been most extensively examined with list-learning tasks and particularly with the paired-associate task. Typically, in a paired-associate task, learners are presented with lists of pairs of items which are not normally associated with each other (e.g., doctor-lemon). The learner is asked to learn the pairs so that when one item is presented at some later time (e.g., doctor), he/she will be able to recall the other item of the pair (e.g., lemon).

Instructional variations consist of instructions to learners to engage in particular activities and of the degree of explicitness in prompting the underlying elaborative process [7]. Thus, "control" instructions simply direct the learner to learn the items for later recall; "prompting" instructions tell the learner to engage in imaginal or verbal elaboration (e.g., "Try to imagine an interaction of the items or create a story involving the items"); "provided" instructions furnish learners with an experimental context for the pairs, such as a picture of the objects interacting or a sentence/story in which the two objects are related in some way (e.g., "The doctor is squeezing the lemon"); "enactment" instructions direct the learner to physically manipulate the objects to be learned in some sort of interactive relation (e.g., a physician doll squeezing the lemon); and "repetition" instructions tell the learner to repeat over and over again the items to be learned (e.g., "doctor-lemon, doctor-lemon"). The repetition method is considered to be antagonistic to the elaboration process, in that it interferes with the creation of shared meanings.

Two other list-learning tasks are free recall and serial learning. In the free-recall task, learners are presented with a list of items to remember and are told that they can remember the items in any order. In the serial task, a list of items is presented and the order of presentation of the items must be maintained. Instructional variations with these tasks include prompting strategies like category clustering, (i.e., grouping items to be recalled by categories) [15] and cumulative-rehearsal procedures (i.e., rehearsing several items together rather than individually) [3].

INSTRUCTIONAL EFFECTS

List Learning

The effect of imagery and elaboration instructions on list learning has been examined across the entire range of school-aged learners. Wolff and Levin attempted to assess at what age children are able to follow instructions to use imagery strategies [16]. They varied instructional conditions for kindergarten and Grade 3 children in a paired-associate task using concrete common objects. The four different instructional conditions included a control condition, an imagery-prompting condition, an experimenter-provided interaction condition, and a learner-enactment condition. The results revealed that the Grade 3 children in all three experimental conditions performed better than those in the control condition. However, kindergarten children, although they remembered more items with experimenter-enacted and subject-enacted instructions, were not able to benefit from instructions to try to imagine the toys "playing together."

Yuille and Catchpole demonstrated, however, that kindergarten children can benefit from imagery instructions if models of appropriate interactions are first provided to the children [17]. The evidence suggests that prior to five years of age children are unable to utilize imagery instructions [18]. Around six years of age, children are able to benefit from visual-imagery instructions in learning verbal materials if it consists of high-imagery pairs and if they are given adequate time for processing [19].

Kindergarten children and educationally mentally retarded children have been shown to benefit from being asked questions, such as "Why is the TABLE sitting on the MOUNTAIN?" or "What is the TABLE doing on the side of the MOUNTAIN?" more than from instructions to generate their own interactions or even from interactions or elaborations provided by the experimenter [20]. Thus, asking young children questions which promote interactional images may stimulate semantic processing of materials or may force children to generate relational meanings to paired objects. Craik and Lockhart suggest that the questioning encourages children not simply to repeat the sentence but to process information at a deeper level [21]. However, the interrogative questioning may be viewed as a variation of prompting the elaborative process; for, as Pressley points out, although the questioning may be beneficial to young children, it still has not been determined if questioning instructions are substantially more effective than simple elaborations for a wide range of ages [5].

Whether the ability to benefit from imagery-prompting instructions is a function of general ability, age, or educational experience was examined by Levin and Pressley [22]. Kindergarten children were randomly assigned to one of four different conditions: an imagery-prompted group and a control group tested in the fall and an imagery-prompted group and a control group tested in the spring of the school year. They found that age was related to performance for the groups given imagery-prompting instructions but not for the control groups even when general ability was partialed out. They concluded that educational experience is not as relevant as children's maturational levels to the ability to benefit from imagery-prompting instructions.

Imagery instructions are not consistently beneficial even for more mature learners in tasks like free recall or serial learning [3, 23]. Adults as well as five- to seven-year-old children, for example, in motoric-enactment conditions have been found to perform better than those in control conditions, in a task involving memory for sentences [24]. Furthermore, enactment conditions prompted better recall than imagery instructions in second- and third-grade children and adults in the free recall of nouns and verbs. However, in this study, imagery instructions consisted of directions to image referents individually rather than in interaction with other items, unlike the instructions used in associative-learning tasks.

The effect of instructions across the entire range of school-aged students was examined by Rohwer and Bean in a concrete paired-associate task with learners from Grades 1, 3, 6, 8, and 11 [25]. Learners at all levels were instructed to listen and to learn the noun pairs (control), to repeat the pairs over and over (repetition), to form sentences containing the pairs (prompted), or to read sentences provided by the experimenter containing the pairs (provided). At the first-, third-, and sixth-grade levels, the control instructions yielded the same results as the repetition instructions but poorer results than the prompted and provided instructions. But at the eleventh-grade level, the effect of the control instructions was equivalent to that produced by the prompted and provided instructions; and at the eighth-grade level, its effect was midway between these two extremes. Rohwer and Bean concluded that there is an increase in the spontaneous generation of elaboration with age, and the critical period of change from nonproduction to production occurs somewhere between the sixth and the eleventh grades [25].

Attempts to replicate these findings, however, have provided some interesting mixed results, which suggest that age alone may not identify spontaneous elaborators. Greer and Suzuki examined the effects of four instructional conditions on the paired-associate learning of sixth-, eighth-, and tenth-grade students using both concrete and abstract nouns [26]. The instructional conditions included an imagery-prompting condition and a verbal-elaboration prompting condition, a control condition and a repetition condition. Spontaneous elaboration was inferred when elaboration training did not yield performance superior to that produced by control instructions, and when repetition instructions led to poorer performance than that which followed control instructions. Consistent with the Rohwer and Bean findings [25], the results indicated that the onset of spontaneous elaboration with concrete items occurred at the eighth-grade level, and spontaneous elaboration of abstract items occurred in tenth grade. However, Kennedy and Suzuki found that while average-I.Q. Mexican-American and Anglo-American Grade 12 students appeared to be engaging in spontaneous elaboration, their low-I.Q. peers appeared to benefit from elaborative prompting instructions [27]. To further complicate matters, Rohwer, Raines, Eoff, and Wagner found that I.Q. was not as predictive of the tendency to spontaneously elaborate as a paired-associate pretest [28]. Also the results suggested that, even among the older adolescents, performance increased with elaboration instructions, indicating that a large number of Grade 11 students were not engaging in spontaneous elaboration activities. More recently, Leung, Suzuki, and Foster found that, when the memory task involves the learning of more difficult abstract noun triplets, even college undergraduates recall more items with prompting instructions than with control instructions, although performance does not differ as a function of instructions for concrete noun triplets [29]. A more detailed discussion of attempts to specify learner characteristics associated with the ability to spontaneously elaborate will be presented in the next section of the chapter.

To summarize briefly the research conducted with list-learning tasks, prompting instructions, such as, "Try to imagine . . . ," are effective in promoting proficient list learning in children as young as kindergarten children, if instructions include examples of appropriate interactions. There are differences related to age in the effectiveness of prompting instructions: In general, the older the student the less likely it is that he/she will need explicit forms of prompting in order to perform well. However, even adults benefit from strategic instruction in remembering sentences, in the free recall of unrelated words, and in the recall of abstract noun triplets. Also, not all adolescents provide evidence of the spontaneous use of strategies.

School-Related Tasks

Keyword method. Researchers have examined imagery and elaboration not only in traditional laboratory learning and memory tasks, but also they have examined developmental questions with a variety of school-related tasks. A variation of the paired-associative task in which imagery processes play a major role is called the keyword method [30]. Initially, the method was shown to facilitate foreign-language vocabulary learning, but also it has been found helpful in the learning of English vocabulary, abstract terms, capitals and states/provinces, cities and products, people and accomplishments [9]. The procedure involves several stages. The initial one consists of the learner pronouncing the stimulus word; in a foreign-language vocabulary lesson, for example, the student pronounces the foreign word and tries to think of an English word that rhymes with it or with part of it. Thus, if in a French vocabulary lesson one of the words to be acquired is "paille" which means "straw," the corresponding English word would be "pail." The key word "pail" is then used in interaction with the translation "straw," in an imaginary scene or event, such as a child drinking milk from a pail with a straw. This event should help the student recover the appropriate translation.

School-aged children as well as adults seem to benefit from keyword techniques [9, 30]. Pressley and Dennis-Rounds found that even eighteen-year-olds benefit from keyword instructions in the learning of city-product pairings [31], (e.g., Buffalo-water-generated power). However, eighteen-year-olds were able to transfer this keyword strategy based on imaginal elaboration to a completely new task, the learning of Latin vocabulary, without specific instructions to do so. In contrast, although twelve-year-old learners benefited from the strategy on the initial task, they were unable to transfer this knowledge without specific instructions which provided the application of the keyword technique to the learning of Latin words (complete instructions) or directions to use a technique like the one utilized in learning cities and their products (general instructions). Additionally, the researchers found that, on the transfer task, the twelve-year-olds and the eighteen-year-olds performed better with complete instructions than with general instructions and no-transfer instructions. The educational implication of the finding that it is necessary to reinstate the original strategy instructions for the new task situation, will be discussed in more detail in the summary section.

Prose learning. Typically, in a prose-learning task, learners are presented with sentences or stories to learn and later are asked to recall information from the materials. Tasks vary with respect to whether recall is prompted (cued) or not (free) and whether specific or general information is required.

In young children associative learning has been shown to be facilitated by the presentation of pairs in meaningful interactive pictures [7, 32]. Researchers working with the prose-learning paradigm have been interested in the effects of pictures which accompany orally presented information, on children's learning. The findings consistently have shown that children in all elementary-school grades benefit from pictorial prompts shown along with story presentations [4, 7, 23, 33, 34]. Also there is some indication that rehearsal processes may facilitate young children's prose learning [35, 36].

Guttman, Levin, and Pressley, in attempting to apply instructional conditions from paired associate learning to prose learning with visual illustrations, presented kindergarten, second- and third-grade children with varying degrees of pictorial support to narratives [33]. They used standard instructions, instructions to attempt to imagine events in the story, instructions which involved the presentation of complete pictures, and instructions which involved the presentation of pictures in which a portion of the content was missing. This later condition was an attempt to induce imagery for missing objects by imposing contextual cues in the form of partial pictures. The story was made up of ten sentences. For kindergarten children, complete pictures promoted better learning than partial pictures, imagery instructions, and control instructions. At the Grade 3 level, all three experimental groups performed better than control subjects. Thus, in the prose-learning task, there were developmental differences in the ability to profit from imagery-prompting instructions.

The relationship of performance to narratives and instructional conditions appears to correspond with that found with associative learning. However, the effect of rehearsal instructions on prose learning has not been clear. Ruch and Levin proposed that pictures and repetition are hierarchically ordered and that pictures provide learners with something more than repetition [35]. They argue that repetition encourages learners to attend to the surface characteristics of the sentences, while pictures provide a context in which information can be processed at a deeper level [21].

Hill examined the effect of pictures and repetition on both free-recall and cued-recall measures [37]. She was interested in the possibility that repetition or rehearsal may have an effect on children's prose learning independent of pictures. Grade 1 children were randomly assigned to one of four different experimental conditions which resulted from the factorial combination of picture presentation and repetition instructions. The picture effect was significant on a paraphrased cued-recall task in one school and approached significance in another school, with the means in the appropriate direction. There was a possibility of a ceiling effect in the latter school. Repetition did not have an effect on the cued-recall task. There were no significant effects on the free-recall task, except on a syntactic-complexity measure, mean length of utterance (MLU), which was affected by repetition instructions in one school only. Thus the evidence is not very strong that repetition and pictures independently facilitate prose learning.

Levin proposed that pictures have several functions [23]. These include reiteration, representation, organization, interpretation, and transformation of information. The reiteration (or repetition) function of pictures is not as beneficial as the other functions. Furthermore, he sees these pictorial functions as not specific to pictures alone but as characteristic of processes or strategies which facilitate children's prose learning. He seems to suggest a single—as opposed to a dual—process hypothesis for prose learning.

Other School-Related Tasks. In an attempt to examine the role of imagery and elaborative processes in solving addition problems by kindergarten children, Grunau varied instructions in the following manner for problems of the form $m + n = \ldots$ [38]. In three different conditions, children were provided with an oral reading of the problem: In a concrete-objects condition, the children were presented with objects (three-dimensional wooden animals) and saw the operation enacted by the experimenter; in a second condition, the children were simply asked to "try to imagine" the number of animals; and in the control condition, children were asked to listen to the problem about the animals. Performance was better in the concrete condition than in the other conditions. However, Grunau did find that the instructions, "try to imagine," did seem to help children in solving the more difficult type of problem relative to the control instructions. The more difficult problems, in this case, were items where $m < n$.

Another school-related task, in which imaginary processes have been examined, is that of understanding instructions. Markman examined whether or not children realize when they do not understand instructions for a task or if they have incomplete instructions [39]. First-, second-, and third-grade children were presented with instructions for two separate games and were asked to help the investigator develop clear instructions so that children their age could play the games correctly. Both sets of instructions were incomplete, in fact, the most critical information had been left out. For example, relative to a card game, the children were told that the person with the "special card" would win the hand

and that, at the end of the game, the person with the most cards would win the game. However, no information was given about the nature of this special card. The dependent variable was where, in a sequence of ten probes from the experimenter, the child asked for more information about the special card. She found that older children recognized that the instructions were incomplete more quickly than younger children. In a second experiment, after aspects of the task had been demonstrated, children were better able to detect that information was missing. Also, when younger children were forced to enact the procedure, they realized that they had insufficient information. Markman concludes that very young children do not spontaneously engage in the mental processing of information and therefore need actual demonstrations or enactments to perform the various necessary transformations.

In summary, the imagery-based keyword method has been shown to be effective with children and adults in a variety of tasks. Although older adolescents more readily than younger adolescents transferred the keyword strategy to a different task, it was necessary to reinstate the training instructions completely for maximal transfer to occur, even with the older students. The evidence from research on prose learning, arithmetic problem solving, and comprehending instructions suggests that imagery and elaborative instructions, in the form of pictures, prompting, or enactment, facilitate learning and understanding of school-related tasks in young children. These results corroborate the findings from list learning.

SELF-ACTIVATED LEARNERS

Spontaneous Elaboration

The first part of this section consists of a review of additional investigations which examined the spontaneous elaboration effect [25], described in the previous section on list learning, and also the learner characteristics underlying the ability to spontaneously generate appropriate strategies for learning and memory tasks. The second part of this section covers investigations of the relationship between metamemory and memory performance.

It is presumed that learners are generating elaboration spontaneously when performance under control instructions does not differ from performance preceded by specific instructions to visually or verbally elaborate, and when performance under repetition instructions is poorer than performance under control instructions. In an attempt to obtain data to establish more concretely this presumed relationship, Pressley and Levin asked learners to report on their strategies [40]. Learners from Grades 5, 7, and 9 first were presented with a list of paired items. After presentation of all pairs, learners were asked whether they could report on how they learned the materials. Further, learners were presented with three new pairs and asked to report on how they would learn these items. Based on learners' reports of overall strategy and of strategy for the three new items, learners were classified as elaborators (users of imagery and verbal elaboration), as users of mixed strategy, or as rehearsers. The researchers reported that the use of repetition as a strategy decreased significantly with age. Also they found that strategy classification was related to performance: Elaborators remembered more items than nonelaborators.

However, various attempts to replicate the original Rohwer and Bean findings [25] have not been successful, as discussed in a previous section [28]. General ability, as indexed by standardized I.Q. tests, is not consistently related to the ability to spontaneously engage in elaborative processes [27, 28]. The possibility that Piagetian developmental levels may be related to the ability to spontaneously generate appropriate strategies was examined by Greer [10]. She attempted to determine the degree to which the presence of the hypothetico-deductive and propositional thinking abilities of the Piagetian formal operational period was related to the ability to spontaneously elaborate.

Students from Grades 6, 8, 10, and 12 first were administered a paper-and-pencil formal-operations instrument. Items included three conservation tasks, a combinatorial-thinking task, and two verbal problems of propositional logic. From each grade, thirty-six students were randomly assigned to one of three memory groups: standard, repetition, and prompted. The memory task consisted of concrete and abstract noun pairs. Only a very modest relationship was found between formal-operations abilities and overall recall (6%); and by Grade 10, learners provided evidence of spontaneous elaboration for both concrete and abstract noun pairs.

Rohwer and Litrownik recently examined instructional effects on the maintenance of elaboration strategies across tasks (dyads and tetrads) and across days, in an effort to distinguish between an "opportunity" and a "capability" explanation of age differences in the use of strategic activities [41]. Training varied within and between learners, and it consisted of rehearsal, elaboration, and control instructions. Maintenance across two days was not significantly different between Grade 5 and Grade 11 students for the dyad task. However, maintenance was much more pronounced with the older age group on the more difficult tetrad task. One source of difficulty in the findings is that elaboration instructions produced significant effects relative to control training for both age groups. The authors interpret the findings as more supportive of a "capability" than an "opportunity" hypothesis, since both age groups had equivalent opportunity to acquire appropriate strategies.

Thus, the research with adolescents provides evidence that memory performance increases with age. There is some suggestion that the maturing learner increasingly engages in elaborative activities and is able to maintain elaboration strategies across a period of time. However, not all mature learners engage in spontaneous elaboration across tasks. It appears that the performance of some adolescents can be modified with elaboration-prompting instructions.

General ability, as indexed by standardized I.Q. tests or Piagetian formal-operations measures, does not seem to adequately account for the presence or absence of spontaneous elaboration in adolescence. An age-related characteristic, which may contribute to observed age differences in strategy behavior, is meta-memorial knowledge.

Metamemory

The term "metamemory" was coined by Flavell to refer to one's knowledge about memory and storage and retrieval variables [42]. Thus, metamemory includes knowledge about person variables (awareness of memory span limits and capacity), about strategy variables (sensitivity to appropriate storage and retrieval strategies), and about task variables (sensitivity to task characteristics and requirements) [43, 44]. Since the original formulation of metamemory, numerous investigations have been conducted to examine potential relationships between memory knowledge and memory performance, because one of the components of metamemory is awareness of the need to engage in strategic activities in anticipation of later recall [44-47].

Much of the recent work on metamemorial development has been conducted with young elementary-school children with various measures of metamemory. For example, for tasks which have been discussed in a previous section of this chapter, measures have included assessment of performance and choice of strategy after performance on paired-associate tasks [48], predictions of performance on a free-recall tasks [49], reporting of form of strategy used for recalling familiar information [50], and judgments of task difficulty and study time allotted [51].

Moynahan examined the effect of prior experience on the awareness of young children of strategic behavior [48]. First-, third-, and fifth-grade students performed paired associate recognition tasks, once under elaborative-interaction instructions and once under rehearsal instructions. On a third task, learners were allowed to choose the strategy they preferred using. Just prior to this third task, they were asked which strategy was better and to give an explanation of their choice. Third and fifth graders were aware that they remembered better with the interactive strategy, but only in the fifth grade did learners refer to the interaction itself as being beneficial for remembering. On the third task, there was no age difference in choice of the interaction strategy; however, performance increased with age and strategy users generally remembered more items than nonusers.

Worden and Sladewski-Awig asked kindergarten, second-, fourth-, and sixth-grade children to predict which items of a free-recall task they would be able to recall [49]. Half of the list consisted of items from three categories, and the other half was made up of uncategorized items. Recall increased significantly with age, and kindergarten children significantly overestimated their performance relative to older children. When children were asked to justify why they thought they would remember particular items, kindergarten children gave justifications referring to their own ability (e.g., "Because I have the smartest brains") [49, p. 346], while sixth-grade children appeared to base their reasoning on item and task characteristics, such as familiarity of items (e.g., "For one reason, my dad's a fireman; I use a saw a lot; my mom uses a pan to cook with; I catch ladybugs; I eat Rice Krispies sometimes; I lost a frog") [49, p. 348].

Evidence that young children may not be able to report on strategies they have used, even when they are able to remember the material, was obtained by Bjorklund and Zeman [50]. First-, third-, and fifth-grade children were asked to recall the names of children in their own classrooms and also to report on the type of strategy they used in order to recall the names of the children. The results suggested that even for very familiar material, like names of children in the class, which they could recall, young children are unaware of possible strategies they may have used. Additionally, when a recognition procedure was used for identifying the possible strategies used, children showed little evidence of awareness. For fifth graders, who had been given some advance metamemory prompting questions, like "Is there any special way you are going to remember the names?" and a thirty-second "thinking period" prior to recall, there was some evidence of metamemorial knowledge of strategy usage.

Owings, Peterson, Bransford, Morris, and Stein examined sensitivity to differences in difficulty of stories and whether or not fifth-grade students are able to respond differentially on a sentence completion task [51]. They classified the students as "successful" and "less successful" on the basis of teachers' judgments and standardized achievement-test scores. Two types of stories were presented to the students, easy and difficult. The easy stories consisted of sentences with appropriate subject-predicate pairings (e.g., "The hungry boy ate the hamburger"). The difficulty stories were inappropriate subject-predicate pairings (e.g., "The hungry boy took a nap"). They found that the successful fifth-grade students were able to monitor their own learning, such that they were aware of the difference between sensible and less sensible stories and, furthermore, could identify the cause of their problem in understanding the more difficult stories. In addition, when given free study time, the successful students allowed more time to the difficult stories than to the sensible stories. Less successful students, however, did not appear to be aware of the differences in the difficulty of the passages and did not vary their study time accordingly. On the sentence completion task, successful students remembered more than the less successful students, and recall scores were higher for sensible than for less sensible stories.

Lodico, Ghatala, Levin, Pressley, and Bell conducted a study with second-grade children to examine the effect of providing children with training in some general principles of strategy monitoring before giving them the opportunity to perform with either of two strategies on a memory task [52]. The training consisted of instructing the children on two example problems: The first was drawing a circle freehand versus tracing one with a cookie cutter, and the second was learning a list of letters versus rearranging the letters to spell their names. The children were instructed that there were many ways to play a game, and that, in order to play well, they must select the method that allows them to perform well. After they had worked through the example problems, they were asked which method had allowed them to do better and why. They were then asked which method they would select if they had to do it again. After the training, the children were presented with either two paired-associate tasks or two free-recall tasks. Both trained and control children were given elaboration instructions for one list and rehearsal instructions for the second paired-associate list. Both trained and control children were given single-item rehearsal instructions for the one free-recall list and multiple-item rehearsal instructions for the other free-recall list. Trained subjects were reminded of the importance of keeping track of their performance. On a third task, children were asked to select a strategy to use. The researchers found that most children were able to identify the strategy which was most effective. However, more children in the group trained in strategy monitoring than in the control group selected to use the more effective strategy on a third task, and their justification for doing so was: They thought it would enhance their performance. Training effects on this third task were significant only for a paired-associate task.

Waters attempted to examine the relationship of metamemory and memory performance in adolescents [53]. She felt that metamemory was present in those learners who could identify the strategy that was the best for remembering items after they had performed a paired associate task. Learners also were asked to indicate which of four strategies they had used for each of the items: repetition, listening, imagery, or sentence elaboration. Eighth and tenth graders who had metamemory used imagery and verbal elaboration for more pairs than those without metamemory. Tenth graders performed better than eighth graders, and those with metamemory performed better than those without. There was an age difference in recall but not in pairs elaborated for these adolescents. In a probability-of-recall analysis in which elaborated pairs recalled was divided by total words recalled, there was a significant age difference. She concluded that the age difference in performance is due to strategy effectiveness, while availability of stimulus materials and frequency of nouns are related to use. "A tenth grader who elaborated was more likely to remember the pair than an eighth grader who reported elaboration" [53, p. 193].

In a recently completed study, the present writer attempted to explore further the relationship between aspects of metamemory and memory performance in adolescent learners [54]. One purpose of the study was to examine the effect of instructions on Grade 7 and Grade 11 students, on two different tasks. The first task involved the learning of sets of two unrelated nouns, and the second task consisted of the learning of sets of five unrelated nouns. In both tasks, the first noun was used as a cue for the recall task. The items within each set were high-frequency, meaningful words. Both tasks were administered under one of three instructional conditions: control, repetition, and prompted-elaboration instructions. Repetition instructions directed learners to repeat the items, and elaboration instructions asked learners to try to imagine an interaction or to make up a story involving all items in each set. Another purpose of the investigation was to examine the relationship between spontaneous elaboration and several measures of metamemory. Aspects of metamemory measured were person variables, strategy variables, and task variables.

The learners were tested individually. The materials were presented via an Apple II microcomputer unit consisting of a monitor, disk drive, keyboard, and printer. The procedure began with general paired-associate instructions to learners and with the presentation of the instructions appropriate to the experimental conditions. Then subjects were asked to predict the number of items they would recall of a list of twenty-four two-item sets. The first learning task, the two-item sets, were then presented for a single study/test trial. Following the learning task, learners were asked to guess the number of items they thought they remembered correctly. They were then asked to report on the way they tried to learn a subset of seven items. These responses were recorded on disk.

During a short break, the learner was asked to leave the room, and the experimenter printed the data from the first half of the session. Then the subject was presented with instructions for the five-item sets. The instructions expanded on the two-item instructions and included examples of five-item sets. The experimental instructions were consistent for learners across the two tasks. Prior to the task, subjects were again asked to predict their performance, this time on a list of six sets of five items. The sets then were presented for one study/test trial. Following the test trial, subjects were asked to guess the number of items they thought they remembered correctly. Finally, subjects were asked to rate seven sets of three statements about memory variables in terms of difficulty (e.g., learning a set of items by listening to them, learning a set of items by repeating them, learning a set of items by imagining or making up a story about them). Students were to rate them as easy, medium, or difficult.

Correct responses were analyzed separately for the two-item and five-item sets. Analysis of variance revealed a significant grade effect for both two-item and five-item sets. The instructional comparisons were examined within each group separately.

For Grade 7 students learning the two-item sets, neither the elaboration versus control contrast nor the repetition versus control contrast was statistically significant; but the elaboration versus control comparison approached significance ($p < .07$) with the means in the appropriate direction (11.1 and 8.5 respectively). The mean for the repetition condition was 6.2.

For Grade 11 students, the elaboration versus control comparison was significant. The means for the elaboration, control, and repetition conditions were 15.7, 15.8, and 9.5 respectively. Thus, spontaneous elaboration can be inferred with Grade 11 students learning the two-item sets.

For the five-item sets, Grade 7 elaboration-instructed learners recalled more words than control learners, and repetition-instructed learners did not recall significantly more words than control learners. The means for the elaboration, control, and repetition groups were 13.5, 7.4, and 8.7 respectively.

For Grade 11 students, elaboration-instructed learners recalled more items than control learners, and control learners recalled more items than repetition-instructed learners. The means for the elaboration, control, and repetition groups were 17.3, 14.3, and 8.2.

Thus, for Grade 7 students, a prompt effect was observed with the more difficult task, and the effect approached significance on the paired-associate task. In both tasks, repetition instructions did not improve performance relative to control instructions. For Grade 11 students, however, the repetition instructions were detrimental to learning relative to control instructions on both tasks. The older students appeared to be engaging in spontaneous elaborative activities with the paired items; however, they still appeared to benefit from elaboration instructions on the more difficult task.

For both Grade 7 and Grade 11 students, posttask predictions of performance on both tasks correlated significantly with actual performance. The difference between the two age levels was apparent in the pretask predictions. None of the correlations was significant for the Grade 7 students, but all of the correlations were significant for the Grade 11 students. For Grade 7 students, the means for predicated and actual score on the two-item sets were 14.0 and 8.6; and for predicated and actual score on the five-item sets, they were 14.0 and 10.0. For Grade 11 students, the means for predicted and actual score on the two-item set were 13.0 and 13.6; and for predicted and actual score on the five-item sets, they were 13.0 and 13.3.

Seven paired items were randomly selected for assessing learner strategies. The same items were used for all subjects. The reported strategies were coded by two individuals and the degree of agreement between the two coders was .93. Three strategy types were identified: elaborators (visual and verbal) who reported some form of interaction between the items to be learned for four or more of the seven items; mixed-strategy users who utilized several strategies, each to the same extent; and rehearsers who reported primarily repetition or no response. In general, there was an increase with age in the number of learners using elaboration strategies and a decrease with age in the number of learners reporting repetition strategies. Eighteen Grade 11 students and eight Grade 7 students were classified as elaborators, while ten Grade 7 students and five Grade 11 students were classified as rehearsers.

On the ratings of difficulty of task and strategy variables, the results consisted of a large number of overlapping ratings. A larger number of these occurred with the Grade 7 students than with the Grade 11 students. Although these results are quite tentative on the majority of items, more Grade 11 students than Grade 7 students judged the difficulty of the statements appropriately.

Thus, the results suggest that Grade 11 students, like the older adolescents in the Bean and Rohwer study [23], appear to be engaging in spontaneous elaboration, particularly on the two-item sets. As Rohwer and Litrownik also found, however, elaborative prompting promoted better learning than control instructions on the more difficult five-item sets [41]. Grade 7 students on the other hand, performed no better in the repetition conditions than in the control conditions on both tasks. The elaborative prompting effect was significant with the more difficult task and approached significance in the simpler task.

Metamemory variables also differentiated the two age groups. There appeared to be more consistency between learners' predictions of performance prior to a task and actual performance for Grade 11 students than for Grade 7 students. In addition, the number of elaboration strategy users increased with age and the number of rehearsal strategy users decreased with age. Also, the results suggested that more Grade 11 than Grade 7 students can rate the items appropriately on task difficulty.

To summarize the research on metamemory, there is evidence to suggest that, with age, learners become more knowledgeable about some variables affecting memory. Furthermore, there is some evidence that this knowledge is related to actual memory performance in young children but that the relationship becomes stronger during adolescence. Grade 10/11 learners have more metamemorial knowledge and perform better than Grade 7/8 learners. If additional research on the role of metamemory in the memory development of self-activated learners produces findings consistent with the present evidence, more specific information will be available concerning the instructional conditions necessary for promoting independent learning.

SUMMARY

As I already mentioned in the introductory section of the chapter, only 28 percent of the sample of sixth-, eighth-, and tenth- and twelfth-grade students reported having received elaboration instruction, and the source of that instruction was not exclusively teachers.

Perhaps this review of research on imagery and the elaborative process will help to change percentages like those reported above.

Five major implications for education will be highlighted as a way of summarizing the reviewed research. The first is that imagery and verbal elaboration-prompting instructions have a powerful effect on learning and remembering. Prompting does facilitate learning. The degree of prompted explicitness required may vary as a function of age: Young learners may need demonstrations or enactments of interactions, and older learners may require only "try-to-imagine" instructions.

Second, elaborative prompting also promotes learning on tasks which bear a close resemblance to school tasks, such as, learning foreign-language vocabulary,

English vocabulary, abstract words, capitals and states/provinces, cities and products, people and accomplishments, sentences/prose, solving simple addition problems, and understanding of instructions.

Third, not all adolescent learners spontaneously elaborate in learning and memory tasks. Neither age nor general ability are reliable predictors of the use of elaboration. Therefore even more mature learners can benefit from prompting instructions. In addition, older adolescents who have been trained in strategic behavior, transfer this training across tasks and over a period of time. However, in order for maximal transfer to occur, both in younger and older adolescents, it is necessary to provide the application of the training strategy in the instructions to the new and different task.

Fourth, metamemorial knowledge appears to be related to learning and memory. Older students know more about variables affecting memory than young students, and some data suggest that this knowledge is related to performance. Results of research in this area still are tentative, and further inquiry is necessary to identify the instructional conditions required for the effective use of metamemorial knowledge to enhance performance.

Finally, much exciting instructional research has been conducted on learning and remembering in school-aged learners. Also, recent formulations of educational frameworks for research on self-monitoring [55] and studying [56] behaviors suggest that the kinds of cognitive activities discussed in this chapter have direct implications for other, more general, behaviors.

REFERENCES

1. A. L. Brown, The Development of Memory: Knowing, Knowing about Knowing, and Knowing How to Know, *Advances in Child Development and Behavior, 10*, H. W. Reese (ed.), Academic Press, New York, pp. 104-152, 1975.
2. R. V. Kail and J. W. Hagen (eds.), *Perspectives on the Development of Memory and Cognition*, Erlbaum, Hillsdale, New Jersey, 1977.
3. P. A. Ornstein and M. J. Naus, Rehearsal Processes in Children's Memory, *Memory Development in Children*, P. A. Ornstein (ed.), Erlbaum, Hillsdale, New Jersey, pp. 69-99, 1978.
4. M. Pressley, Imagery and Children's Learning: Putting the Picture in Developmental Perspective, *Review of Educational Research, 47*:4, pp. 585-622, 1977.
5. M. Pressley, Elaboration and Memory Development, *Child Development, 53*: 2, pp. 296-309, 1982.
6. M. Pressley, B. E. Heisel, C. B. McCormick, and G. V. Nakamura, Memory Strategy Instruction with Children, *Verbal Processes in Children: Progress in Cognitive Development Research*, C. J. Brainerd and M. Pressley (eds.), Springer-Verlag, New York, pp. 125-159, 1982.
7. W. D. Rohwer, Jr., Elaboration and Learning in Childhood and Adolescence, *Advances in Child Development and Behavior, 8*, H. W. Reese (ed.), Academic Press, New York, pp. 1-57, 1973.

8. K. L. Higbee, Recent Research on Visual Mnemonics: Historical Roots and Educational Fruits, *Review of Educational Research*, 49:4, pp. 611-629, 1979.

9. J. R. Levin, The Mnemonic '80s: Keywords in the Classroom, *Educational Psychologist*, 16:2, pp. 65-82, 1981.

10. R. N. Greer, Spontaneous Elaboration of Paired Associates and Formal Operational Thinking: A Developmental Analysis, (doctoral dissertation, University of British Columbia, 1978), *Dissertation Abstracts International*, 39:9, pp. 5410A-5411A, 1979.

11. A. Paivio, *Imagery and Verbal Processes*, Erlbaum, Hillsdale, New Jersey, 1971.

12. H. W. Reese, Imagery and Associative Learning, *Perspectives on the Development of Memory and Cognition*, R. V. Kail, Jr., and J. W. Hagen (eds.), Erlbaum, Hillsdale, New Jersey, pp. 113-175, 1977.

13. J. D. Bransford, *Human Cognition*, Wadsworth, Belmont, California, 1979.

14. J. C. Yuille and M. Marschark, Imagery Effects on Memory: Theoretical Interpretations, *Imagery: Current Theory, Research and Application*, A. Sheikh (ed.), John Wiley and Sons, New York, pp. 131-155, 1982.

15. B. E. Moely, Organizational Factors in the Development of Memory, *Perspectives on the Development of Memory and Cognition*, R. V. Kail, Jr. and J. W. Hagen (eds.), Erlbaum, Hillsdale, New Jersey, pp. 203-236, 1977.

16. P. Wolff and J. R. Levin, The Role of Overt Activity in Children's Imagery Production, *Child Development*, 43:2, pp. 537-547, 1972.

17. J. C. Yuille and M. J. Catchpole, Associative Learning and Imagery Training in Children, *Journal of Experimental Child Psychology*, 16:3, pp. 403-412, 1973.

18. J. R. Levin, R. E. McCabe, and B. G. Bender, A Note on Imagery-inducing Motor Activity in Young Children, *Child Development*, 46:1, pp. 263-266, 1975.

19. M. Pressley and J. R. Levin, Task Parameters Affecting the Efficacy of a Visual Imagery Learning Strategy in Younger and Older Children, *Journal of Experimental Child Psychology*, 24:1, pp. 53-59, 1977.

20. J. Turnure, N. Buium, and M. Thurlow, The Effectiveness of Interrogatives for Promoting Verbal Elaboration Productivity in Young Children, *Child Development*, 47:3, pp. 851-855, 1976.

21. F. I. M. Craik and R. S. Lockhart, Levels of Processing: A Framework for Memory Research, *Journal of Verbal Learning and Verbal Behavior*, 11:6, pp. 671-684, 1972.

22. J. R. Levin and M. Pressley, A Test of the Developmental Imagery Hypothesis in Children's Associative Learning, *Journal of Educational Psychology*, 70:5, pp. 691-694, 1978.

23. J. R. Levin, *On Functions of Pictures in Prose*, theoretical paper No. 80, University of Wisconsin, Wisconsin Research and Development Center for Individualized Schooling, Madison, 1979.

24. E. Saltz and D. Dixon, Let's Pretend: The Role of Motoric Imagery in Memory for Sentences and Words, *Journal of Experimental Child Psychology*, 34:1, pp. 77-92, 1982.

25. W. D. Rohwer, Jr. and J. P. Bean, Sentence Effects and Noun-pair Learning: A Developmental Interaction during Adolescence, *Journal of Experimental Child Psychology*, 15:3, pp. 521-533, 1973.

26. R. N. Greer and N. S. Suzuki, *Development of Spontaneous Elaboration in Concrete and Abstract Noun Pair Learning*, paper presented at the annual meeting of the American Educational Research Association, San Francisco, April, 1976.

27. S. P. Kennedy and N. S. Suzuki, Spontaneous Elaboration in Mexican-American and Anglo-American High School Seniors, *American Educational Research Journal*, *14*:4, pp. 383-388, 1977.

28. W. D. Rohwer Jr., J. M. Raines, J. Eoff, and M. Wagner, The Development of Elaborative Propensity in Adolescence, *Journal of Experimental Child Psychology*, *23*:3, pp. 472-492, 1977.

29. J. J. Leung, N. S. Suzuki, and S. F. Foster, Imagery Values, Instructional Prompts, and Noun Recall, *Journal of Mental Imagery*, 7:2, pp. 87-90, 1983.

30. R. C. Atkinson, Mnemotechnics in Second-language Learning, *American Psychologist*, *30*:8, pp. 821-828, 1975.

31. M. Pressley and J. Dennis-Rounds, Transfer of a Mnemonic Keyword Strategy at Two Age Levels, *Journal of Educational Psychology*, *72*:4, pp. 575-582, 1980.

32. W. D. Rohwer, Jr., M. S. Ammon, N. S. Suzuki, and J. R. Levin, Population Differences and Learning Proficiency, *Journal of Educational Psychology*, *62*:1, pp. 1-14, 1971.

33. J. Guttman, J. R. Levin, and M. Pressley, Pictures, Partial Pictures, and Young Children's Oral Prose Learning, *Journal of Educational Psychology*, *69*:5, pp. 473-480, 1977.

34. W. D. Rohwer, Jr. and W. J. Harris, Media Effects on Prose Learning in Two Populations of Children, *Journal of Educational Psychology*, *67*:5, pp. 651-657, 1975.

35. M. D. Ruch and J. R. Levin, Pictorial Organization Versus Verbal Repetition of Children's Prose: Evidence for Processing Differences, *AV Communication Review*, *25*:3, pp. 269-280, 1977.

36. T. C. Dunham and J. R. Levin, Imagery Instructions and Young Children's Prose Learning: No Evidence of "Support," *Contemporary Educational Psychology*, *4*:2, pp. 107-113, 1979.

37. L. Hill, The Functions of Pictures and Repetitions in Children's Oral Prose Learning, unpublished master's thesis, University of British Columbia, 1982.

38. R. V. E. Grunau, Effects of Elaborative Prompt Condition and Developmental Level on the Performance of Addition Problems by Kindergarten Children, *Journal of Educational Psychology*, *70*:3, pp. 422-432, 1978.

39. E. M. Markman, Realizing that You Don't Understand: A Preliminary Investigation, *Child Development*, *48*:3, pp. 986-992, 1977.

40. M. Pressley and J. R. Levin, Developmental Differences in Subjects' Associative Learning Strategies and Performance: Assessing a Hypothesis, *Journal of Experimental Child Psychology*, *24*:3, pp. 431-439, 1977.

41. W. D. Rohwer, Jr. and J. Litrownik, Age and Individual Differences in the Learning of a Memorization Procedure, *Journal of Educational Psychology*, *75*:6, pp. 799-810, 1983.

42. J. H. Flavell, First Discussant's Comments: What Is Memory Development the Development Of?, *Human Development*, *14*, pp. 272-278, 1971.

43. J. H. Flavell, Cognitive Monitoring, *Children's Oral Communication Skills*, W. P. Dickson (ed.), Academic Press, New York, pp. 35-60, 1981.

44. J. H. Flavell and H. M. Wellman, Metamemory, *Perspectives on the Development of Memory and Cognition*, R. V. Kail, Jr. and J. W. Hagen (eds.), Erlbaum, Hillsdale, New Jersey, pp. 1-33, 1977.

45. J. C. Campione and A. L. Brown, Memory and Metamemory Development in Educable Retarded Children, *Perspectives on the Development of Memory and Cognition*, R. V. Kail, Jr. and J. W. Hagen (eds.), Erlbaum, Hillsdale, New Jersey, pp. 367-406, 1977.

46. J. C. Cavanaugh and J. G. Borkowski, Searching for Metamemory–Memory Connections: A Developmental Study, *Developmental Psychology*, *16*:5, pp. 441-453, 1980.

47. J. C. Cavanaugh and M. Perlmutter, Metamemory: A Criticial Examination, *Child Development*, *53*:1, pp. 11-28, 1982.

48. E. D. Moynahan, Assessment and Selection of Paired Associate Strategies: A Developmental Study, *Journal of Experimental Child Psychology*, *26*:2, pp. 257-266, 1978.

49. P. E. Worden and L. J. Sladewski-Awig, Children's Awareness of Memorability, *Journal of Educational Psychology*, *74*:3, pp. 341-350, 1982.

50. D. F. Bjorklund and B. R. Zeman, Children's Organization and Metamemory Awareness in Their Recall of Familiar Information, *Child Development*, *53*:3, pp. 799-810, 1982.

51. R. A. Owings, G. A. Peterson, J. D. Bransford, C. C. Morris, and B. S. Stein, Spontaneous Monitoring and Regulation of Learning: A Comparison of Successful and Less Successful Fifth Graders, *Journal of Educational Psychology*, *72*:2, pp. 250-256, 1980.

52. M. G. Lodico, E. S. Ghatala, J. R. Levin, M. Pressley, and J. A. Bell, The Effects of Strategy-monitoring Training on Children's Selection of Effective Memory Strategies, *Journal of Experimental Child Psychology*, *35*:2, pp. 263-277, 1983.

53. H. S. Waters, Memory Development in Adolescence: Relationships between Metamemory, Strategy Use, and Performance, *Journal of Experimental Child Psychology*, *33*:2, pp. 183-195, 1982.

54. N. S. Suzuki, Semantic Elaboration and Memory Knowledge, unpublished manuscript, University of British Columbia, 1983.

55. A. L. Brown, J. C. Campione, and J. D. Day, Learning to Learn: On Training Students to Learn from Texts, *Educational Researcher*, *10*:2, pp. 14-21, 1981.

56. W. D. Rohwer, Jr., An Invitation to a Developmental Psychology of Studying, *Advances in Applied Developmental Psychology*, *1*, F. J. Morrison, C. A. Lord and D. P. Keating (eds.), Academic Press, New York, in press.

CHAPTER 9
Imagery Research with Adults: Implications for Education
KATHRYN LUTZ ALESANDRINI

INTRODUCTION

Internal visualization can be thought of as a basic cognitive process, a mental skill, or a learning strategy [1]. As a basic cognitive process, internal visualization will be referred to as mental imagery. Mental imagery presumably can be elicited in a learner by various instructional techniques, such as presenting the learner with pictures or concrete language. One purpose of this review is to summarize the research on imagery-eliciting strategies for adults. As a mental skill, internal visualization may refer to a person's ability to create and control mental images [2, 3]. This review deals with individual differences in mental imagery only as those differences affect the impact of imagery-eliciting strategies on learning. Internal visualization as a learning strategy refers to the application of mental imagery to a particular learning task. Another purpose of this chapter is to review the research findings on the success of directing or training adult learners to use learning strategies involving mental imagery. The term imagery will be used to refer to the broad range of visualization, including that which is internal (mental imagery) and that which is external (pictures, graphs, concrete words, visual analogies, etc.). Research on pictures and adult learning has been summarized previously [4, 5].

Empirically based conclusions will be drawn about the usefulness of imagery in facilitating adult learning. It should be noted that research results are not the only source of information about imagery and its effectiveness. Much knowledge in the field comes from the intuitions, skills, and knowledge of experts, such as educators, instructional designers, and graphic artists. Some reviewers have combined knowledge from both researchers and practitioners in summarizing what is known about various aspects of imagery [6, 7, 8]. This review and discussion will be restricted to knowledge that is empirically based, except when dealing with areas where little or no research has been conducted.

Categories of Imagery in Education

The research findings and discussion on imagery are organized according to three broad categories of pictures, including representational, analogical, and abstract. These categories also have been termed realistic, analogical, and logical (or arbitrary) (see Figure 1) [9, 10]. Previous reviewers of imagery in education have dealt primarily with only the first category of imagery—that is, mental images or external visuals that are isomorphic with the objects or concepts that they represent [4, 11, 12]. Yet there is a growing body of research on the educational effects of analogical imagery and abstract imagery, and those findings should be considered in an integrative review on imagery. This chapter will review research on all three types of imagery and discuss how each type may play a crucial, yet different, role in the learning process. The chapter emphasizes imagery's effect on adult meaningful learning, such as concept learning, learning from prose materials, and learning from expository text. The review does not cover imagery strategies that serve only to control attention, such as visual cueing and prompting techniques [13]. The primary focus is on imagery strategies that effectively communicate information and facilitate meaningful learning in adults.

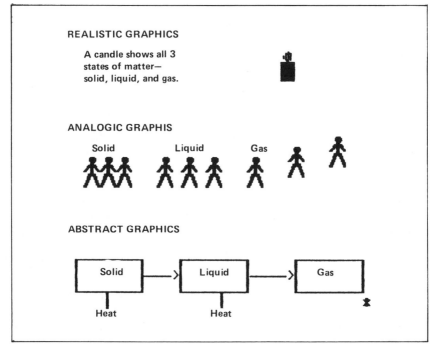

Figure 1. Three types of images used to represent the topic "states of matter" including representational, analogical, and abstract.

REPRESENTATIONAL IMAGERY

Definition and Limitations

The representational image is one that shares a physical resemblance with the thing or concept that the image stands for. Use of representational images is supported by the research and theory on the potency of visual memory [14] and the importance of providing examples when teaching concepts [15, 16]. Some researchers, such as Dwyer, have investigated the variable of realism in representational pictures [17]. Since this category also has been termed realistic [10], some confusion has resulted. Dwyer uses the term "realism" to refer to a continuous variable that reflects the amount of realistic detail in a picture. However, Knowlton uses the term "realistic" to denote a category rather than a continuum. The amount of realistic detail is recognized here as a potentially important variable in visuals, but the variable of realism is treated as distinct and separate from the category of representational imagery. Some representational images are highly realistic, such as models and colored photographs; whereas, simple line drawings and concept-related graphic symbols [18] are simplified representation images.

Representing Tangible Objects. Salomon [19] has raised an important theoretical question about the objectivity versus the subjectivity of representing objects. Is there really a fixed objective standard of reality against which representations can be compared? An example is that a representational image for the concept of "home" would be vastly different for Eskimos, early native American tribes, and modern urban dwellers. Much research on cognitive processes indicates that the perception of meaning is subjective rather than objective. Fortunately, certain norms do exist for creating meaning from visuals among learners sharing a common culture. Salomon's concern does serve to emphasize the importance of the learner's subjective interpretation of the meaning of a visual. Some studies have compared viewers' subjective perceptions of meaning with the designer's intended meaning of a visual and have discovered significant discrepancies [20, 21]. Educators are, therefore, somewhat limited in providing objective, external images that may be termed representational, because representations are subjective. One response to this limitation is to rely on cultural and social norms to devise representational images that have the intended impact on the learner [22, 23].

Representing Intangibles. Simple, tangible objects or concepts can be represented directly. However, what does it mean to represent a concept that has no tangible existence in the phenomenological realm? Gropper has pointed out that although abstract principles cannot be directly portrayed, they may be indirectly portrayed by showing any effects, results, instances, or examples [9]. It may be impossible to directly portray the wind, for example, but its effect on the movement of objects, such as trees and leaves, can be visualized. Similarly, an abstract concept such as generosity may be visually portrayed by showing a generous person donating to a worthy cause. Another approach to illustrating abstract concepts representationally is to portray a concrete associate of the concept [24]. An example is to show the Statue of Liberty to represent "freedom." Others have made up pseudoexamples that portray what the designer thinks the concept might look like if it were tangible [25]. Research has yet to address the question of how learning is affected by images that differ in the degree to which they are isomorphic with the referent. Whitehead has raised the concern of the "fallacy of misplaced concreteness" [26], but research has not fully explored whether or not it is harmful to concretize abstract concepts and ideas.

External Representational Pictures

Photos and Drawings. Most studies on external imagery have tested the effect of supplementing verbal material with representational pictures. In one study, college students who read a passage about revolutions with supplemental pictures remembered more than learners in a read-only control condition [27]. However, the strategy of instructing learners to form internal mental imagery appeared to be more effective than the picture strategy. A second study suggested a similar pattern of results with high-school seniors, but no significant effects were observed. Perhaps adult readers ignore supplemental pictures when the passage is easily comprehended.

Supplemental pictures, however, do appear to help adults learn new concepts from expository text. Dwyer and his associates have conducted over 100 studies involving more than 40,000 adult learners since 1965 to investigate the effects of representational pictures that varied in the amount of detail, from highly detailed colored photos to simple line drawings [17, 28]. The results of those studies will be generally summarized here. Dwyer provides descriptions and discussion of individual studies [17]. The results of that research effort generally have shown that pictures facilitate adult learning. Based on the results, Dwyer concluded that when visuals are used to supplement verbal information with which the learner is already familiar, no facilitation will occur. On the other hand, if the material to be learned is too complex, presenting a representational visual may not facilitate learning either. For certain learning outcomes, visual presentation can be facilitative. For example, a representational visual can aid learning if the learning outcome involves requiring the learner to draw or otherwise identify location and interrelations among parts, specific patterns or functions, or content relationships.

Research findings from other studies are similar to Dwyer's results. A study using science materials in biology found that supplemental line drawings helped high-school students learn new concepts [29]. Simple line drawings presented via computer-assisted instruction also facilitated science learning by college students: Students in the line drawings condition performed better than those in a read-only control condition [30] but no better than learners' who used the verbal strategy of answering inserted questions [31]. Line drawings also helped high-school students of several developmental stages learn an abstract concept in chemistry [25]. Since the concept was abstract and had no perceptible instances, the authors devised line drawings to provide what they termed pseudo-examples. Similar results were found when portraying an abstract concept in mathematics with drawings. A visual treatment of the geometric topic of symmetry facilitated learning, especially for learners with greater visualization ability [32]. It may be difficult to devise representational visuals for certain topics but this type of imagery can facilitate adult learning.

Several other studies considered the role of individual differences in determining the effects of representational visuals on learning. In one study, young adults saw abstract diagrams in biology that either contained only abstract visual elements or contained representational visuals in the form of line drawings [33]. Learners with low verbal ability scored higher on the posttest after they had seen the diagram containing the line drawings. However, in another study with young adults, no interaction was found between presentation of representational visuals and verbal ability of the learner [34].

Models and Manipulatives. Several researchers have investigated the effects of concrete models or manipulatives on learning. In one study, learner construction of concrete models facilitated learning for high-school students who were identified as formal-operational thinkers [35]. Learners in the experimental groups constructed models to represent important topics, such as the combining of hydrogen and oxygen molecules to form water. Manipulating models also helped other high-school chemistry students of several cognitive stages of development [36], as well as college learners studying high-level concepts in chemistry [37]. The act of manipulation appears to be important: One study found that students who were allowed to manipulate models throughout the school year exhibited greater achievement than students who watched their teachers manipulate the models [38]. One problem with the studies on model manipulation is that they are evaluations rather than tightly controlled research comparisons. Also, most of these studies used classes as the unit for treatment group assignment but used individual learners as the unit of analysis in assessing the effects.

Effects of Realistic Detail. One issue concerning representational pictures in learning has been whether their effectiveness is influenced by the amount of realistic detail they contain. Dwyer attempted to address this question by comparing visuals of the human heart that differed in the amount of realistic detail—the visuals ranged from simple line drawings in black and white to color photographs [17]. Several studies focused directly on the question of the effects of varying degrees of realistic detail in the visuals. Results of those studies showed that the more detailed visuals (i.e., the shaded drawings and colored photographs) were least effective in supplementing verbal instruction, adding no facilitation beyond the verbal treatment alone. Dwyer concluded that simple line drawings are most helpful to learners, while overly detailed visuals, such as photographs, do not aid learning. However, the effects depend on the objectives to be achieved. Detailed visuals, such as photographs, may be interesting to view and provide the learner with an accurate portrayal of reality, but they may have limited instructional potential unless the learner is already familiar with the content or is adept at interpreting visual information. Research with other materials has confirmed that younger learners prefer viewing visuals that contain more detail [39, 40]. The variable of color, in particular, adds to the realistic detail of a picture and elicits more attention, although it sometimes distracts attention from more relevant information [41, 42]. Several studies supported Dwyer's findings directly by showing that the addition of detail to simple line drawings did not facilitate learning [43, 44].

Learner-Drawn Pictures. None of the studies investigating learner-drawn pictures reported whether or not the pictures were representational. However, it seems unlikely that learners would produce analogical or abstract drawings when told to illustrate passage contents. Support for this assumption comes from research on learner-illustrated concepts. When asked to draw concepts that were either concrete or abstract (i.e., above or below concreteness ratings of 3.50 [45]), college learners drew concrete representations even for highly abstract concepts [24]. The learners drew representational images for 96 percent of the more concrete concepts and for 86 percent of the more abstract concepts. According to the study's author, learners tended to illustrate the highly abstract concepts by drawing an associate of the referent of the concept; for example, for "disease," they drew a box of pills or a thermometer.

Research indicates that adult learners may benefit from drawing their own pictures. In one study, college students who had to illustrate prose passages performed better on a criterion test than a control group and also performed as well as students who answered inserted questions [46]. However, learners in the drawing conditions spent more time than learners in the control group. Therefore, group differences could be attributable to time differences. In another study, college students remembered a prose passage better when they spent five minutes illustrating the passage after reading it [47]. Unfortunately, time was again a confounding factor, because control-group learners spent the five-minute intervals either drawing unrelated figures or alphabetizing the words in the passage rather than reviewing the content.

Several studies investigated the effects of drawing with time-on-task controlled. College students who were told to draw pictures to illustrate science concepts performed better on the posttest than learners who either wrote verbal paraphrases or repeatedly read the content [48]. Also in that study, some learners were told to be either analytic, by focusing on details, or holistic, by relating specifics to more inclusive concepts. See Figure 2a for an example of a

Figure 2. Learner-drawn pictures are either: 1) analytic, by focusing on details, or 2) synthetic, by relating details to the bigger picture.

drawing that focused on the specific concept and Figure 2b for one that related the concept to the bigger picture. The study revealed weak effects favoring the drawing strategy for all learners and the holistic strategy for females only. A related study investigated a learner-manipulated visual strategy rather than a drawing strategy [30]. In that study, college learners either reread the lesson content or manipulated graphics that were designed to relate specific concepts to the bigger picture. Rearranging and manipulating the graphic representation of the content facilitated performance on a picture recognition test but not on a verbal, multiple-choice test. Finally, illustrating passage content does not always facilitate learning of the material. Compared to a group using a verbal learning strategy (paraphrasing), learners who illustrated concepts in passages from a number of subject areas did not perform as well [49]. Taken together, the studies on learner-drawn pictures offer weak support favoring this imagery-eliciting strategy.

Concreteness of Verbal Material

Another type of imagery strategy that has been investigated is concreteness or "imagery value" of verbal material—that is, the ease with which a word elicits a mental image. Imagery values for hundreds of words have been established by having readers rate how well a word arouses sensory images. These ratings are available for nouns [45] and for verbs [50]. Although a number of studies have investigated various aspects of concreteness effects on cognition, only a few have investigated the effects of concreteness on meaningful learning.

Studies show that concreteness correlates highly with recall for both experimenter-constructed sentences [51] and for published expository text segments [52]. Several researchers manipulated concreteness by constructing passages which varied on the basis of imagery values. Concrete versions of prose passages were better remembered than otherwise equivalent, abstract passages [53, 54]. The relevance of these studies to meaningful learning is limited, however, because the materials were contrived by the experimenters.

A recent study provides more convincing evidence that concreteness facilitates meaningful learning [49]. The materials used in the study were passages from textbooks in several fields. Independent ratings indicated that the expository passages were equivalent in terms of comprehensibility but differed on the concrete-abstract dimension. The concrete passages were comprehended better than the abstract passages according to the short-answer tests; but concreteness did not affect scores on verbal, multiple-choice tests. The results of the studies discussed here have sufficient consistency to permit the conclusion that concreteness is an instructional strategy that can facilitate meaningful learning.

Imagery Instructions

Learning also can be facilitated by using mental imagery to visualize the material being studied. Imagery instructions have facilitated memory for easy material, such as sentences and narratives [27, 55, 56]. Imagery instructions *per se* appeared to have no effect on memory in one study, but closer examination revealed that mental imagery at least was correlated with learning [57] : Students who reported that they learned the text passage by using "mental pictures" remembered more than students who reported not using mental imagery. Another study showed no overall benefit from imagery instructions during a limited time period [58]. However, adults who received the imagery instructions remembered more from the first half of the passage than did control subjects, suggesting that the imagery strategy was beneficial but required more time. The authors, however, felt that imagery should not be considered a useful strategy if it produces no learning gains per unit time.

Directing adults to use mental imagery while learning new concepts may not facilitate their learning. In several studies, college learners were directed to mentally imagine passage contents on science topics, but the directions had no effect on learning [59, 60]. Mental-imagery instructions also failed to facilitate the solving of insight problems [61]. Learners who had been given more extensive training in the use of an imagery strategy for studying expository material, performed better on a delayed-retention test, although not on an immediate test as compared to a control group [62]. However, they did not differ from a group who had used a paraphrasing strategy. The failure of mental-imagery instructions to aid new-concept learning in some cases may be due to learners' inability to create realistic imagery for concepts that have not been adequately introduced.

Mental imagery has been used successfully to facilitate adult performance in other areas than learning new information. Imagery has been used to enhance or correct performance in sports [63], to facilitate artistic expression or appreciation [64], and as a tool for therapeutic intervention in psychotherapy [65], to name only a few applications. The research evidence from a number of areas indicates that mental imagery can have a major influence on adult learning and performance. The question is no longer whether or not mental imagery facilitates learning but rather how it can best be used to produce the optimum facilitation.

Taken together, the studies on representational imagery indicate that this strategy can be effective in facilitating adult learning. External strategies, such as pictures and concrete language, have aided recall, although not necessarily for material that is highly abstract or complex. Perhaps, the problem lies with educators and learners who do not know how to use visuals that indirectly yet effectively represent abstract concepts. Picture drawing and mental imagery, which require more learner elaboration than external strategies, also can be successful strategies. Training programs have achieved some success in helping learners apply mental imagery and drawing strategies. Again, these strategies have not always proved useful in learning new concepts or abstract material. Perhaps more effective training for applying mental imagery and drawing strategies to the learning of abstract content could be devised. Learners also may benefit from instruction on how to select the most appropriate type of imagery given certain materials and task requirements. Analogical or abstract imagery may be more appropriate under certain learning conditions.

ANALOGICAL IMAGERY

An analogical image represents an object or concept by presenting something else and implying a similarity. If this type of image is to be successful, the learner must recognize or be able to comprehend the object used as the analogy. Analogical images might be especially useful when the concept or topic to be communicated is abstract or has no tangible existence so that direct portrayal is difficult. An example of an analogical image used in computer science is a recursive drawing by Escher to represent the concept of "loop" in a program.

According to learning theorists, new information will be better remembered if the learner relates it to prior knowledge [66, 67]. Therefore, to facilitate learning, analogical images should help the learner interpret new information in light of prior knowledge.

Analogies and Learning

Research evidence indicates that concrete analogies can be very helpful in adult learning. Several studies tested the learner's ability to transfer information gained from a concrete analogy to understanding subsequent abstract information. In an initial study, college students learned about two topics (i.e., heat flow and electrical conductivity) that are more understandable if the student has a basic knowledge of the internal structure of metals [68]. The passages were presented in either a concrete or an abstract style, and half contained physical analogies (presented verbally) to explain portions of the content. For example, the analogy for metallic crystalline structure was a tinker toy model with sticks between the discs to present chemical bonds between the molecules of a metal. Learners who read the concrete passages with analogies remembered more of the new information than those who had read the abstract passages with no analogies. Furthermore, learners who read an initial concrete passage with relevant analogies, learned more from a subsequent abstract passage, presumably due to exposure to the helpful analogies in the first passage. One problem with the study is that the concrete style of the passage was confounded with the inclusion of concrete analogies. To provide a better test of the use of analogies, another study was conducted with college learners who again had to read two passages [69]. In all conditions, the second passage was abstract, and the study was testing the facilitative transfer effects of the first passage that contained either physical analogies, concrete style of writing, or analogies with accompanying illustrations. In the control condition, both the initial and the subsequent passage were abstract. The results again confirmed the facilitative effects of physical analogies on learning, but no differential effects were observed among the various imagery-eliciting conditions of the first passage.

Analogies also have been used successfully in other subject areas. Adult non-programmers were given instruction in programming that either used a diagram model of a computer expressed in familiar terms or contained no such model [70]. The diagram used familiar objects as analogies for computer components; for example, "input" was related to a ticket window and "output" was represented by a pad of message paper. Learners who saw the analogical diagram were better at interpreting programs, while those who did not see the model were better at generating programs. In two subsequent studies, the analogy was particularly helpful in facilitating performance of low-ability learners.

In a related series of studies, adult nonprogrammers used the analogy model to explain, in their own words, how the new information related to the analogy [71]. Performance was facilitated when learners read concrete analogies and also when they had to relate the new information to these familiar analogies, relative to a read-only control or a group that saw the analogical model after instruction.

Some evidence suggests that it may not be necessary for learners to be familiar with the analogy if an easily comprehended picture of the analogical object is presented. In one study, college students read "The Mat Maker" chapter from Melville's *Moby Dick* under one of three conditions: 1) read-only control with no accompanying picture, 2) irrelevant picture in which the passage was accompanied by a nonanalogical but otherwise equivalent picture or 3) analogical picture in which the learners saw a picture and read a verbal description of a sword-mat loom [72]. In the analogical condition, the parts of the loom were compared to the abstract concepts in the chapter. For example, warp and woof were compared to necessity and free will; the sword was related to the concept of chance, etc. Results indicate that learners in the analogical-image condition made fewer errors in identifying assertions based on the text.

Several studies were unsuccessful in manipulating analogy generation in adult learners. One study directed learners to write verbal analogies to science concepts after studying a twenty-minute lesson presented via computer, but the strategy did not aid learning [60]. A visual inspection of the analogies created by the learners in that study reveals that they tended to write paraphrases of the content rather than analogies. Training in analogy generation probably requires a good deal of time and practice, but both studies used simple, short directions. Learning-strategy training involving analogy generation might facilitate learning. One learning-strategy training program for students in college physics, which emphasized comparing and contrasting new information with prior knowledge, resulted in significant learning gains [73]. Although the program did not train the students in analogical imagery *per se*, it is noteworthy because its success suggests that training learners to create analogies is feasible.

Analogies and Problem Solving

Another series of studies investigated the effects on creative problem solving of giving a relevant analogy either verbally via a story or visually via an abstract diagram [74, 75]. One problem used in the studies was the classic "radiation problem" in which a tumor must be destroyed by radiation of high intensity; yet, low-intensity rays must be used to avoid hurting healthy tissue. Reading a story that contained an analogous solution to the problem facilitated solution, relative to reading a control story containing no relevant analogy: The solution rates were 71 percent for the analogical group versus 20 percent for the control groups. One analogous story used was "The General," describing how a successful military attack was accomplished via dispersion of troops in order to attack from numerous sides. An analogous abstract diagram was helpful but only when learners were given an explicit hint that the diagram should be helpful in solving the problem (7% vs. 60% solution rates before and after the hint, respectively). Interestingly, results showed that after reading an analogous story, a learner received no additional benefit from being specifically told the underlying abstract principle, except when the principle was portrayed via an abstract picture. In fact, the most effective means for facilitating analogical transfer in the series of studies was to give the learner two analogical stories, an abstract picture representing the principle needed for solution, and a hint to apply the information gained in the stories and picture. Learners in that treatment condition did nine times better in problem solution than the base-line solution rate for learners trying to solve the problem with no facilitation. The authors point out that the amount of facilitation is close to the maximum amount that any manipulation could achieve.

In summary, a small number of studies on analogical imagery indicates that this type of imagery can be beneficial to learning when it is presented to the learner or when the learner is allowed to manipulate or elaborate upon the analogy provided. However, the effect of using analogical imagery as a learner-generated strategy remains a question for future research.

ABSTRACT IMAGERY

Another category of images can be termed abstract, because these highly schematized visuals do not look like the things they represent. Knowlton [10] termed abstract images as "logical," not isomorphic with elements portrayed but isomorphic with the "pattern and/or order of connection" of the represented state of affairs. Based on that definition, abstract images include graphs, flowcharts, networks, maps, tree diagrams, and other schematized charts and diagrams.

Graphic Organizers

Graphic organizers serve as a way to structure the main points or concepts in textual material. This type of abstract image presumably helps communicate the hierarchical organization of the content. Most approaches to graphic organizers are based on the semantic network models of memory [76, 77]. Graphic organization schemes for representing text information have taken a variety of specific forms and include structured overviews, networks, structural outlines, hierarchical mapping, and tree diagrams, to name a few.

Structured Overviews and Hierarchies. One main type of graphic organizer is the structured overview, which graphically presents the key vocabulary from a new passage, showing the relationships between concepts [78]. A meta-analysis of studies investigating structured overviews found that graphic organizers do tend to facilitate learning [79, 80]. In four of the studies, learners constructed their own graphic organizers, and this resulted in substantial learning gains. The reviewers concluded that learners probably should construct their own organizers, and that graphic organizers may be most suitable for high-ability learners and expository texts. Several more recent studies have confirmed earlier results by showing that structured overviews facilitate immediate and delayed recall [81], as well as lower- and upper-level comprehension [82].

Several other types of graphic organizers have been used to facilitate adult learning. In one study, college learners saw a structural outline consisting of a hierarchical word tree with four levels of specificity, proceeding from the most general to the most specific concepts [83]. Learners who saw the structural outline before reading a fifteen-paragraph passage on the topic of minerals from an encyclopedia, remembered more specific facts but not general facts from the passage than did learners who saw no organizer. Another approach used has been termed conceptual hierarchy, where each node of the hierarchy represents one or more features that lower-level nodes have in common [84]. In several studies, showing a diagram of the conceptual hierarchy of the topic facilitated adult learning [85, 86].

Learner-generated Networks and Maps. A number of studies have investigated the effects of training learners to generate their own graphic organizers for textual material. One approach to generating graphic organizers has been termed networking by Dansereau [62]. The networking strategy is a hierarchical mapping technique that helps the learner organize passage information into node-link diagrams: The nodes contain paraphrases and images of the key information and the links indicate their interrelationships. Learners who received five and one-half hours of training in using the networking strategy recalled more main points from a 3000-word passage based on a geology textbook than did learners not trained in networking [87]. The two groups did not differ, however, on the basis of number of details recalled from the passage. The networking strategy proved to be more helpful to lower achievers. In another study, the same networking technique was tested in the context of a semester-long learning-strategy training course [88]. In that study, college students applied various learning strategies to a variety of subject areas. At midcourse, one group was given special training in networking, while two other groups received training in other strategies, such as paraphrasing and imagery generation. The group which had received the training in networking increased its advantage relative to the group of students, who had received no special additional training, while groups trained in other strategies at midcourse did not show any comparative benefits over control-group students.

Mapping is another way for learners to graphically organize text. It involves graphically representing important relationships in the text, such as comparing and contrasting concepts. After twelve hours of training in the use of a mapping strategy, young adults recalled more idea units from an expository text, especially ideas that had been included in the maps [89]. In another study with young adults, low achievers were trained in the use of several study strategies, including the creation of dimensional-tabular structures to represent comparisons and contrasts in the text [90]. Learners who were taught how to use the mapping strategy performed better than those in the control condition. However, due to the fact that the training involved several study techniques, the results cannot be attributed to the use of graphic organizers specifically.

A related technique called flowcharting also has been shown to facilitate learning. Flowcharting is similar to networking and mapping in that the nodes consist of idea units and propositions, while the links represent the connection of nodes to each other or to the entire structure of the passage. The difference is that the flowcharting technique emphasizes the use of conjunctions in detecting text structure. In several studies, college students who were trained in the flow-charting technique showed significant improvements in reading comprehension. The improvement was shown for both skilled and less skilled readers [91].

How important is it that learners generate their own graphic organizer rather than merely view one that has been provided to them? College learners who created a maplike representation of passage contents about a fictitious African tribe learned more than learners who only read the passage [92]. Then, using a composite graphic based on those generated in the first study, a second study was conducted with three conditions; learners either viewed the graphic organizer, added labels to it, or read the passage without the accompanying graphic. Only learners who labeled the maplike graphic remembered more passage contents than the read-only control group. The results suggest that a graphic organizer will not be very helpful unless the learners generate it themselves or manipulate it in some way.

Graphic Organizers and Mental Imagery. The graphic-organizer studies reviewed so far have dealt with abstract images that are external to the learner. There is some evidence that graphic organizers can also facilitate learning when they are mental images. In one study, learners were trained to generate a mental image of a tree structure by analyzing prose into sets of superordinate-subordinate idea units, transforming the idea units into mental images, and embedding those images in a loci mnemonic for purposes of free or serial recall [93]. Low-achieving learners who used this mental tree diagram technique remembered twice as much information as those who used traditional learning strategies, such as notetaking.

The strategy of graphic organizers, whether applied as external or internal imagery, appears to be effective in facilitating learning.

Graphs, Charts, and Diagrams

Graphs. Few recent studies have investigated the effectiveness of graphic presentation to communicate numerical information. Several reviews summarize what is known about the effective use of graphs based on both research and practice [7, 94]. One recent textbook provides numerous examples of graphs and also reviews the state of the art in the design of graphs [95]. A useful alphabetical listing of graph formats with examples is given by Macdonald-Ross [94]. In general, reviewers have concluded that graphs are more effective than tables or text for communicating numerical information. The reviews also provide more specific findings in regard to design features and the relative effectiveness of the various graph formats.

Diagrams. There is also a lack of research on the effects of charts and diagrams on adult learning. The series of studies by Gick and Holyoak discussed earlier investigated the use of an abstract diagram [75]. They found that showing learners the abstract diagram described earlier helped them solve a problem whose solution could be abstractly represented by the diagram. Interestingly, however, the diagram was facilitative only when learners were specifically instructed to use it in arriving at a solution.

The effects of showing adult learners charts or diagrams may vary with the learner's ability. In one study, learners of low verbal ability learned more from a flow diagram that contained realistic visuals (line drawings), while high-ability learners did equally well with the abstract flow diagram and the more concrete version of the diagram containing line drawings [33]. In another study with young adults, learners with high verbal ability performed better on an identification task when critical attributes in the visual material were highlighted via arrows, and they also made fewer errors when a two-dimensional chart was shown [96].

Flowcharts. There has been some research on the use of flowcharts and other schematized visuals to represent directions and other algorithmic information. Most of the studies in this area have focused on how flowcharts facilitate the learner's speed in performing the visually described procedures and also how they affect the number of errors made. Several studies have shown that directions communicated by flowcharts were better understood than directions given in a prose format [97-99]. However, a more recent study found that flow-charts used to represent algorithmic information about lab procedures in a college chemistry course did not facilitate critical-thinking ability, time required to complete laboratory assignments, and final course grade [100].

Arbitrary Graphics and Mental Imagery. The effects of training learners to create abstract images mentally also has been investigated. In one study, learners had to read several passages that contained information about set relations, such as "exclusion," in which two sets share no common elements [72]. One group received a short training program in creating Venn diagrams to represent set relations asserted in sentences and short passages. This group was then instructed to form mental images of Venn diagrams while reading the experimental passages, one control group read the passages and took the post-test, while another group served as a test-only control. Results indicate that learners who created the abstract mental images did not differ from the controls on the basis of total amount of information recalled from the passages, but they did remember significantly more set relations than did the read-only group. These results suggest that abstract imagery did indeed facilitate recall of the information to which it was applied.

Taken together, the studies on the effects of abstract imagery indicate that learning and performance can be facilitated by this type of imagery. Gick and Holyoak's studies suggest that an abstract diagram representing essential information can be as helpful as an analogy. As applied to learning new information, abstract imagery may serve to portray the logical essence of new concepts, thereby facilitating learning.

IMPLICATIONS FOR EDUCATION

One Textbook's Use of Imagery

A recent college-level textbook in data processing has been touted for its heavy reliance on colorful photographs and visuals [101]. An analysis of the external images (also called visuals) used in the text was conducted for purposes of illustrating and discussing the role of the various types of imagery reviewed in this chapter. A count of the visuals used in the book was conducted, excluding completely verbal or numeric "figures." In the 472-page book, there are 316 external images, more than three images for every five pages. Nearly two-thirds of the visuals are representational images (212 out of 316). Most of those are photographs (177). The remaining visuals are abstract images (i.e., graphs, flowcharts, schematic diagrams, etc.). The book contains no analogical images. A lack of analogical images also has been observed in science textbooks [102] and computer-based instruction lessons in a variety of topic areas [103]. Although no systematic attempt was made to determine the use of verbal analogies in the book, it was noted that some key concepts are introduced by abstract images or representational images rather than by analogical images. One notable example is the concept of data input, processing, and output. An abstract image in the form of a flow diagram introduces the topic. No verbal or visual analogies to familiar concepts are provided. Then representational line drawings of an input device, processing unit, and output device are given along with verbal explanations in the text. Finally, colored photographs of actual input, processing, and output devices are shown. Contrast this approach with Mayer's use of visual and verbal analogies to teach the same information.

Recommendations for Using Imagery in Education

The results of the studies discussed in this chapter suggest that analogical and abstract imagery deserve much more attention by both practitioners and researchers because these types of imagery may play an important role in instruction. A small but convincing core of studies has demonstrated that both analogical and abstract imagery can facilitate learning. With training, learners may be able to generate their own imagery to represent information in the most helpful way. More attention should also be given to representing complex and abstract topics pictorially. There are several ways to indirectly represent complex material, and research on the value of portraying complex topics representationally is encouraging. Based on the studies discussed here, it is recommended that imagery play the following role in teaching or learning new information: 1) Begin with analogical imagery to relate new information to prior knowledge; 2) follow with abstract imagery to convey the essence of the new information and distinguish it from the analogous information; and 3) conclude with representational imagery that serves to further define and distinguish the new information.

REFERENCES

1. W. Winn, Visualization in Learning and Instruction: A Cognitive Approach, *Educational Communications and Technology, 30*, pp. 3-25, 1982.
2. D. F. Marks, Mental Imagery and Consciousness: A Theoretical Review, in *Imagery: Current Theory, Research, and Application*, A. A. Sheikh (ed.), Wiley, New York, 1983.
3. P. W. Sheehan, R. Ashton, and K. White, Assessment of Mental Imagery, in *Imagery: Current Theory, Research, and Application*, A. A. Sheikh (ed.), Wiley, New York, 1983.
4. K. L. Alesandrini, Imagery and Meaningful Learning, *Journal of Mental Imagery, 6*, pp. 125-140, 1982.
5. K. A. Alesandrini, Pictures and Adult Learning, *Instructional Science, 13*, pp. 63-77, 1984.

6. K. L. Alesandrini and A. A. Sheikh, Research on Imagery: Implications for Advertising, in *Imagery: Current Theory, Research, and Application*, A. A. Sheikh (ed.), Wiley, New York, 1983.

7. M. Macdonald-Ross, Graphics in Text, in *Review of Research in Education* No. 5, L. S. Shulman (ed.), Peacock, Itasca, Illinois, 1977a.

8. P. Wright, Presenting Technical Information: A Survey of Research Findings, *Instructional Science, 6*, pp. 93-134, 1977.

9. G. L. Gropper, Why is a Picture Worth a Thousand Words? *AV Communication Review, 11*, pp. 75-79, 1963.

10. J. Knowlton, On the Definition of "Picture," *AV Communication Review, 14*, pp. 157-183, 1966.

11. J. R. Leven and A. M. Lesgold, On Pictures in Prose, *Educational Communication and Technology Journal, 26*, pp. 233-243, 1978.

12. W. H. Levie and R. Lentz, Effects of Text Illustrations: A Review of Research, *Educational Communications and Technology, 30*, pp. 195-232, 1982.

13. J. Hartley, S. Fraser, and P. Brunhill, A Selected Bibliography of Typographical Research Relevant to the Production of Instructional Materials, *AV Communication Review, 22*, pp. 181-190, 1974.

14. J. C. Yuille and M. Marschark, Imagery Effects on Memory: Theoretical Interpretations, in *Imagery: Current Theory, Research, and Application*, A. A. Sheikh (ed.), Wiley, New York, 1983.

15. H. Mandl, W. Schnotz, and S. Tergan, On the Function of Examples in Instructional Texts, paper presented at the annual meeting of the American Educational Research Association, New Orleans, April 1984.

16. R. D. Tennyson and O. C. Park, The Teaching of Concepts: A Review of Instructional Design Research Literature, *Review of Educational Research, 50*, pp. 55-70, 1980.

17. F. M. Dwyer, *Strategies for Improving Visual Learning*, Learning Services, State College Pennsylvania, 1978.

18. R. E. Wileman, *Exercises in Visual Thinking*, Hastings House, New York, 1980.

19. G. Salomon, *Communication and Education: An Interactional Approach*, Sage, Los Angeles, 1982.

20. M. C. Cahill, Interpretability of Graphic Symbols as a Function of Context and Experience Factors, *Journal of Applied Psychology, 60*, pp. 376-380, 1975.

21. S. Spaulding, Communication Potential of Pictorial Illustrations, *AV Communication Review, 4*, pp. 31-46, 1956.

22. J. Mangan, Cultural Conventions of Pictorial Representations: Iconic Literacy and Education, *Educational Communications and Technology, 26*, pp. 245-267, 1978.

23. R. Pettersen, Cultural Differences in the Perception of Image and Color in Pictures, *Educational Communications and Technology, 30*, pp. 43-53, 1982.

24. S. Jones, Stereotype in Pictograms of Abstract Concepts, *Ergonomics, 26*, pp. 605-611, 1983.

25. L. Cantu and J. Herron, Concrete and Formal Piagetian Stages and Science Concept Attainment, *Journal of Research in Science Teaching, 15*, pp. 135-143, 1978.

26. A. N. Whitehead, *Process and Reality: An Essay in Cosmology*, Macmillan, New York, 1929.

27. R. V. Rasco, R. D. Tennyson, and R. C. Boutwell, Imagery Instructions and Drawings in Learning Prose, *Journal of Educational Psychology, 67*, pp. 188-192, 1975.

28. F. M. Dwyer, *International Journal of Instructional Media, 10*, pp. 23-38, 1982-83.

29. W. G. Holliday, The Effects of Verbal and Adjunct Pictorial-verbal Information in Science Instruction, *Journal of Research in Science Teaching, 12*, pp. 77-83, 1975.

30. J. W. Rigney and K. A. Lutz, Effect of Graphic Analogies of Concepts in Chemistry on Learning and Attitude, *Journal of Educational Psychology, 68*, pp. 305-311, 1976.

31. K. L. Alesandrini and J. W. Rigney, Pictorial Practice and Review Strategies in Science Learning, *Journal of Research in Science Teaching, 18*, pp. 465-474, 1981.

32. V. J. DuRapau and L. R. Carry, Interaction of General Reasoning Ability and Processing Strategies in Geometry Instruction, paper presented at the meeting of the National Council of Teachers of Mathematics, Seattle, 1980.

33. W. G. Holliday, L. L. Brunner, and E. L. Donais, Differential Cognitive and Affective Responses to Flow Diagrams in Science, *Journal of Research in Science Teaching, 14*, pp. 129-138, 1977.

34. W. Winn, The Role of Diagrammatic Representation in Learning Sequences, Identification and Classification as a Function of Verbal and Spatial Ability, *Journal of Research in Science Teaching, 19*, pp. 79-89, 1982.

35. M. Goodstein and A. Howe, The Use of Concrete Methods in Secondary Chemistry Instruction, *Journal of Research in Science Teaching, 15*, pp. 261-366, 1978.

36. A. C. Howe and B. Durr, Using Concrete Materials and Peer Interaction to Enhance Learning in Chemistry, *Journal of Research in Science Teaching, 19*, pp. 225-232, 1982.

37. L. H. Talley, The Use of Three-dimensional Visualization as a Moderator in Higher Cognitive Learning Concepts in College Level Chemistry, *Journal of Research in Science Teaching, 10*, pp. 263-269, 1973.

38. D. Gabel and R. Sherwood, The Effect of Student Manipulation of Molecular Models on Chemistry Achievement According to Piagetian Level, *Journal of Research in Science Teaching, 17*, pp. 75-81, 1980.

39. B. Myatt and J. M. Carter, Picture Preferences of Children and Young Adults, *Educational Communications and Technology, 27*, pp, 45-53, 1979.

40. R. M. Travers and V. Alvarado, The Design of Pictures for Teaching Children in Elementary School, *AV Communication Review, 18*, pp. 47-64, 1970.

41. A. G. Chute, Analysis of the Instructional Functions of Color and Monochrome Cuing in Media Presentations, *Educational Communications and Technology, 27*, pp. 251-263, 1979.

42. D. J. Reid and G. J. A. Miller, Pupils' Perceptions of Biological Pictures and Its Implications for Readability Studies of Biology Textbooks, *Journal of Biological Education, 14*, pp. 59-69, 1980.

43. D. A. Gorman, Effects of Varying Pictorial Detail and Presentation Strategy on Concept Formation, *AV Communication Review, 21*, pp. 337-350, 1973.

44. W. R. Borg and C. F. Schuller, Detail and Background in Audiovisual Lessons and Their Effect on Learners, *Educational Communications and Technology, 27*, pp. 31-38, 1979.

45. A. Paivio, J. C. Yuille, and S. A. Madigan, Concreteness, Imagery, and Meaningfulness Values for 925 Nouns, *Journal of Experimental Psychology Monograph, 76*:1 (pt. 2), pp. 1-25, 1968.

46. J. Snowman and D. J. Cunningham, A Comparison of Pictorial and Written Adjunct Aids in Learning from Text, *Journal of Educational Psychology, 67*, pp. 307-311, 1975.

47. A. M. Lesgold, J. R. Levin, J. Shimron, and J. Guttman, Pictures and Young Children's Learning from Oral Prose, *Journal of Educational Psychology, 67*, pp. 636-642, 1975.

48. K. L. Alesandrini, Pictorial-verbal and Analytic-holistic Learning Strategies in Science Learning, *Journal of Educational Psychology, 73*, pp. 358–368, 1981.

49. W. C. Tirre, L. Manelis, and K. L. Leicht, The Effects of Imaginal and Verbal Strategies on Prose Comprehension by Adults, *Journal of Reading Behavior, 11*, pp. 99-106, 1979.

50. M. Z. Lippman, Enactive Imagery in Apried-associate Learning, *Memory and Cognition, 2*, pp. 385-390, 1974.

51. P. A. Devilliers, Imagery and Theme in Recall of Connected Discourse, *Journal of Experimental Psychology, 103*, pp. 263-268, 1974.

52. R. E. Johnson, Learners' Predictions of the Recallability of Prose, *Journal of Reading Behavior, 28*, pp. 339-350, 1974.

53. W. E. Montague and J. F. Carter, Vividness of Imagery in Recalling Connected Discourse, *Journal of Educational Psychology, 64*, pp. 72-75, 1973.

54. J. C. Yuille and A. Paivio, Abstractness and Recall of Connected Discourse, *Journal of Experimental Psychology, 82*, pp. 467-471, 1969.

55. R. C. Anderson, Encoding Processes in the Storage and Retrieval of Sentences, *Journal of Experimental Psychology, 91*, pp. 338-340, 1971.

56. R. C. Anderson and J. L. Hidde, Imagery and Sentence Learning, *Journal of Educational Psychology, 62*, pp. 526-530, 1971.

57. R. C. Anderson and R. W. Kulhavy, Imagery and Prose Learning, *Journal of Educational Psychology, 63*, pp. 242-243, 1972.

58. A. M. Lesgold, M. E. Curtis, H. Degood, R. M. Golinkoff, C. McCormick, and J. Shimron, *The Role of Mental Imagery in Test Comprehension: Preliminary Studies*, University of Pittsburgh, Learning Research and Development Center, Pittsburgh, 1974.

59. K. L. Alesandrini, J. J. Langstaff, and M. C. Wittrock, Visual-verbal and Analytic-holistic Strategies, Abilities and Styles, *Journal of Educational Research, 77*, pp. 151-157, 1983.

60. K. A. Lutz and J. W. Rigney, *The Effects of Student-generated Elaboration During Acquisition of Concepts in Science*, No. 82, University of Southern California, Behavioral Technology Laboratories, Los Angeles, (NTIs #ADA 047088), 1977.

61. F. W. Wicker, D. E. Weinstein, C. A. Yelich, and J. D. Brooks, Problem-reformulation Training and Visualization Training with Insight Problems, *Journal of Educational Psychology*, *70*, pp. 372-377, 1978.

62. D. Dansereau, The Learning-strategy Training Program, in *Learning Strategies*, H. F. O'Neil Jr. (ed.), Academic Press, New York, 1978.

63. R. M. Suinn, Imagery and Sports, in *Imagery: Current Theory, Research, and Application*, A. A. Sheikh (ed.), Wiley, New York, 1983.

64. M. S. Lindauer, Imagery and the Arts, in *Imagery: Current Theory, Research, and Application*, A. A. Sheikh (ed.), Wiley, New York, 1983.

65. A. A. Sheikh and C. S. Jordan, Clinical Uses of Mental Imagery, in *Imagery: Current Theory, Research, and Application*, A. A. Sheikh (ed.), Wiley, New York, 1983.

66. M. C. Wittrock, Learning as a Generative Process, *Educational Psychologist*, *11*, pp. 87-95, 1974.

67. C. M. Reigeluth, Meaningfulness and Instruction: Relating What is Being Learned to What a Student Knows, *Instructional Science*, *12*, pp. 197-218, 1983.

68. J. M. Royer and G. W. Cable, Facilitated Learning in Connected Discourse, *Journal of Educational Psychology*, *67*, pp. 116-123, 1975.

69. J. J. M. Royer and G. W. Cable, Illustrations, Analogies, and Facilitative Transfer in Prose Learning, *Journal of Educational Psychology*, *68*, pp. 205-209, 1976.

70. R. E. Mayer, Different Problem Solving Strategies Established in Learning Computer Programming With and Without Meaningful Models, *Journal of Educational Psychology*, *67*, pp. 725-734, 1975.

71. R. E. Mayer, Elaboration Techniques that Increase the Meaningfulness of Technical Text: An Experimental Test of the Learning Strategy Hypothesis, *Journal of Educational Psychology*, *72*, pp. 770-784, 1980.

72. R. E. Davidson, The Role of Metaphor and Analogy in Learning, in *Cognitive Learning in Children Theories and Strategies*, J. R. Levin and V. L. Allen (eds.), Academic Press, New York, 1976.

73. J. H. Larkin and F. Reif, Analysis and Teaching of a General Skill for Studying Scientific Text, *Journal of Educational Psychology*, *68*, pp. 431-440, 1976.

74. M. L. Gick and K. J. Holyoak, Analogical Problem Solving, *Cognitive Psychology*, *12*, pp. 306-355, 1980.

75. M. L. Gick and K. J. Holyoak, Schema Induction and Analogical Transfer, *Cognitive Psychology*, *15*, pp. 1-38, 1983.

76. J. R. Anderson and G. H. Bower, *Human Associative Memory*, Winston, Washington, D.C., 1973.

77. D. A. Norman and D. E. Rummelhart, *Explorations in Cognition*, Freeman, San Francisco, 1975.

78. R. F. Barron, The Use of Vocabulary as an Advance Organizer, in *Research in Reading in the Content Areas: First Year Report*, H. L. Herber and P. L. Sanders (eds.), Syracuse University, Syracuse, New York, 1969.

79. D. W. Moore and J. E. Readence, A Meta-analysis of the Effect of Graphic Organizers on Learning from Text, in *Perspectives in Reading Research and Instruction*, M. L. Kamil and A. J. Moe (eds.), Twenty-ninth Yearbook of the National Reading Conference, National Reading Conference, Washington, D.C., 1980.

80. D. W. Moore and J. E. Readence, A Quantitative and Qualitative Review of Graphic Organizer Research, paper presented at the annual meeting of the American Educational Research Association, Montreal, 1983.

81. D. E. Alvermann, The Compensatory Effect of Graphic Organizers on Descriptive Text, *Journal of Educational Research, 75*, pp. 44-48, 1981.

82. N. K. Snouffer and L. L. Thistlethwaite, The Effects of the Structured Overview and Vocabulary Pre-teaching upon Comprehension Levels of College Freshmen Reading Physical Science and History Materials, *Journal of the Association for the Study of Perception*, Fall, pp. 11-16, 1983.

83. S. M. Glynn and F. J. DiVesta, Outline and Hierarchical Organization as Aids for Study and Retrieval, *Journal of Educational Psychology, 69*, pp. 89-95, 1977.

84. M. D. Merrill and R. D. Tennyson, *Teaching Concepts: An Instructional Design Guide*, Educational Technology Publications, Englewood Cliffs, New Jersey, 1977.

85. W. C. Wilcox and M. D. Merrill, Effect of Teaching a Conceptual Hierarchy on Concept Classification Performance, *Journal of Instructional Development, 5*, pp. 8-13, 1981.

86. B. G. Wilson and M. D. Merrill, Effects of Structural Instruction and Sequence in Learning a Conceptual Hierarchy, paper presented at the annual meeting of the American Educational Research Association, Montreal, 1983.

87. C. D. Holley, D. F. Dansereau, B. A. McDonald, J. C. Garland, and K. W. Collins, Evaluation of a Hierarchical Mapping Technique as an Aid to Prose Processing, *Contemporary Educational Psychology, 4*, pp. 227-237, 1979.

88. D. F. Dansereau, K. W. Collins, B. A. McDonald, C. D. Holley, J. Garland, G. Diekhoff, and S. H. Evans, Development and Evaluation of a Learning Strategy Training Program, *Journal of Educational Psychology, 71*, pp. 64-73, 1979.

89. B. B. Armbruster and T. H. Anderson, *The Effect of Mapping on the Free Recall of Expository Text* Technical Report No. 1960, University of Illinois, Center for the Study of Reading, Urbana, 1980.

90. A. Collins, D. Gentner, and A. Rubin, *Teaching Study Strategies*, Report No. 4794, Bolt, Beranek and Newman Inc., October, 1981.

91. E. Geva, Facilitating Reading Comprehension through Flowcharting, *Reading Research Quarterly, 18*, pp. 384-405, 1983.

92. R. S. Dean and R. W. Kulhavy, Influence of Spatial Organization in Prose Learning, *Educational Psychology, 73*, pp. 57-64, 1981.

93. J. Snowman, E. W. Krebs, and L. Lockhart, Improving Recall of Information from Prose in High-risk Students through Learning Strategy Training, *Journal of Instructional Psychology, 7*, pp. 35-40, 1980.

94. M. Macdonald-Ross, How Numbers are Shown: A Review of Research on the Presentation of Quantitative Data in Texts, *AV Communication Review, 25*, pp. 359-404, 1977.

95. E. R. Tufte, *The Visual Display of Quantitative Information*, Graphics Press, Cheshire, Connecticut, 1983.

96. W. Winn, Effect of Attribute Highlighting and Diagrammatic Organization on Identification and Classification, *Journal of Research in Science Teaching, 18*, pp. 23-31, 1981.

97. R. Kammann, The Comprehensibility of Printed Instructions and the Flowchart Alternative, *Human Factors, 17*, pp. 183-191, 1975.

98. B. N. Lewi, I. S. Horabin, and C. P. Gane, *Case Studies in the Use of Algorithms*, Pergamon Press, New York, 1973.

99. P. Wright and F. Reid, Written Information: Some Alternatives to Prose for Expressing the Outcomes of Complex Contingencies, *Journal of Applied Psychology, 57*, pp. 160-166, 1973.

100. W. C. Coscarelli and T. M. Schwen, Effects of Three Algorithmic Representations on Critical Thinking, Laboratory Efficiency, and Final Grade, *Educational Communications and Technology, 27*, pp. 58-64, 1979.

101. G. B. Shelly and T. J. Cashman, *Introduction to Computers and Data Processing*, Brea, Anaheim, California, 1980.

102. K. L. Alesandrini, Three Kinds of Pictures in Science Instruction, paper submitted for publication.

103. K. L. Alesandrini, Types of Instructional Graphics in Courseware, paper presented at the Annual Meeting of Association for the Development of Computer-based Instructional Systems, Columbus, Ohio, May 1984.

CHAPTER 10
The Enhancement of Imaging Ability

ANEES A. SHEIKH, KATHARINA S. SHEIKH
AND L. MARTIN MOLESKI

As researchers are furnishing more evidence of the effectiveness of imagery-based methods in the educational process, educators are becoming increasingly interested in implementing them in the classroom. But, of course, the success of these procedures is dependent upon the learner's ability to form vivid images. A number of studies have demonstrated that significant changes in experiential, behavioral, and physiological measures can be produced in subjects who experience vivid images, but not in those who can muster only weak ones [1-3]. The crucial question that comes to mind at this point is: Are weak imagers condemned to remain so, or can they learn to reduce or even to eliminate their handicap?

Already in 1883, Sir Francis Galton, in his *Inquiries into Human Faculty*, indicated that practice in forming mental images can strengthen this ability [4]. Galton referred to a French educator who trained his students to visualize objects so clearly, that they could draw these images. He began by urging his students to examine the object carefully, so that they could form a clear visual image. Next, he directed them to "draw" it in the air, so that they might retain "muscular memories" of it. Finally, he required them to draw the object from memory. He claimed that after his students had been trained in this manner for three to four months, they could summon images with ease and could hold them steady enough to draw them.

Imagery researchers agree that everyone has the capacity to image. Marks comments, "While the ability to generate and employ mental imagery varies across people, the potential to do so is probably universal. Given appropriate and optimal conditions of thinking and performance, it is likely that all persons could utilize imagery-encoded information [in 5, p. 61]. Kroger and Fezler state, "Many believe that once sensations have been experienced, they are retained somewhere within the system and that the ability to recall and reexperience the situation and its associated sensations is available to all of us, although we rarely take advantage of these possibilities" [in, 5, p. 61]. Imagery ability is an innate potential like drawing or the use of language, or any other skill that improves with practice. Since the potential is there, it is possible to develop it through training. Of course, not all people can become superimagers, any more than they can learn to draw like Leonardo da Vinci or write like Shakespeare, but everyone can improve his/her skill over what it is at the present [6]. In short, the main ingredient in improving imagery appears to be "practice, practice, and more practice" [6, p. 139].

Conversely, neglect eventually will lead to the inability to summon images. Korn states, "Any system or ability that is not nurtured tends to atrophy. When we do not utilize the birthright of imagery experience, we eventually 'forget' the experience entirely" [5, p. 62].

The next question that arises is: Have researchers provided evidence that practice can improve imagery ability, and have they identified specific methods? Unfortunately, systematic research in the area of the enhancement of imagery has been very limited, but a number of useful suggestions and some indirect evidence are scattered throughout the literature. The purpose of this brief review is to bring these together and to offer recommendations for further research.

METHODS FOR IMPROVING IMAGERY VIVIDNESS

The salient factors that seem to lead to improved imagery vividness include: relaxation, concentration, body position and sensory input, sensory training, practice in imaging, multimodal training, convincing the client, developmentally determined images, increased right-hemisphere activity, somato-affective states, overcoming resistances, drugs, and certain developmental factors. This section provides a brief discussion of all of these factors.

Relaxation

Relaxation appears to be one of the most important prerequisites for the experience of vivid imagery [7, 8]; for, it seems to allow the process of becoming aware of internal states to begin.

Imagery, a symbolic mode of representation, to be distinguished from the verbal symbolic mode [9], is produced throughout the waking hours. But generally we are unaware of our imagery because it has to compete with the live broadcasting of everyday experience. We constantly are bombarded by stimuli, and the preoccupation with filtering out the superfluous ones among them renders us unaware of the internal stimuli which are of a relatively less dramatic nature. Furthermore, in Western cultures, the tendency has been to emphasize verbal, rational, secondary thought processes at the expense of imaginal experience—most people literally lose sight of their imagery.

During relaxation, the noisy, hectic world is shut out, and the inner world, the realm of imaginal experience, has a chance to become the focus of attention.

Gendlin notes, "Imagery comes very well and very richly during highly relaxed states" [8, p. 71]. Singer concludes that relaxation is "conducive to the occurrence or awareness of imagery and ongoing daydreaming" [10, p. 226]. Relaxation reduces "hyperalertness to external stimulation that would blur the vividness of imagery and overload the visual system which must handle both imagery derived from long-term memory and incoming stimulation" [10, p. 226]. Bakan, too, focuses on the central role of relaxation: "It is evident to people who work with imagery that relaxation is conducive to the experience of imagery." He explains, "The left hemisphere appears to have a closer relationship to motor activity than does the right hemisphere. Perhaps imagery activity, associated with the right hemisphere, is incompatible with a high degree of motor activity" [7, p. 40]. It may be more accurate to say that imagery is incompatible with *changes* in sensory input or in motor activity. Many long-distance runners have reported that they have experienced highly vivid imagery, often of a creative or problem-solving nature, while running. Their imaginal experience appears to be related not to speed or distance but to length of time: Generally it occurs when they maintain a steady pace. This finding is in harmony with Shapiro's observation relative to the psychology of meditation. He states that meditation involves habituation to any single stimulus which has been the primary focus of attention [11].

Numerous relaxation procedures have been developed over the years. For detailed information about these methods the reader is referred to other sources [5, 12, 13].

Concentration

Relaxation is a necessary preliminary step to visualization; it clears the mind and dispels distracting muscular tension. But another prerequisite for vivid imagery is the ability to concentrate. Generally, an endless procession of thoughts files through our mind, and we seem to have little control over their occurrence or their nature. But obviously this lack of thought control must be overcome by anyone who wishes to focus on one image.

Yoga offers a variety of suggestions to develop the powers of concentration [12]:

1. Concentration on a small external object: The student attempts to think only of the object, and each time a different thought intrudes, he/she pushes it aside and returns to the object.
2. Counting breaths: The student tries to ban all thoughts and to focus on counting breaths. Every time a thought does arise, he/she returns to the count. One way of dealing with these unbidden thoughts is to cut them off as quickly as possible, before they have a chance to unfold. Another approach is to let the intrusive thoughts pass unheeded, as if they belonged to someone else. A Zen metaphor likens thoughts to birds flying across the sky of one's mind—one simply watches them appear and then disappear.

Regular practice of such exercises enables a person to better ward off intrusive thoughts and to hold an image for a longer period [12, pp. 111-113]. Detailed discussions of numerous exercises in concentration are available elsewhere [12, 14, 15].

Body Position and Sensory Input

The supine body position has been found to facilitate the experience of vivid imagery, and it probably was by design that Freud directed his patients to the analytic couch. Pope has stated that the recumbent posture can markedly increase the experience of visual imagery and influence the flow of consciousness and the quality of our imagining experience [16]. Kroth reported that individuals who were reclining, free-associated more freely, more spontaneously, and generally more effectively than those who sat up [17]. Unfortunately, Kroth did not present data on imagery *per se*. Morgan and Bakan determined that subjects who were lying down produced reports that rated much higher in vividness of imagery than subjects who were sitting [18]. In a subsequent study, Berdach and Bakan elicited memory material from subjects in a reclining or sitting position, and they found that the reclining subjects produced earlier and more copious memories than the comparison group [19].

Segal and Glickman produced some very objective evidence by means of the Perky phenomenon [20]. Subjects, who were either lying down or sitting, gazed at a blank white screen onto which they were directed to project certain images. Unknown to them, the experimenter projected comparable images onto the screen. The investigators found that reclining subjects were much less likely to become aware that an external image had been projected. That is, their own images were sufficiently vivid to preclude awareness of the external ones.

A number of researchers have proposed explanations why imagery is enhanced in the reclining position. Berdach and Bakan suggest that this is so due to the decrease of tension in the head and neck muscles, a condition which prevails also at the onset of rapid eye movement sleep [19]. Singer points out that the reclining position is associated with sleep and hence with dreaming and daydreaming. Most people report that the greatest part of their daydreaming occurs while they are preparing for sleep [21].

Rychlak proposes that the effect may be due not to the reclining position as such, but rather to the reduction in complex external stimulation that accompanies this posture—a blank ceiling simply is not very distracting [22]. As Richardson indicates, imagery is more likely to manifest itself when we are awake and when external stimuli are not functionally operative [23].

Sensory Training

On the basis of extensive interviews of women who had been rated as excellent hypnotic subjects, Wilson and Barber concluded that a hallmark of these individuals is their profound fantasy life [24, 25]. These people (who constitute approximately 4% of the population) fantasize much of the time, and they do so very intensely—that is, they generally can "see," "hear," "smell," "feel," and fully experience what they are imagining.

These fantasy-prone individuals experience more vividly in all the sense modalities not only their fantasies but also the real world around them. Wilson and Barber hypothesize "that vivid sensory experiences, vivid memories, and vivid fantasies are causally interrelated as follows: individuals who focus on and vividly feel their sensory experiences, have relatively vivid memories of their experiences; and individuals with vivid memories of their experiences are able to have relatively vivid fantasies because they can use their vivid memories as raw material from which they can creatively construct their fantasies" [25, p. 380].

This relationship is corroborated by what is known about the manner in which creative persons approach the world. It seems that they experience the world with a certain innocence and consequently more intensely. Vivid sensory experience engenders vivid sensory-based memory, which in turn provides the material for vivid fantasies.

In other words, it appears that sensory training leads to improved imagery abilities [4, 23, 25]. Samuels and Samuels state, "The better people train their minds to perceive external images, the easier it becomes for them to imagine internal images as well" [12, p. 114]. For instance, "learning to see directly affects the ability to visualize. In seeing the images are external; in visualizing the images are internal. But the process and effects are similar" [12, p. 116].

Many psychologists believe that congenitally blind persons have no visual images. Similarly, those who see blindly will have difficulty in forming visual mental images. And it is indeed possible to see blindly. All of us probably have had the experience of walking right past a friend on the street without noticing him/her, because we were preoccupied by our thoughts. Another type of blind seeing occurs when we view an object solely with regard to a specific function and ignore all its other attributes. For example, when we are tired, we may regard a chair only as a place to rest and not notice anything else about it [12].

Samuels and Samuels suggest that the first step in developing the ability to see is becoming fully alert and aware as we look around, and, of course, this suggestion is applicable also to the cultivation of the other senses [12]. A number of specific exercises toward that end have been proposed:

1. It is beneficial to focus upon the various traits of an object, one after the other. One should take note of the way the light strikes the object, the highlights and shadows, and the color variations it creates. One should focus on the texture of the object, its color, its perspective, and its many other properties [12].
2. It is very helpful to stare at an object and to attempt to experience it. This means trying not to react verbally or to label, but rather to admit the object into one's consciousness [12].
3. The ability to perceive is improved by looking at an object from different physical perspectives and from different mental points of view. For instance, one could

consider an apple from the viewpoint of an artist, a hungry man, a migrant worker picking the apple, etc. With each shift, different aspects of the object will come to the fore. Witnessing this rich procession of attributes helps one to become aware of the labels and associations which one unconsciously uses in ordinary seeing; and this awareness prompts one to break out of the habitual manner of viewing familiar things and to see them again with a degree of innocence [12].

4. Hooper believes that clarity of perception can be improved by sketching and photographing objects from various angles not; but, attentively listening, smelling, tasting, and touching objects [in 6].

5. Petitclere suggests that it is useful to describe an object that one can feel but not see [in 6].

6. McKim uses puzzles and games to improve visual recognition. For instance, he may present five playing cards, of which four contain errors and one is correct. In order to find the minor errors, such as a spade which is upside down or a 10 written 01, the player must pay close attention to details. Analogous puzzles targeting the other senses, could easily be devised. For example, a succession of tones could be played, and the player would be required to identify the one that was of a different pitch. Also, different fabrics or spices could be presented to a blindfolded person for identification [26].

7. Parmenter maintains that one can improve one's powers of observation by pretending to be a reporter on a news assignment [in 6].

Numerous other exercises designed to sharpen one's awareness of the world have been outlined, and the interested reader can find those elsewhere [6, 12, 26, 27].

Practice in Imaging

Practice in imaging seems to yield improvement in imaging ability, and a number of apparently useful exercises have been devised for that purpose.

1. McKim proposes the following: A person closes his/her eyes and visualizes a wooden cube whose sides are painted red. Then he/she images two parallel vertical cuts through the cube, dividing it into thirds, and two more vertical cuts perpendicular to the first ones, dividing it into ninths. Next, he/she visualizes two parallel, horizontal cuts through the cube, dividing it into 27 cubes. Now, he/she tries to imagine how many cubes are red on three sides, on two sides, on one side, and how many cubes are unpainted on all sides [26].

2. McKim suggests the use of two-dimensional designs which can be folded together to make three-dimensional figures. The task consists of mentally folding a design and then indicating which one of several test figures has been created [26].

3. McKim recommends sketching to promote thinking schematically. The student starts with free doodling, then he/she progresses to disciplined doodling, then to realistic drawing, and finally to drawing his/her images. Later still, he/she draws things which are felt rather than seen, such as objects concealed in a bag. McKim's exercises focus on vision; however, they could be adapted without difficulty to involve the other senses. The guiding principle which runs through all these procedures is that practice promptly followed by feedback will improve performance [26].

4. Parmenter, a reporter, found the search for similes to sharpen his powers of observation. He stumbled upon this technique during an airplane trip—as he discerned a certain feature in the landscape, he asked himself, "What does it recall?" And he attempted to answer in a different material, species, or modality every time. For example, a winding road reminded him of a tortoise shell hairpin, and he compared a brook to worm tracks in wood [in 6].

5. Lazarus has found the blackboard exercise to be effective [27]. The student relaxes, closes his/her eyes, visualizes a blackboard, and imagines writing the letter

"A" on it, followed by "B" and so forth. Throughout the process, the student tries to retain a clear image of all the letters on the board. Initially, most people find that, as they add more letters, the beginning ones tend to fade. But with practice, the clarity of the letters improves.

6. Lazarus also recommends the light bulb technique. The student closes his/her eyes and imagines a dim light bulb suspended in front of him/her. While focusing on the light, he/she attempts to make it grow brighter and brighter until it illuminates everything, and then dimmer and dimmer [27].

7. Another technique involves careful study of a common object. The student scrutinizes the object until he/she is familiar with it. Then he/she closes his/her eyes and pretends to still be studying the object. He/she tries to see it as clearly as possible and studies it as he/she did the real object. Next, he/she opens his/her eyes and reexamines the real object to compare the difference between it and its image. Then he/she closes his/her eyes again and repeats the exercise, taking care to add to the image those traits which were missed the first time [27].

8. Lazarus also claims to have used the seashore exercise with success. The student relaxes, closes his/her eyes, and imagines that he/she is strolling along a quiet beach on a balmy day. He/she is wearing a swim suit, and he/she feels the warm sun on the skin and the sand between the toes. He/she smells the fresh sea air and listens to the waves breaking on the sand. He/she summons other soothing images associated with a stroll on the beach and enjoys the serenity that accompanies them [27].

9. Samuels and Samuels recommend the following sequence for improving visualization ability: A) With the eyes closed, imagine a two-dimensional object, such as a geometrical shape. Then close the eyes and try to visualize it. B) Repeat Exercise A with a three-dimensional object. C) Visualize your childhood room. D) Image a large object, such as a house, and move around and through it. E) Visualize a complicated, three-dimensional object from various angles. F) Return to the childhood room of Exercise C, and imagine that you are doing several things in it, such as picking up items, switching the lights off, etc. G) Visualize a person. H) Image yourself as if you are looking in a mirror [12].

There is some evidence that hypnotic suggestions can lead to more vivid imagery; hence, many of the above exercises may be more effective when they are performed under hypnosis [5, 12]. Also, some clinicians claim that listening to concrete descriptions of scenes, either recorded ones or ones presented live by the therapist, can stimulate imagery.

Many other procedures have appeared in the popular literature. But "what is lacking for all these techniques is information on how they work. As parlor games, they are fun and harmless. However, before they are included in school curricula or mnemonics workshops, some efforts must be made to measure their effectiveness" [6, p. 147].

Multimodal Training

Related to the ideas discussed in the preceding section are Cautela and McCullough's suggestion concerning the involvement of all sense modalities [28, p. 236]:

> Vividness must not be equated solely with visual imagery, for the greatest effectiveness is obtained when the client reports a vividness in all sense modalities. For example, if a client had trouble imagining

or visualizing an airplane, the sound of the plane would be described, the kinaesthetic feeling of the takeoff or the seatbelt, the physiological responses such as increased heartbeat or shortness of breath, and the appropriate affective state such as anxiety or exhilaration. It is emphasized that the client not simply imagine the scene, but try to feel that he is actually experiencing it. Recent research suggests that the largest and most consistent physiological responses occur in response to imagining somato-motor and visceral responses and to imagining "being there" rather than just imagining detailed descriptions without affective components.

Convincing the Client

Imaging ability probably is universal; yet, some clients claim that they lack it. An important preliminary step with such individuals is convincing them of the contrary. Korn proposes a simple yet effective procedure [5] : The client is directed to imagine that the therapist is a window washer contracting to clean the windows of the client's residence. In order to quote a price, the window washer must know how many windows are involved. The client is asked to furnish this information. In response to this request, the client's eyes will turn to the side opposite the nondominant hemisphere, which may indicate stimulation of the nondominant hemisphere, and if the client is questioned at this point, he/she will reveal that he/she actually was counting the windows. But "how can one count the windows without visualizing them, even if the image is not clear and tends to be a mind's eye image? This will demonstrate to even the most recalcitrant of subjects that imagery is not only possible, but that he or she uses it every day for the solution of many of life's problems" [5, p. 62].

Shorr mentions another method of demonstrating to clients that they are capable of producing imagery: "When people tell me they never have images, I ask them to imagine sexual scenes. . . . So far this has resulted in no failures" [28, p. 157].

Developmentally Determined Images

Images of past key events seem to be effective in rendering the individual aware of his/her images in general. Even those individuals who do not have vivid imagery, with some encouragement and concentration, can visualize developmentally determined images from significant life situations in the past. These images tend to open up the general imagination and fantasy processes [30].

Enhancing Right-Hemisphere Activity

Research on cerebral specialization has revealed that "the left hemisphere seems to be more concerned with the temporal analysis of incoming information which it labels verbally, for storage and for later retrieval and manipulation in recall or problem solving. The right hemisphere on the other hand, seems to deal with organizing incoming information on the basis of complex wholes, and acts as a synthesizer rather than analyzer" [31, p. 112]. Paivio proposes that verbal or mathematical processes, which involve sequential processing, occur in the left hemisphere; spatial or imaginal processes, which entail parallel processing, take place in the right hemisphere [9]. Oyle expresses the differentiation of the hemispheres in this manner: "The self is hermaphroditic. Each one of us is two individuals, a male and a female. The former is rational, can speak and think thoughts. The female side makes the pictures, dreams, mental images, and empirical reality" [32, p. 99]. Ley stresses that the right hemisphere "seems to predominate in a variety of states of consciousness, such as dreaming (day and night), hypnosis and meditation, as well as in religious and drug-induced states, in which emotional and imagery components are salient" [33, p. 42].

Since right-hemisphere functions are linked to imagery, enhancement of the former would be expected to produce amelioration of the latter. Thus, participation in activities which generally are regarded as right hemispheric, such as music, art, poetry, dancing, humor, and meditation, would be expected to lead to enhanced imagery production. Although some support for this contention can be found in the literature, there is an obvious need for further empirical validation.

Oyle suggests two general approaches to imagery enhancement which are relevant to this section: "The left hemisphere can be put at rest by a variety of techniques. These have by and large been formalized as religious rituals, hypnotic suggestions, or sensory deprivation among others. Another way to shift the balance in favor of the image-making right brain is to overload the thinker in the left brain" [32, p. 87]. This may be accomplished by the use of Zen Buddhist koans, insoluble problems, like, "What is the sound of one hand clapping?" Oyle feels that "if the thinker is quiescent or overloaded to the point of exhaustion, energy flows from the right cerebral hemisphere to form an image" [32, p. 87].

The Role of Somato-Affective States

Imagery has long been thought to have a direct relationship to emotions. Many psychologists have noted that images possess an amazing ability to effect extensive affective and physiological changes [3, 34]. A recent memory image may elicit an emotional response and a physiological arousal whose intensity rivals and even surpasses that of the reaction to the actual event [35, 36]. Bauer and Craighead state: "A basic assumption underlying the use of imagery techniques in behavioral therapy has been that the patterns of physiological response to imagined and real stimuli are essentially isomorphic. For example, Wolpe [37] suggested that the pattern of arousal elicited by visualization of fearful scenes in desensitization directly corresponded to that brought about by actual contact with an anxiety-eliciting stimulus" [38, p. 389].

Recently, attempts have been made to integrate three fundamental aspects of all human experience [39-41]. These include: the image (I), the somatic response—including emotional arousal (S), and the meaning—including affective signification (M). It seems that all significant images are a triadic unity (ISM). Clinicians often work with the image component of this triangle. They ask the client to concentrate and to repeatedly project an image that originally had been weak or vague, until it becomes vivid, precise, detailed, and stable. Through the image, the individual attempts to recreate the original experience, that is to re-experience the affect and meaning and the accompanying bodily responses, which form the memory in its entirety. If the concept of the ISM is valid, then focusing on any aspect of this triangle, not only on the image, should bring the entire experience into relief. In other words, concentrating on the image's meaning or on the affect and bodily response it evokes, should render the whole event more real. For example, if the focus is on an aggressive image, the production of bodily responses involved in agresssion may help to make the image more vivid.

Support for the ISM approach to the enhancement of imagery can be found in the research of several investigators. For instance, Ley considers imagery and emotions to be inseparable: "Given sufficient, affective potency, stimulus salience, and the vast and elusive differences in imaging ability and cognitive styles (*i.e.*, 'picture' thinkers vs. 'word' thinkers), imagic and emotional stimulus components may be inextricable in practice" [33, p. 47]. Perhaps these imagic and emotional components are inextricable because they are bound together by the meaning they convey. Gendlin, who has developed a form of therapy called "focusing" which relies substantially on imagery, recommends emphasizing the somatic component to enhance imagery; for, he has observed that a by-product of doing so is increased *meaning* for the individual. "In summary, I believe that whatever your way of working with imagery may be, you will find your method enhanced quite powerfully, if you employ focusing. . . . Imagery and body-sense are inherently related, but on different planes. It is much more powerful if one not only works with the body and imagery, but devotes specific attention to the formation of something directly sensed in the body, yet implicitly meaningful" [40, p. 72].

Lang's brainformational theory of emotional imagery is also relevant here [42]. Lang conceives the image in the brain to be a "conceptual network, controlling specific somatovisceral patterns, in constituting a prototype for overt behavioral expression" [in 5, p. 73]. He believes that instructions to the client would be more effective if they consisted not only of the usual stimulus propositions but also of response propositions. Therefore, a statement such as, "The wooden walls of the small room surround you, closing you in . . ." would change to "You tense all your muscles of your forehead, squinting . . . your eyes . . . dart left and right to glimpse the exit" [in 5, p. 73].

Overcoming Resistances

In some cases, the inability to image or to image vividly may be a function of certain kinds of resistances on the part of the client. These resistances may affect imaging ability in specific areas, or they may inhibit the total imaging process. Such resistances need to be identified and understood before proper evolvement of imagery can take place. Shorr offers an explanation for these resistances: "It is inevitably the fears, anxieties, or frustrations inherent in people's internal conflicts, which lead to the curtailment of an imaginary capacity, in order to shrink the boundaries of their self-hood to more manageable dimensions" [43, p. 15].

A detailed discussion of various types of resistances is beyond the scope of this chapter and the reader is referred to other sources [5, 30, 44-47].

Drugs

It has been known for centuries, for instance by participants in religious rituals, that certain psychoactive drugs stimulate mental imagery [48]. For example, the religious rites of the American Indians culminated in the ingestion of psychoactive drugs, such as peyote and psilocybin, which prompted intense religious experiences mediated by remarkably vivid imagery [49, 50]. In the 1960s, thousands of American youths made the expansion of their mind and conscious awareness a top priority. The means they most commonly chose were LSD, marijuana, and cocaine, and their major shared experience was intensification of sensory awareness through hallucinations [51].

Subject accounts indicate that the drug experience often involves an attitudinal shift or change in level of awareness that fosters the production of imagery or the greater awareness of imagery. For example, ordinary awareness has been compared to spotlighting: This focused lighting is like our linear, logical thinking—specific and task oriented. Drug-induced awareness represents a shift toward floodlighting; it is more global, more panoramic [52]. The analogy parallels comparisons of left- and right-brain functioning, which are different but complimentary types of perception [7]. Holt too links the attitudinal changes, such as weakened defenses, which accompany drug-induced conditions, to increased imagery [53].

The image-enhancing quality of certain drugs may be due also to their relaxing effect on the system. For instance, Segal found that subjects who were under the influence of tranquilizers displayed a stronger Perky effect than those who were not [54].

Obviously, drugs are not a recommended means of enhancing imagery. Nevertheless, it is possible that some subjects who have experienced vivid imagery by means of drugs, will be more highly motivated to enhance their imagery, simply because they already have had a taste of the experience.

Developmental Factors

Qualls and Sheehan believe that "the origins of imaginal skills and the readiness to spontaneously utilize imaginal capacities lie in the imaginative, make-believe play and fantasy experiences of childhood" and that "early childhood may represent a sensitive period for the development of imaginal abilities" [55, p. 91]. Investigators have identified a number of factors that seem to enhance make-believe play in children which in turn may lead to better imagery abilities later in life:

1. Positive interpersonal experiences early in life are beneficial [56].
2. Security of attachment is an important factor [56].
3. A parental model who enjoys artistic pursuits and verbal and other forms of inventiveness enriches the child's play activities [56].
4. Opportunities for space and time to be alone, accompanied by the approval of a parent figure, contribute to meaningful play [56].
5. The child should be encouraged to engage in role-taking activities and to *behave* toward an object as if it were something other than what it actually is [57].
6. Storytelling by parents and other significant individuals can be helpful [58].
7. Television viewing in moderate degrees also can be a useful catalyst for imaginative play. However, the presence of an adult to encourage the creative use of television rather than passive viewing, is very important [59].
8. Both sociodramatic play, which involves themes and events within the realm of the child's everyday experience (*e.g.*, playing school or pretending to go to the doctor), and thematic fantasy play, whose themes and events are remote from personal experience (*e.g.*, fairy tales), are effective in stimulating the child's imaginal abilities [55].

DIRECT RESEARCH EVIDENCE

Although numerous techniques to enhance imagery have been proposed, research directly investigating their efficacy is extremely limited. However, the results of the few existing studies are encouraging.

Walsh, White, and Ashton found that imagery training can be beneficial and that marked improvements can take place in a relatively short time [60]. They identified vivid and weak imagers by means of the Betts Test and then formed three groups, each consisting of six vivid and six weak imagers. Every group met for twenty minutes on four successive days. One group was not exposed to any imagery-related activities. Another group discussed the therapeutic uses of imagery but did not undergo any formal training. The experimental group practiced visual, kinesthetic, and auditory imaging on the first day, gustatory and olfactory on the next day, tactile and organic on the third day, and an exercise which involved all seven modalities on the last day. Also, they were assigned exercises to practice at home between sessions.

The posttest revealed no significant change in the first two groups. Of the third group, the vivid imagers revealed no change, but the weak imagers exhibited a very significant change. Not only did they rate their imagery as markedly more vivid, which may represent simply a response to the demand characteristics of the situation, but also, when they were asked to imagine their favorite food, they salivated as copiously as untrained vivid imagers.

Richardson and Patterson felt the need to extend and refine the study of Walsh *et al.*, for a number of reasons [61]. First, Walsh *et al.* had not separated the effects of sensory-awareness training from the effects ascribable to relaxation. Richardson and Patterson took care to do so. Second, the earlier study invited the question whether training in a single major modality (vision) would suffice to produce the reported amelioration in imagery vividness. Consequently, Richardson and Patterson exposed two groups to multimodal training, and they gave the other group practice solely in the visual modality. Third, Walsh *et al.* had conducted the evaluation only immediately after the training period. Richardson and Patterson added a follow-up test administered two months after the conclusion of training. That is, Richardson and Patterson evaluated the relative effectiveness of three training procedures: multimodal imagery training with relaxation (RMM), multimodal imagery training by itself (MM), and visual imagery training with relaxation (RV).

They found an increase in imagery vividness for the RMM and MM training groups both on experiential (Betts Questionnaire) and on physiological (salivation) measures. However, the posttest two months later did not reveal significant differences. It is possible that weak imagers need periodic refresher training sessions to maintain their gain in imagery vividness and to prevent the relapse to their habitual modes of thought [2].

There are several other recent studies which have implications for the enhancement of imagery, which the reader may wish to consult [62, 63].

THE ISSUE OF IMAGERY CONTROL

The success of imagery procedures is determined not only by the ability to form vivid images but also by the ability to control them. If the individual can produce vivid images but is unable to control them, the prospects for effective use of imagery techniques are dim. "In fact, the most difficult state in which to cause behavioral change is one in which the client experiences intensely vivid imagery but cannot control or maintain adaptive thoughts and continues to revert to maladaptive images" [28, p. 237]. According to Richardson, the combination of high vividness and high controllability correlates the most with behavioral change, while the combination of high vividness and low controllability correlates the least with behavioral change [23].

Quite typically, an individual who lacks control over his/her images, will experience difficulty in focusing on beneficial images. He/she may begin by imagining a very positive situation but then find himself/herself constantly interrupted by aversive thoughts; for example, he/she may visualize himself/herself skiing downhill on a sunny day, only to fall. Cautela and McCullough propose a number of procedures that seem to aid in controlling and redirecting negative imagery [28]:

1. The individual is reminded that the fantasy is his/hers, that he/she has created it and hence also can change it in any way. Then he/she is asked to descibe the scene again but with a positive outcome (*e.g.*, he/she skis down the hill without a mishap). Sometimes this exercise suffices, and the person is able to control his/her imagery.
2. If the above exercise is not effective, then undesirable images are modified gradually by shaping. For instance, the individual proceeds to imagine falling down while skiing, but the fall does not hurt. He/she visualizes the skiing scene repeatedly, and each time he/she images that he/she is able to maintain better balance or to stop before falling.
3. The person keeps a log of all the situations which cause tension, anxiety, or depression. After a week of recording these incidents, he/she learns to identify them quickly. He/she attempts to relax in the face of aversive thoughts and to interrupt them at the onset, when they are easier to control and stifle.

CONCLUDING REMARKS

A survey of the literature relevant to the enhancement of imagery reveals that investigators share the persuasion that everyone possesses the potential for imaging. Furthermore, it appears that even if the imaging ability has withered due to neglect, it can be revived. The literature contains a number of methods which have been used for stimulating mental imagery. Nevertheless, little research has been carried out to establish the efficacy of these various methods and also to determine their relative merit under different circumstances.

Furthermore, it appears that investigators have been disproportionately fascinated by visual imagery. Although visual images are the most common kind, they are not the only type or even the preferred one for some individuals. Undoubtedly, the other modalities deserve more of the investigators' attention than they have hitherto received.

Also, researchers seem preoccupied with the issue of vividness, and, although they recognize the importance of control of imagery, they have made little attempt to explore this area. More sophisticated measures of control as well as scientifically developed procedures to improve control are sorely needed.

If the increase of interest over the last ten years in imagery-related topics can be used as an indicator, then it seems virtually certain that within the next ten years a host of pressing questions will be answered, and clearer guidelines will be available to educators.

REFERENCES

1. D. F. Marks, Imagery and Consciousness, *Journal of Mental Imagery*, 2, pp. 275-290, 1977.
2. A. Richardson and C. C. Taylor, Vividness of Mental Imagery and Self-induced Mood Change, *British Journal of Clinical Psychology*, *21*, pp. 111-117, 1982.
3. A. A. Sheikh and R. G. Kunzendorf, Imagery, Physiology, and Psychosomatic Illness, in *International Review of Mental Imagery*, Vol. 1, A. A. Sheikh (ed.), Human Sciences Press, New York, pp. 95-138, 1984.

4. F. Galton, *Inquiries into Human Faculty*, McMillan, London, 1883.
5. E. R. Korn, *Visualization: Uses of Imagery in the Health Professions*, Dow Jones-Irwin, Homewood, Illinois, 1983.
6. R. Sommer, *The Mind's Eye: Imagery in Everyday Life*, Delacorte Press, New York, 1978.
7. P. Bakan, Imagery, Raw and Cooked: A Hemispheric Recipe, in *Imagery: Its Many Dimensions and Applications*, J. E. Shorr, G. E. Sobel, P. Robin, and J. A. Connella (eds.), Plenum, New York, pp. 35-53, 1980.
8. E. T. Gendlin, *Focusing*, Bantam Books, New York, 1981.
9. A. Paivio, *Imagery and Verbal Processes*, Holt, Rinehart, Winston, New York, 1971.
10. J. L. Singer, *Imagery and Daydream Methods in Psychotherapy and Behavior Modification*, Academic Press, New York, 1974.
11. D. L. Shapiro, The Significance of the Visual Image in Psychotherapy, *Psychotherapy: Theory, Research, and Practice*, 7, pp. 209-212, 1974.
12. M. Samuels and N. Samuels, *Seeing with the Mind's Eye*, Random House, New York, 1975.
13. *Imagination and Healing*, A. A. Sheikh (ed.), Baywood Publishing Company, New York, 1984.
14. D. Goleman, *The Varieties of the Meditative Experience*, E. P. Dutton, New York, 1977.
15. S. Ostrander, L. Schroeder, and N. Ostrander, *Superlearning*, The Dell Publishing Company, New York, 1979.
16. K. Pope, How Gender, Solitude and Posture Influence the Stream of Consciousness, in *The Stream of Consciousness*, K. S. Pope and J. L. Singer (eds.), Plenum, New York, 1978.
17. J. A. Kroth, The Analytic Couch and Response to Free Association, *Psychotherapy: Theory, Research, and Practice*, 7, pp. 206-208, 1970.
18. R. Morgan and P. Bakan, Sensory Deprivation Hallucinations and Other Sleep Behavior as a Function of Position, Method of Report, and Anxiety, *Perceptual and Motor Skills*, 20, pp. 19-25, 1965.
19. E. Berdach and P. Bakan, Body Position and Free Recall of Early Memories, *Psychotherapy: Theory, Research, and Practice*, 4, pp. 101-102, 1967.
20. S. J. Segal and M. Glickman, Relaxation and the Perky Effect: The Influence of Body Position and Judgments of Imagery, *American Journal of Psychology*, 60, pp. 257-262, 1967.
21. J. L. Singer, Experimental Studies of Daydreaming and the Stream of Consciousness, in *The Stream of Consciousness*, K. S. Pope and J. L. Singer (eds.), Plenum, New York, 1978.
22. J. Rychlak, Time Orientation in the Positive and Negative Free Phantasies of Mildly Abnormal versus Normal Highschool Males, *Journal of Consulting and Clinical Psychology*, 41, pp. 175-190, 1973.
23. A. Richardson, *Mental Imagery*, Routledge and Kegan Paul, London, 1969.
24. T. X. Barber, Changing "Unchangeable" Bodily Processes by (Hypnotic) Suggestions: A New Look at Hypnosis, Cognitions, Imagining, and the Mind-Body Problem, in *Imagination and Healing*, A. A. Sheikh (ed.), Baywood Publishing Company, New York, pp. 69-127, 1984.

25. S. C. Wilson and T. X. Barber, The Fantasy-Prone Personality: Implications for Understanding Imagery, Hypnosis, and Parapsychological Phenomena, in *Imagery: Current Theory, Research, and Application*, A. A. Sheikh (ed.), Wiley, New York, 1983.
26. R. H. McKim, *Experiences in Visual Thinking*, Brooks/Cole, Monterey, California, 1980.
27. A. Lazarus, *In the Mind's Eye*, Rawson Associates, New York, 1977.
28. J. R. Cautela and L. McCullough, Covert Conditioning, in *The Power of Human Imagination*, J. L. Singer and K. S. Pope (eds.), Plenum, New York, pp. 227-254, 1978.
29. J. E. Shorr, *Go See The Movie in Your Head*, Popular Library, New York, 1977.
30. A. A. Sheikh, Eidetic Psychotherapy, in *The Power of Human Imagination*, J. L. Singer and K. S. Pope (eds.), Plenum, New York, pp. 197-224, 1978.
31. A. Richardson, Verbalizer-Visualizer: A Cognitive Style Dimension, *Journal of Mental Imagery, 1*, pp. 109-126, 1977.
32. I. Oyle, *The New American Medicine Show*, Celestial Arts, Millbrae, California, 1979.
33. R. G. Ley, Cerebral Asymmetries, Emotional Experience, and Imagery: Implications for Psychotherapy, in *The Potential of Fantasy and Imagination*, A. A. Sheikh and J. T. Shaffer (eds.), Brandon House, New York, pp. 41-65, 1979.
34. A. A. Sheikh and N. C. Panagiotou, Use of Mental Imagery in Psychotherapy: A Critical Review, *Perceptual and Motor Skills, 41*, pp. 555-585, 1975.
35. A. Ellis, *Reason and Emotion in Psychotherapy*, Lyle Stuart, Inc., New York, 1962.
36. M. J. Horowitz, *Image Formation and Cognition*, Appleton Century Crofts, New York, 1970.
37. J. Wolpe, *Psychotherapy by Reciprocal Inhibition*, Stanford University Press, Stanford, California, 1958.
38. R. Bauer and E. Craighead, Psychophysiological Responses to the Imagination of Fearful and Neutral Situations: The Effects of Imagery Instructions, *Behavior Therapy, 10*, pp. 389-403, 1979.
39. A. Ahsen, *Basic Concepts in Eidetic Psychotherapy*, Brandon House, New York, 1968.
40. E. T. Gendlin, Imagery is More Powerful with Focusing, in *Imagery: Its Many Dimensions and Applications*, J. E. Shorr, G. E. Sobel, P. Robin, and J. A. Connella (eds.), Plenum, New York, pp. 65-73, 1980.
41. *Imagery: Current Theory, Research, and Application*, A. A. Sheikh (ed.), Wiley, New York, 1983.
42. P. J. Lang, Imagery in Therapy: An Information Processing Analysis of Fear, *Behavior Therapy, 8*, pp. 862-886, 1977.
43. J. E. Shorr, *Psychotherapy Through Imagery*, Thieme-Stratton, New York, 1983.
44. A. Ahsen, *Eidetic Psychotherapy: A Short Introduction*, Nai Matbooat, Lahore, 1965.

45. A. Bry, *Visualization: Directing the Movies of Your Mind*, Barnes and Noble, New York, 1972.
46. J. E. Shorr, Clinical Uses of Categories of Therapeutic Imagery, in *The Power of Human Imagination*, J. L. Singer and K. S. Pope (eds.), Plenum, New York, pp. 95-121, 1978.
47. M. M. Watkins, *Waking Dreams*, Harper and Row, New York, 1976.
48. P. McKellar, Imagery from the Standpoint of Introspection, in *The Function and Nature of Imagery*, P. W. Sheehan (ed.), Academic Press, New York, pp. 36-61, 1972.
49. C. Castaneda, *The Teachings of Don Juan: A Yavui Way of Knowledge*, Simon and Schuster, New York, 1968.
50. C. Castaneda, *Journal to Ixtlan*, Simon and Schuster, New York, 1972.
51. T. Leary, R. Metzner, and R. Alpert, *The Psychedelic Experience*, University Books, New York, 1964.
52. *Altered States of Consciousness*, C. Tart (ed.), Doubleday, New York, 1969.
53. R. R. Holt, On the Nature and Generality of Mental Imagery, in *The Function and Nature of Imagery*, P. W. Sheehan (ed.), Academic Press, New York, pp. 6-33, 1972.
54. *Imagery: Current Cognitive Approaches*, S. J. Segal (ed.), Academic Press, New York, 1971.
55. P. J. Qualls and P. W. Sheehan, Imaginative, Make-Believe Experiences and Their Role in the Development of the Child, in *Mental Imagery and Learning*, M. L. Fleming and D. W. Hutton (eds.), Educational Technology Publication, Englewood Cliffs, New Jersey, pp. 75-97, 1983.
56. R. B. Tower, Imagery: Its Role in Development, in *Imagery: Current Theory, Research, and Application*, A. A. Sheikh (ed.), Wiley, New York, pp. 222-251, 1983.
57. E. Saltz, D. Dixon, and J. Johnson, Training Disadvantaged Preschoolers on Various Fantasy Activities: Effects on Cognitive Functioning and Impulse Control, *Child Development*, *48*, pp. 367-380, 1977.
58. J. Hilgard, *Personality and Hypnosis: A Study of Imaginative Involvement*, University of Chicago Press, Chicago, 1980.
59. J. L. Singer, Imagination and Make-Believe Play in Early Childhood: Some Educational Implications, *Journal of Mental Imagery*, *1*, pp. 127-144, 1977.
60. F. J. Walsh, K. D. White, and R. Ashton, Imagery Training: Development of a Procedure and Its Evaluation, unpublished research report, University of Queensland, 1978.
61. A. Richardson and Y. Patterson, An Evaluation of Three Procedures for Increasing Imagery Vividness, in *International Review of Mental Imagery*, Vol. 2, A. A. Sheikh (ed.), Human Sciences Press, New York, in press.
62. H. J. Crawford and C. McLeod-Morgan, Hypnotic Investigations of Imagery, in *International Review of Mental Imagery*, Vol. 2, A. A. Sheikh (ed.), Human Sciences Press, New York, in press.
63. J. Heil, Visual Imagery Change During Relaxation Meditation Training, doctoral dissertation, Lehigh University, 1982, *Dissertation Abstracts International*, *43*, p. 2338B, 1982.

SUBJECT INDEX

ACKNOWLEDGMENTS

Permission to reproduce material from the following sources is gratefully acknowledged:

1. B. Catton, *This Hallowed Ground*, Doubleday and Company, New York, 1963.

2. L. C. Ehri, N. D. Deffner, and L. S. Wilce, Pictorial Mnemonics for Phonics, *Journal of Educational Psychology* (in press).

3. J. R. Levin, C. B. McCormick, G. E. Miller, J. K. Berry, and M. Pressley, Mnemonic versus Nonmnemonic Vocabulary-Learning Strategies for Children, *American Educational Research Journal, 19*, pp. 121–136, 1982.

4. W. P. Wharton, Higher Imagery and the Readability of College History Texts, *Journal of Mental Imagery, 4*, pp. 128–147, Fall 1980.

CONTRIBUTORS

Kathryn Lutz Alesandrini, Ph.D.
Instructional Media & Technology
 Department
California State University,
 Los Angeles
5151 State University Drive
Los Angeles, CA 90032

Beverly-Colleene Galyean, Ph.D.
Deceased
Formerly Director
Center for Integrative Learning
767 Gladys Avenue
Long Beach, CA 90804

Tore Helstrup, Ph.D.
Department of Psychology
University of Bergin
5000 Bergin, Norway

Geir Kaufmann, Ph.D.
School of Cognitive Psychology
University of Bergin
5000 Bergin, Norway

Melvin Kaushansky, Ph.D.
Department of Psychology
Simon Fraser University
Burnaby, B.C.
V5A 1S6, Canada

Joel R. Levin, Ph.D.
 Wisconsin Center for Education
 Research
School of Education
University of Wisconsin-Madison
1025 West Johnson Street
Madison, WI 53706

Robert G. Ley, Ph.D.
Department of Psychology
Simon Fraser University
Burnaby, B.C.
Canada Z5A 1S6

L. Martin Moleski, MA
Marin General Hospital
Greenbrae, CA 94902

Anees A. Sheikh, Ph.D.
Department of Psychology
Marquette University
Milwaukee, WI 53233

Katharina S. Sheikh, MA
Institute for Human Enhancement
PO Box 13453
Milwaukee, WI 53213

Diana Shmukler, Ph.D.
Department of Psychology
University of Witwatersrand
1 Jan Smuts Avenue
Johannesburg 2001, South Africa

Gisela E. Speidel, Ph.D.
Language and Learning Center for
 Development of Early Education
Kamehamexa Schools
1850 Makuakame Street
Honolulu, HI 96817

Nancy S. Suzuki, Ph.D.
School of Education
University of British Columbia
Vancouver, B.C.
V5A 1S6 Canada

Mark E. Troy, Ph.D.
Language and Learning Center for
 Development of Early Education
Kamehamexa Schools
1850 Makuakame Street
Honolulu, HI 96817

William P. Wharton, Ph.D.
Emeritus Professor of Education
Allegheny College
415 North Main Street
Meadville, PA 16335

BOOKS IN THIS SERIES

Imagery and Human Development Series
Series Editor: Anees A. Sheikh

Volume 1   Imagination and Healing
edited by *Anees A. Sheikh*

Volume 2   Imagery in Education—Imagery in the Educational Process
edited by *Anees A. Sheikh and Katharina S. Sheikh*

Forthcoming

Volume 3   Imagery in Sports
edited by *Errol Korn, M.D. and Anees A. Sheikh*

Volume 4   Death before Life—Therapeutic Potential of Death Imagery
edited by *Anees A. Sheikh*